COMPUTING
THE NEWS

SYLVAIN PARASIE

COMPUTING THE NEWS

Data Journalism and the Search for Objectivity

Columbia University Press / *New York*

Columbia University Press
Publishers Since 1893
New York   Chichester, West Sussex
cup.columbia.edu
Copyright © 2022 Columbia University Press
All rights reserved

Library of Congress Cataloging-in-Publication Data
Names: Parasie, Sylvain, author.
Title: Computing the news data : journalism and the search for objectivity / Sylvain Parasie.
Description: New York : Columbia University Press, 2022. | Includes bibliographical references and index.
Identifiers: LCCN 2022009172 (print) | LCCN 2022009173 (ebook) | ISBN 9780231199766 (hardback) | ISBN 9780231199773 (trade paperback) | ISBN 9780231553278 (ebook)
Subjects: LCSH: Computer-assisted reporting. | Journalistic ethics. | Journalism—Data processing.
Classification: LCC PN4784.E5 P37 2022 (print) | LCC PN4784.E5 (ebook) | DDC 070.40285—dc23/eng/20220304
LC record available at https://lccn.loc.gov/2022009172
LC ebook record available at https://lccn.loc.gov/2022009173

Cover design: Noah Arlow

To Elsa and Abel

CONTENTS

List of Figures ix

Acknowledgments xi

Introduction: Trying to Be Nonjudgmental 1

PART I
TWO PATHS TO DATA JOURNALISM

1 Revealing Injustice with Computers, 1967–1995 27

2 Rankings; or, The Unintended Consequences of Computation, 1988–2000 51

CONTENTS

PART II
A CHALLENGE FOR JOURNALISM

   3 Rebooting Journalism 79

   4 A Tale of Two Cultures? 105

   5 The Tensions Facing Data Journalism 125

PART III
DATA JOURNALISM IN THE MAKING

   6 The Making of a Revelation 153

   7 How Not to Get Academic 177

   8 The Art of Bringing About Publics 201

Conclusion: An Ethics of Reflexivity 235

Notes 245

Bibliography 279

Index 293

FIGURES

Figure 0.1 Proportion of *New York Times* and *Le Monde* articles featuring at least one percentage figure in them since 1945   15

Figure 1.1 Bill Dedman, a computer-assisted reporter, at his desk   28

Figure 1.2 "The Top 38 List of Excuses Government Agencies Give for Not Being Able to Fulfill Your Data Request"   41

Figure 1.3 "Cleaning Up Data from a File on Diskette"   41

Figure 2.1 "America's Best Colleges," rankings for 1994   66

Figure 3.1 The government activity of a French MP exposed through data, 2016   87

Figure 5.1 Comparing daily air quality in Paris and San Francisco   143

Figure 6.1 The investigation process initially imagined by the California Watch team   158

Figure 6.2 Adapting the data to "real-life evidence"   167

LIST OF FIGURES

Figure 6.3   Writing an ethical consideration into the mapping algorithm for the investigation of California schools' seismic safety   174

Figure 7.1   Word counts for French presidential candidates' speeches shown as raw occurrences, not frequencies, 2017   192

Figure 7.2   The infrastructure underpinning "The Weight of Words" project   197

Figure 8.1   The Homicide Report: an interactive map and a searchable database   206

Figure 8.2   One homicide covered in the Homicide Report in 2011   207

Figure 8.3   Distribution of the authors who posted comments on the Homicide Report according to the number of their comments, 2010–2016   210

Figure 8.4   Measuring agency in Homicide Report comments, 2010–2016   212

Figure 8.5   Distribution of the number of comments received with respect to homicides on the Homicide Report, 2010–2016   214

Figure 8.6   Radar chart comparing how superposters and nonsuperposters make sense of homicides, 2010–2016   217

Figure 8.7   Radar chart showing how occasional posters make sense of homicides involving police officers, 2010–2016   221

Figure 8.8   Radar chart showing how occasional posters make sense of homicides before and after their interaction with superposters, 2010–2016   225

Figure 8.9   Title and title-page photograph of "South Vermont Avenue: L.A. County's 'Death Alley,'" 2014   226

Figure 8.10 Graph locating the homicides committed on Vermont Avenue since 2007   227

ACKNOWLEDGMENTS

This book would not exist without the involvement of many others. It all started in Paris in 2008 with a conversation with Patrice Flichy, who suggested I look into the way journalists used the growing amount of data available to them. At the time, especially in France, the idea seemed a bit far-fetched. Nevertheless, over the years many people allowed me to follow this initially rather thin thread and ultimately to explore practices that were taking on growing importance.

Three people were critical to the success of the project. Éric Dagiral was the first. He believed in it enough to spend several weeks with me in Chicago in 2010 and again in San Francisco in 2012. Together we conducted half of the interviews for this book, which owes much to Éric's enthusiasm and involvement. Jean-Philippe Cointet also played a major part, investigating with me the data that provided the basis for chapter 8. His expertise in computational sociology and his great generosity allowed me to experience what data journalists were doing—renewing their methods with the hope of becoming better professionals. I have published several research articles with Éric and Jean-Philippe in which we tested some of the arguments made in this book.

ACKNOWLEDGMENTS

Around 2013, when it became clear that I wanted to extend these analyses and turn them into a book, Cyril Lemieux's support was decisive. For four years, we met regularly as part of my accreditation to supervise research, as it is called in the French academic system. I benefited greatly from his stimulating theoretical suggestions and advice on the organization of the book.

I would also like to express my gratitude to the many American and French journalists, activists, and developers who welcomed me, gave me their time, and shared their experiences with me. I especially think of Brian Boyer, Chase Davis, Adrien Gaboulaud, Nicolas Kayser-Bril, Alexandre Léchenet, Anne-Sophie Lechevallier, Darnell Little, and Pierre Falga.

Furthermore, this book owes much to ongoing discussions with several researchers over the past decade, including Jean-Samuel Beuscart, Dominique Boullier, Dominique Cardon, François Dedieu, Kevin Mellet, Ashveen Peerbaye, and my colleagues at Sciences Po's médialab. I also benefited from the feedback I received during and after work-in-progress presentations from Madeline Akrich, Yannick Barthe, Valérie Beaudouin, Bilel Benbouzid, Nicolas Benvegnu, Pablo Boczkowski, Sylvain Bourmeau, Romain Huret, Pierre-Benoît Joly, Seth Lewis, Juliette de Maeyer, Olivier Martin, Dominique Pasquier, Nathalie Pignard-Cheynel, Zvi Reich, Nikos Smyrnaios, and Jean-Marc Weller. I thank Angèle Christin, Vincent Lépinay, Grégoire Mallard, and Ignacio Siles as well for their encouragement and advice on the elaboration of the book.

French institutions also supported this project by giving me the resources to investigate in the United States: the Agence nationale de la recherche, the Ministry of Culture, and the Conseil national des universités.

My editor at Columbia University Press, Philip Leventhal, was a tremendous help throughout the prepublication process. He championed the project from our very first conversation and provided excellent guidance during the revision. I also thank the two reviewers who so generously helped me with the manuscript while remaining anonymous. Finally, my gratitude goes to Nonta Libbrecht-Carey, who was so helpful and efficient in polishing my English.

Paris, October 25, 2021

INTRODUCTION

Trying to Be Nonjudgmental

How can we try to be nonjudgmental by just showing?" This was the question Mark asked in September 2012 in the meeting room of a news organization based in the financial district of San Francisco. Mark and the two other people in the room were journalists, but of an unusual kind. Trained at journalism schools, they specialized in web development and data analysis, which led them to work for several major newspapers across the United States. On that day, they were discussing an online application that could allow users to compare local-government salaries in California. Their aim was to enable citizens to check whether their cities were well managed and whether some employees received abnormally high salaries. For Mark and his team, collecting and processing digital data constituted a way to contribute to the monitoring of local governments while keeping their own judgments at bay.

Their discussion seemed far removed from the conversations usually heard in newsrooms. It was about *variables, probability, unsupervised learning, input strings, statistical clustering,* and *linear algebra.* As the meeting went on, issues emerged that were closely linked to computer or statistical considerations. "Just showing" local-government salaries turned out to be a

INTRODUCTION: TRYING TO BE NONJUDGMENTAL

delicate operation—and not just because it required statistical and computer skills. Mark's primary concern was that this application might fuel "voyeuristic motivations" in users who wanted to "find out how much [their] neighbor[s] make[] so [they] can either make fun of them or hate them." How could the journalists ensure that more civic-oriented users would find this application helpful to hold their local government to account? A second concern related to the sources on which the journalists relied to compare the salaries of hundreds of thousands of employees across California. A fair comparison would require factoring in the cost of living in each city, for instance, which the team could ascertain using digital data from public authorities or think tanks. But how could these journalists be sure they were not relying on biased ways of describing the world? Throughout the meeting, the question arose as to which kind of statistical models would be appropriate for such a project. Some of these models were commonly used in marketing or biology, but at this point Mark and his colleagues were unsure about how these models could be used for journalistic purposes.

Since the outbreak of COVID-19 in 2020, computational approaches to journalism are no longer of concern solely to start-ups or news organizations seeking to be at the forefront of digital innovation. The pandemic has prompted many journalists and news organizations around the world to think about their work in computational terms. Journalists have found new ways to assess the virus's fatality rate without relying on official death counts,[1] developed epidemiological-modeling expertise to analyze the inequalities affecting underprivileged populations and racial minorities,[2] and designed visualization formats that afford citizens a more accurate and human representation of the epidemic beyond the abstraction of numbers.[3] However, employing these practices has brought journalists face to face with the following questions: How can they ensure the quality of data when the institutions that produce them are also being challenged? What forms of calculation are not only reliable but also likely to produce editorial content that allows people to make the right decisions and address the problems brought on by the pandemic?

This book focuses on the collective endeavor of journalists who have embraced computing as a means to demonstrate greater objectivity and,

INTRODUCTION: TRYING TO BE NONJUDGMENTAL

ultimately, increase journalism's contribution to democracy. Rallying around the term *data journalism*, which emerged in the United Kingdom in the late 2000s, a coalition of journalists has leveraged the growing availability of data and algorithms to address the multifaceted crises facing their profession. The major economic turmoil afflicting the news industry, the high level of public mistrust of journalism, and the relentless suspicion of partisanship by news professionals are all problems that greater investment in computational practices and technology has been expected to mitigate. More specifically, so-called data journalists have argued that integrating data practices and computational skills into newsrooms will allow the whole profession to better fulfill its mission to make governments more transparent, shed light on social issues, and help citizens make more informed decisions. Their goal has been to make newsrooms actual "calculation centers" rather than simply repositories for calculations performed by governments, research institutions, and think tanks. By building computational capabilities, these journalists aim to become less dependent on the agendas of authoritative actors and powerful interests.

Since the late 2000s, this movement has been led by new organizations and dedicated teams within established media in the United States (e.g., ProPublica, FiveThirtyEight, the *New York Times*' blog *The Upshot*), Europe (*Guardian, Le Monde, Die Zeit*), South America (*La Nación, Estadão*).[4] More recently, data journalism has spread to new outlets, and in 2019 one of the "data journalism awards" went to *FactChecker.in*, a small Indian newsroom that designed a database of religious hate crimes in India to cover an issue not recorded by official statistics.[5] The growth of this movement has also led to new forms of cooperation between journalists around the world to investigate transnational issues through the collection, processing, and release of massive databases. The most notable example has been the International Consortium of Investigative Journalists' projects around global tax evasion.[6]

"Computational journalism"—that is, the application of computation and computational thinking to journalistic activities[7]—now encompasses a diversity of practices: the use of data infrastructure to renew news-production practices; the integration of forms of computation drawn from academia or the digital industries to provide the public with robust analyses or compelling news products; the automation of the whole news-production process, reducing the resources needed to broaden the scope of news coverage and make it more timely; and the more intensive use of audience metrics and customer data to better satisfy audience preferences. Among these various computational practices, this book focuses on those that are initiated by journalists and not by media managers, consulting firms, or technology providers and that are carried out primarily within media organizations. I therefore use the term *data journalism*, which many journalists across the world currently use to present themselves to their peers and to the public. By embracing this umbrella term, they emphasize that the impetus to adopt these computational practices must come from journalists, with the aim of better fulfilling journalism's core missions. Accordingly, journalistic uses of audience metrics do not qualify as data journalism because those practices have mostly been imposed on journalists. For the same reason, the most common forms of "robot journalism" are not addressed here, for they are rarely initiated by journalists and are employed mainly for cost-cutting purposes.

THE PROMISES OF DATA JOURNALISM

Data journalism advocates have argued that the pursuit of greater objectivity would allow the profession to better fulfill its mission and that this can be achieved through computational methods.[8] They have pushed for the adoption of material and technological practices that strive for neutrality and factuality and avoid personal judgment and interpretation.[9] Simon Rogers, who coined the term *data journalism* in 2009 when he was an editor at the *Guardian*, emphasized this claim. In his book *Facts Are Sacred* (2013), Rogers declares that the journalistic ideals of the early twentieth century are now more necessary than ever, arguing that "ninety years later, publishing those sacred facts has become a new type of journalism in itself: data journalism."[10] U.S. advocates of data journalism have also stressed the need for journalists to show greater rigor in their news coverage. Nate Silver, the founder of the website FiveThirtyEight, has urged his fellow journalists to be more open to scientific method. In a series of tweets posted in 2017 in which he tried to define data journalism, he stated that "bolder claims require a higher burden of proof. Stories should not cherry-pick evidence."[11] This stance, widely shared by data journalists, exemplifies what the science historians Loraine Daston and Peter Galison have called "mechanical objectivity," referring to late nineteenth-century scientists' attempt to capture nature with as little human intervention as possible.[12]

Beyond these rather sweeping statements, it is possible to identify specific promises made by data journalism in its claims to contribute to democracy.[13] A first promise is that through interactive maps, search engines, and other web applications, data journalism provides citizens with a set of research tools that allow them to make more informed decisions—be it a voter deciding on a candidate, parents wondering which school will be best for their child, a resident seeking to know about the health risks of drinking tap water,[14] or a patient checking how much money her doctor is receiving from the pharmaceutical industry.[15] This claim is in line with the liberal justification for the importance of journalism in informing citizens and giving them the resources to make independent judgments. Yet while this is consistent with the standards of journalists around the world, data journalists have also been influenced by open-software communities and open-data advocates. Both movements have advocated giving citizens the broadest and easiest possible access to data on the grounds that web applications afford citizens greater agency.[16] In some Western countries, these movements have led some journalists to view data-driven applications as a way to ultimately get them more involved in public life.[17]

A second promise is that data journalism contributes to democracy by empowering news organizations to scrutinize those in power. The increasing availability of public and government data and the easier access to computational resources are expected to help data journalists more effectively monitor governments as well as powerful private organizations and people.[18] In addition to the legal mechanisms for access to administrative documents established in most Western countries in the 1960s and 1970s, data

INTRODUCTION: TRYING TO BE NONJUDGMENTAL

journalists have taken advantage of the tools offered by open-data activists (through the development of data portals, code libraries, etc.). Examples of this promise being fulfilled range from investigations conducted by national news organizations into how elected officials spend public money[19] to investigations, as already mentioned, carried out by international coalitions of journalists that have used massive databases to uncover tax-evasion schemes that benefited high-profile figures and companies in Western and non-Western countries.[20]

The third promise relates to the analysis of complex or systemic phenomena within society. As Michael Schudson argues, "Journalists aid democracy when they explain a complicated event or process in a comprehensible narrative."[21] Data analysis allows journalists new ways to identify and explain systemic processes within society by using statistical or visualization techniques. This is what the American pioneers of data journalism did in the 1970s when they collected data on lawsuits and bank loans and used quantitative social science techniques to uncover the discrimination suffered by African Americans.[22] Journalists are still doing this today when they seek to identify inequalities in how different social groups are affected by COVID or when they analyze how temperatures in a variety of cities have increased over the past fifty years.[23] The databases and the means of calculation make it possible to put a large number of different events in series and to identify patterns. This aspect of data journalism draws on the scientific disciplines and offers journalists resources for identifying systemic phenomena. But the journalists' specific task is to take this raw information and find clear ways to explain complex phenomena through visualization and other techniques.

A final promise, albeit less often stated, is that this form of journalism will cover events or populations previously excluded from the mainstream media. This aspect of data journalism takes as its starting point the criticism that the media select news they consider worthy of coverage by privileging institutional sources (e.g., the police, government officials, etc.) and pay less attention to disadvantaged populations or minorities. For example, journalists at the *Los Angeles Times* have maintained a popular platform since 2010 that collects data on all homicides in the city with a view to breaking with the established practice of prioritizing coverage only of homicides

INTRODUCTION: TRYING TO BE NONJUDGMENTAL

affecting white middle- and upper-class people.[24] Through this platform, the murders of young Black and Latinx men gain greater visibility and recognition throughout the city. Similarly, several journalistic projects have mobilized data and computation to give visibility to the prejudice and abuse experienced by women[25] and the tragedies confronted by migrants across the world.[26] These efforts, which often rely on gathering and collecting data with the help of citizens, allow journalists to use data and computational means to reduce their dependence on official institutions for information about marginalized groups.[27]

All of these promises have built on and reformulated conventional understandings of how journalism contributes to democracy. However, despite some of the successes of data journalism, its practices are not without their shortcomings.

PITFALLS AND CRITIQUES

Data journalism's emphasis on objectivity may seem at odds with the current media climate—especially in the United States, where many voices have been raised within the profession to denounce the fact that what is considered objective truth is decided almost exclusively by a journalistic establishment historically dominated by white male reporters and editors.[28] Black journalists, other journalists of color, female journalists, and transgender journalists have criticized the way in which the notion of objectivity has been used to define how news stories are framed and whose voices get heard. Data-driven and computational forms of journalism have sometimes been viewed as a way to further promote this "view from nowhere" that journalists have long claimed as their own but that is also entangled in a white male perspective. One of the strongest voices in this critique, Wesley Lowery, an award-winning American reporter known for his investigations of police violence, has called for the industry to "abandon the appearance of objectivity as the aspirational journalistic standard."[29] Not all of these voices have argued against the use of data in journalistic work, and Lowery himself built a national database of police killings and won a Pulitzer Prize for it in 2016. However, computational approaches have been criticized for being invented and championed primarily by white men, resulting in bias and little attention being paid to the perspectives of women, Blacks and other minority groups, and transgender people.[30] From this perspective, data journalism would only deepen the "coding gap" at play in the digital industry at large.[31] Thus, under the guise of seemingly neutral general values, the development of data journalism practices would in fact contribute to reinforcing the lack of diversity in the perspectives in journalism.

Furthermore, data journalism's emphasis on objectivity as an ideal does not guarantee neutrality when it comes to important public debates. In the United States, this was exemplified by several stories about climate change published by FiveThirtyEight. This news organization, which has been one of the most ambitious proponents of data journalism, was widely criticized for opening its columns to a contrarian environmental scientist whose controversial statements relied on data.[32] Thus, instead of providing clear-eyed analysis based on facts, FiveThirtyEight's use of data led to distortion and confusion.[33] As the economist Allison Schrager has written, there is concern that data may give journalists "a false sense of authority since data analysis is inherently prone to bias." Highlighting her own expertise as a data analyst, Schrager convincingly warns reporters that "anytime you use data it is subject to bias and it can be manipulated to push a particular point of view."[34]

Beyond analysis, the data always need to be questioned by journalists. Although at first glance databases may provide valuable facts and figures for reporters, it is not at all clear that they provide neutral information. First, statistical data, like any source of information, are produced by individuals and organizations who have certain interests and seek to promote a particular perspective on the world. In particular, leaks of digital data—like all leaks of documents—are an opportunity for the people behind the leaks to push their own agenda. Second, as science and technology studies have shown, data infrastructures are never neutral but convey political and moral choices and reflect power imbalances in society. By stabilizing categories and naturalizing differences, data infrastructure tends to promote certain entities or social groups over others.[35] This suggests that reusing data produced by institutions can make journalists dependent on classifications that are beyond their control. The claim that computational tools help journalists to produce and analyze "value-free" facts is therefore in no way self-evident.

Finally, other concerns have emerged about how citizens use applications or tools designed by data journalists. The rationale for these applications, as discussed earlier, is that individuals will be better informed thanks to these tools and consequently will make better decisions as citizens, which would eventually benefit society. But it is not at all obvious that these tools in fact enable citizens to make better decisions or even be more engaged in public life.[36] Moreover, in many cases these applications are used primarily by those whose education and jobs provide the access and skills to use, analyze, and understand statistics. Other concerns have been raised about whether these practices empower citizens to address collective problems—be it neighborhood crime or poor air quality. Journalists and critics have argued that this information does not necessarily lead citizens to mobilize because they may be more inclined to adopt what Albert Hirschman has called an "exit strategy":[37] instead of organizing to address a problem, they may simply move to another neighborhood or city. Some scholars have echoed these concerns, arguing that the growing availability of personalized information through the web and social media lead people to pay attention only to information that affects them personally or confirms their ideological preferences.[38]

Thus, despite the many accomplishments of data journalism, the promise of contributing to a stronger democracy through computational practices—by providing better information, monitoring those in power, offering analysis, and expanding media coverage—faces many obstacles. These doubts about data journalism raise several questions for the journalistic profession: Should it delve into these practices that use data and computational technology with a claim to objectivity at the risk of imposing a dominant perspective or failing to help citizens address major issues collectively? Or should journalism distance itself from these practices, stick to its more established working practices, and resist having data scientists, developers, and designers take a more active part in the production of news? The answers to these questions, as we shall see, are far from being agreed upon not only among journalists but also among social scientists, who study the increasing use of calculation and quantification by journalists and more widely in public affairs.

SOCIAL SCIENCE AND THE JOURNALISTIC SEARCH FOR OBJECTIVITY

In social scientific studies of journalism's objectivity, three different traditions emerge, each offering a particular albeit unsatisfactory way of approaching journalists' claim to objectivity though computational practices.

A first tradition, rooted in the history and sociology of statistics, posits that statistics are not always a "tool of power" in the hands of dominant classes who seek to defend their interests but can be a "tool of weakness" in the hands of dominated or resistant groups.[39] Theodore Porter's book *Trust in Numbers*, published in 1995, showed that statistical argumentation gives the more educated middle class the ability to challenge the social order and make injustice visible. More recently, this argument was further developed in research on "data activism," a contemporary form of protest that takes advantage of the abundance of digital data to monitor powerful actors and uncover social, economic, or environmental problems.[40] This research argues that easier access to a wider range of computational resources afforded by open-data policies and the development of digital technologies has allowed social movements and media organizations to gain more leverage with governments and institutions.

A second stream of research offers a more critical perspective on the journalistic claim to objectivity. Rooted in the sociology of journalism, it argues that data journalists' claim to objectivity should be seen as a facade or "strategic ritual" aimed at deflecting criticism.[41] The journalistic impetus to define standards—such as the requirement to present supporting evidence in a news story—is driven primarily by a desire to minimize the risk of lawsuits or attacks against the profession. In *Apostles of Certainty* (2018), Christopher Anderson argues that the claim of objectivity reaffirmed by data journalists is partly delusional in its response to the epistemic, cultural, and political crisis facing the profession. Although he recognizes journalism as a knowledge-producing institution, he argues that instead of "doubling down on objectivity," journalists ought to "become more humble and more willing to admit the complexity and uncertainty of more situations, rather than . . . aggressively shouting about their own professional confidence in the face of doubt."[42]

A last tradition, rooted in the "sociology of quantification," has investigated the growing public demand for numbers in the name of transparency and accountability in Western countries, studying how these numbers are produced and used to assess individuals and organizations in areas as diverse as politics, health, and education.[43] Although not interested primarily in journalism, a few sociologists have examined the impact of journalistic products such as university and hospital rankings on institutions and society. For example, Wendy Espeland and Michael Sauder found that the production of rankings by news organizations had profoundly transformed institutions by imposing standardization through "reactivity": "the idea that people change their behavior in reaction to being evaluated, observed, or measured."[44] Thus, rather than making institutions more transparent and accountable, such journalistic quantification practices—for example, the rating of colleges by *U.S. News & World Report*—would weaken institutions by making them reallocate a significant part of their resources and often manipulate the figures to improve their ranking.[45] More broadly, it is argued that these journalistic practices reflect and serve the rise of neoliberalism, in which individuals and organizations are systematically compared and put in competition with each other. Far from contributing to democracy, these data-driven rankings run the risk of weakening institutions for the sake of a false transparency.

This book enters into these debates regarding data journalism by, first, rejecting the notion that the primary purpose of these computational efforts is to protect the journalistic profession by emphasizing its objectivity.

INTRODUCTION: TRYING TO BE NONJUDGMENTAL

Although the crisis facing the profession is a key driver in the growth of data journalism, we must take data journalism's methods and aims seriously with real consequences beyond its impact on journalism's reputation. I see news organizations as knowledge-producing institutions. The information produced by journalists is not in itself of a different nature than that produced by scientists. More specifically, this book adopts a perspective rooted in science and technology studies[46] and so does not assess whether data journalists' claims to objectivity are valid or not. Rather, I analyze how journalists make knowledge claims that they collectively find acceptable.

I also recognize that quantification and computation can be a resource for news organizations to increase their contribution to democracy. However, the methods of data journalists in and of themselves do not guarantee that citizens will be better informed or that governments will be more controlled or that society's systemic problems will be revealed. Rather than focusing solely on the technology itself, I emphasize the importance of organizational cultures in the articulation of digital technology within journalism.[47] When implemented in particular organizational settings and embedded with a set of moral and political expectations, computational methods and digital technologies shape the relationship among journalists, their sources, and their audiences in different ways. More specifically, turning the newsroom into a "calculation center" involves relying on data providers, computational resources (such as algorithms, software, and statistical models), and their designers. Depending on organizational contexts and professional cultures, these relationships can take specific forms that produce news with varying emphases and effects.

Finally, I recognize that data journalism practices are part of a larger context, where a significant part of the population and authorities demand services that compare individuals, organizations, and institutions. Yet I do not consider that journalists' adoption of computational practices will necessarily lead to the weakening of institutions through a process of standardization. Because these practices are diverse and their effects on society are largely undetermined, I draw on pragmatic sociology to focus on how journalists evaluate these editorial products according to their own professional standards,[48] how they criticize and justify the work of data journalists, and how they build rules to ensure that these computational practices allow them to fulfill their democratic mission.

FIXING THE ETHICS OF JOURNALISM

To understand how data journalism can increase journalism's contribution to democracy, it is crucial to examine the ethics of data journalism—that is, the application of the standards that journalists set for their profession to data journalism. Specifically, by importing computational techniques and ways of knowing new to journalism, data journalists have come to depend on a broader array of human and nonhuman actors.[49] Turning the newsroom into a "calculation center" implies relying on data providers (the organizations and infrastructures that produce and communicate the data), computational resources (algorithms, software, and statistical models), as well as experts and practitioners (web developers, data scientists, social scientists). It also entails other ways of engaging the audience to allow citizens to access and interpret the data through interactive applications. Through the process of relying more on computational methods, news organizations have consequently come to depend on a broader set of actors—citizens, activists, social media platforms, application developers, and so on—who do not necessarily share their values regarding what constitutes worthy, useful, or responsible information.

This change in the division of journalistic labor is closely linked to the rise of the web. The development of online journalism over the past two decades has brought new actors into the news-production process—citizens, activists, social media platforms, application developers, and others. As a result, activities once viewed as inherently journalistic—collecting information, verifying it, interpreting it, and forming publics around it—are increasingly distributed across a range of actors.[50]

Moreover, this change in the division of labor has destabilized the professional ethics of journalists,[51] who are now faced with the following questions: How can we ascertain the quality of data? How can we be sure that the data are not biased? Under what conditions can data processing reduce the weight of biases in news production? What professional qualities should data journalists demonstrate? How should data work be distributed within and outside the newsroom? When and how does the publishing of data allow or not allow citizens to organize to address a problem? These questions point to the need for some new rules specifically for data journalists in their role as providers of news.

To determine which direction the ethics of data journalism might take, this book considers how U.S. and French data journalists as well as the professional groups in both countries have responded to professional standards that no longer seem adequate with respect to this form of journalism.

A FRENCH-U.S. COMPARISON

Although journalism in both France and the United States developed around a set of principles inspired by political liberalism,[52] media sociologists often contrast U.S. journalism's emphasis on facts and objectivity with European and particularly French journalism's tendency to give greater weight to politics and values.[53] The spread of data journalism appears to confirm this difference in professional culture. Computational practices in journalism have long been more widespread and more visible in the United States than in France. Yet journalists in both countries have a strong interest in numbers, as is evident in the articles published in the *New York Times* and *Le Monde* since 1945 (figure 0.1). Although percentages have long been more prevalently used in the U.S. newspaper, they have become comparably and even slightly more present in the French newspaper since the 1980s. Furthermore, French and American journalists have been able to access larger quantities of data than in many other countries because their governments have produced a wide range of statistics for decades. The journalists in these two countries have also adopted the web and digital technology within fairly similar timeframes.[54]

INTRODUCTION: TRYING TO BE NONJUDGMENTAL

—— Ratio of percentages in *Le Monde*   —— Ratio of percentages in the *New York Times*

FIGURE 0.1 Proportion of *New York Times* and *Le Monde* articles featuring at least one percentage figure since 1945.

Source: This graph was built from the complete *New York Times* archive using the newspaper's application programming interface and from a query of *Le Monde*'s internal database.

This book therefore does not assume that the difference in the spread of data journalism in the two countries can be explained by a different relationship to objectivity in French and U.S. journalism. To argue that the varying importance given to data journalism in France and the United States is simply the product of different attitudes toward objectivity in the two countries' professional groups would fall into the essentialist trap of culturalism. French journalism has undergone a series of significant transformations since the 1980s, including the rise of investigative reporting and the growing importance of commercial considerations, which have challenged the long-standing image of it as opinion-based journalism with little concern for facts. I argue that differences in data journalism practices are the product of a set of cultural arrangements in each country that either make or do not make such practices desirable, practical, and accountable. Such practices are desirable if journalists can see a benefit to themselves and their organization, whether from a civic or a commercial standpoint. They are practical not only if data collection is practically and materially possible but also if the data come with quality guarantees and can be linked to journalistic interests. Finally, these practices are justifiable when journalists are able to share them within their professional group to make them intelligible.

The comparison between the two countries sheds light on why data journalism practices have long flourished more in the United States than in France or any other country. For a long time, the autonomy of the French bureaucracy and its ability to monopolize expertise as well as the highly centralized nature of the French state made data journalism less desirable, less practical, and less accountable. Moreover, French journalism did not have individuals within its own ranks capable of translating computational technology for journalistic purposes. In the United States, by contrast, a distinct movement developed within journalism beginning in the 1970s to leverage computers and the growing availability of data. This movement wanted to reassert a kind of objectivity in the profession that was being increasingly challenged by "New Journalism" approaches and a more activist approach to reporting coming out of the social movements of the 1960s and 1970s. Under the label of "computer-assisted reporting," this movement carved out a segment of its own within U.S. journalism in the early 1990s, paving the way for the spread of data journalism in news organizations.

The comparison between France and the United States also highlights how data journalism challenges journalistic practices. In the United States, the division of journalistic labor around data is more pronounced than in France. Major U.S. news organizations hire a set of people with specialized skills (data analysis, visualization, web development, etc.), whereas French news organizations usually recruit a single person to perform a range of tasks—primarily for budgetary reasons and because technical profiles are viewed with suspicion. Moreover, data journalists' focus on technology is more of a problem in France, where the profession gives less importance to technique in the definition of the journalistic craft.[55] The implications for the ethics of journalism in France are twofold. On the one hand, this organization of labor gives less visibility to controversies within the profession in France because data journalists are often seen as handling technical tasks and less able to impose themselves on more "legitimate" journalists. On the other hand, French data journalists are viewed more skeptically by their colleagues, forcing them to find creative ways of setting new practical ethical standards. Ultimately, France and the United States do not offer two different models of how data journalism can be employed in news organizations; rather, the difference between the two countries is more one of degree than of nature. Yet the comparison does afford a better understanding of how data journalism practices are in the future likely to extend far beyond the United States, where they have flourished for several decades.

To analyze the different approaches to data journalism in both countries, I employ several research methods. The book provides a historical analysis by examining a variety of sources, including handbooks, biographies, and training materials for journalists. I also interviewed seventy-five people, including journalists, data journalists, programmers, and directors of technology in established news organizations in the United States (the *Chicago Tribune*, *U.S. News & World Report*, Center for Investigative Reporting, *Mother Jones*) and in France (*Le Monde*, *Libération*, *L'Express*, *Paris Match*) as well as in organizations specializing in computational journalism (EveryBlock.com, OWNI) and open government activism (MAPLight.org, NosDéputés.fr, etc.). Finally, I also draw on computational methods to study how data journalists manage to bring about publics through data-driven news products.

AN ETHICS OF REFLEXIVITY

By studying the United States and France from the late 1960s to the present day, this book illuminates a set of standards that have developed within data journalism. These rules outline what can be called an "ethics of reflexivity," aimed at ensuring that journalists' computational efforts align with the more traditional mission of the journalistic profession. Such an ethics is intended to foster a high degree of reflexivity on the part of news organizations in their handling of data and their assessment of the editorial products that result from the data. In other words, news organizations and professionals take into account the actions of all the human and nonhuman actors who contribute to the production of data and calculations.

This ethics of reflexivity involves several dimensions. First, journalists should not take the data for granted or assume that they reflect unbiased and unambiguous reality. Both in the United States and in France, journalists already have a set of ethical rules that prevent them from taking documents at face value. However, the issue of bias is far more pronounced with respect to data due to their more fluid circulation, the higher number of actors involved in their production, and the greater opacity of the choices that inform the production process. This book shows that certain ways of organizing journalistic work protect against the risk of bias by maintaining collective vigilance over the epistemic status of the data. Thus, news organizations need to resist the tendency to increase the division of labor surrounding data. As work on data becomes more segmented, news workers end up losing visibility over the choices made throughout the different data-processing stages.

Second, this renewed ethics calls for a rethinking of the relationship between journalists and the actors who have access to computational resources. The core principle of data journalism is that journalists should not delegate technological choices to actors who are alien to their values and concerns. However, the constant change in technologies and skills makes this principle difficult to guarantee in practice, and so journalists must accept a certain degree of delegation. The key is therefore to create the conditions for the profession as a whole to gain an understanding of technologies so that the technologies can be integrated into and put at the service of journalism. This requires establishing the conditions to open up the profession to technological profiles and to set up trading zones between journalists, data scientists and practitioners, industry technologists, and social scientists (e.g., through conferences). But it also requires that journalists be collectively aware of the constraints of their profession and of news organizations in order to make explicit what they collectively value in their interactions with other actors.

INTRODUCTION: TRYING TO BE NONJUDGMENTAL

Third, this set of standards moving toward greater reflexivity also applies to the relationship between journalists and their audience. It encourages journalists to identify the effects of their data and analysis on the shaping of publics. Sharing information in the form of data in no way guarantees that citizens will be able to make sense of this information and organize themselves collectively to address a problem. Again, this issue is not new to journalism in either France or the United States, but, given the volume of accessible data and the personalization possibilities afforded by web applications, it has taken on unprecedented significance. Journalists need to recognize the fact that the design of data news products shapes how publics might use them.

OUTLINE OF THE BOOK

The book is organized in three parts. The first looks at the history of how a handful of French and U.S. journalists pioneered a computational approach to news making between the late 1960s and the 1990s. The two chapters in this section identify two distinct paths to what is now considered "data journalism." In the decades before the internet era, journalists developed new ways of producing news with computers and the collection and analysis of data. However, several of these journalists faced resistance or skepticism from sources, colleagues, technologists, social scientists, and audiences. As part of their efforts to overcome these challenges, they designed standards that still currently inform how U.S. and French news organizations approach computational tools for journalism.

Chapter 1 retraces the first path to data journalism. In the late 1960s, a few U.S. investigative reporters began using computers to perform statistical data processing. At a time when journalistic objectivity was in crisis, their goal was to find new ways for the profession as a whole to make more robust claims. First under the label *precision journalism* and then later under the label *computer-assisted reporting*, they imported social science techniques into journalism to reveal injustices in the United States (socioeconomic

INTRODUCTION: TRYING TO BE NONJUDGMENTAL

inequalities, legal discrimination, etc.), achieving widespread professional recognition by the 1990s. This chapter shows how "computer-assisted reporters" developed a "politics of computation" by creating professional and organizational standards to help journalists maintain their independence from the government and to enhance their contribution to public debate.

Chapter 2 focuses on a second path to data journalism that has been mostly overlooked: the rise of journalistic rankings of hospitals and universities in the 1980s and 1990s. Building on consumer journalism, the U.S. and French journalists who pioneered this computational practice sought to provide readers with an objective evaluation of the quality of service they would receive in a university or hospital. Their goal was to provide information about and scrutiny of frequently opaque institutions. But this use of computation has come under strong criticism both inside and outside the profession on both sides of the Atlantic. Nevertheless, this chapter argues that these "ranker journalists" offer a valuable lesson for today's data journalists: the use of computation in journalism in no way guarantees a greater contribution to democracy, and it is paramount that journalists consider the consequences of their own computational practices.

The second part of the book analyzes the challenge that the growth of data journalism in the United States and France has raised for journalism as a profession since the mid-2000s. As discussed earlier, this technology-driven approach to journalism has challenged the profession as a whole. The three chapters in this section show how data journalism has formed as a new segment within the profession, crystallizing around the issue of journalistic objectivity. Data journalists have sought to make governments more transparent and news organizations more open, while trying to mitigate the role of personal judgment in reporting and analyzing the news. These efforts by data journalists have often prompted strong and legitimate reactions from more traditional journalists skeptical of the promises being made. Although this dispute has materialized differently in France and the United States due to professional and institutional differences, critics of data journalism on both sides of the Atlantic have raised important ethical questions.

INTRODUCTION: TRYING TO BE NONJUDGMENTAL

Chapter 3 investigates how data journalism has emerged as a more defined professional segment in the United States and France in recent years, with the primary purpose of "rebooting journalism." Such emphasis on technology is often at odds with the way the profession established itself in both countries, rooting its identity in the mastery of general skills such as writing and news gathering. This chapter demonstrates that the rise and characteristics of data journalism are closely linked to a series of developments that have affected the web since the mid-2000s. By creating data-driven infrastructures and services, web companies, open-source communities, and open-data activists have enabled people with computer skills to claim a more active role in the production of editorial content. Rather than passively observe the growing role of these actors and in a context where journalism has seen its social role and working conditions profoundly weakened, a group of journalists has promoted an alternative vision of how technology can be used in journalism. Arguing that news organizations should set up dedicated units staffed with people equally familiar with both journalism and code, they have attracted a growing number of individuals eager both to change journalism and to secure a place for themselves in a very competitive job market.

Chapter 4 considers the differing importance that the profession has given data journalism in France and the United States, challenging the tale of two different professional cultures. I argue that although data journalism has developed both more recently and less extensively in France and remains far less visible, this is not due primarily to French journalists attributing greater value to the expression of opinions and less to facts. This chapter proposes an alternative perspective of the cultural differences underlying the development of data journalism in both countries. Drawing on pragmatic sociology, I argue that France has long displayed particularities that made it rather inhospitable to journalistic practices involving the collection and processing of digital data. The considerable autonomy of the French bureaucracy and its ability to monopolize expertise, combined with the highly centralized nature of the French state and the absence of translators within the journalistic profession, made such practices at once less

INTRODUCTION: TRYING TO BE NONJUDGMENTAL

desirable, more impractical, and less accountable. I then show that the dynamics of the web, in particular the rise of the open-data movement, has allowed the rise of these practices in French journalism by increasing their desirability, practicability, and accountability.

Chapter 5 examines the epistemological claims made by data journalists regarding their ambition to reboot journalism and how these claims have fueled controversy within journalism. Because the debates have been more pronounced in the United States than in France, this chapter focuses on U.S. journalism. Data journalists have urged fellow journalists to change their practices in four different ways with a view to increasing their contribution to democracy by placing an even great emphasis on (1) making governments more accountable, (2) keeping reporters' personal opinions out of their work, (3) being more transparent about news production, and (4) providing more services to readers. Although data journalists rely heavily on technology and knowledge drawn from outside journalism (web development, algorithms, statistical modeling, data science, etc.), each of these shifts builds on standards that are widely shared within the profession. As soon as data journalists started producing news guided by this new approach, however, other fellow journalists began sounding the alarm. Those shifts, the latter argued, were going too far either because they had an effect opposite to the one initially intended or because they conflicted with other standards equally important to the profession, such as not harming individuals or undermining the organization's resources. The core argument of this chapter is that data journalism has been deeply affected by ethical, epistemological, and organizational tensions, which has provided the opportunity to set limits on how computing technology could and should be used without jeopardizing professional values. This chapter concludes by discussing how in neither the United States nor France is there consensus on how data and algorithms might help journalism better contribute to democracy and how their dangerous effects might be curtailed.

The last part of the book scrutinizes "data journalism in the making." Because data journalism is affected by tensions between objectivism (the attitude of considering the data as reflecting reality) and constructivism (the attitude of questioning the conditions of data production), it is helpful

INTRODUCTION: TRYING TO BE NONJUDGMENTAL

to investigate how some news organizations have successfully overcome that divide. I focus on three widely lauded individual news projects in the United States and France. Each chapter identifies the organizational, practical, ethical, and cognitive conditions in which the use of data and algorithms can strengthen the voice of journalists in their coverage and analysis of public issues. Chapter 6 focuses on an investigation by the San Francisco–based Center for Investigative Reporting. Processing data from California public authorities, the center revealed that the State of California had failed to enforce earthquake-safety standards in public schools. The story reached millions of readers and was a finalist for a Pulitzer Prize. This organization overcame the tension between the effort to make government more transparent and the fact that the data used for the investigation was produced by the government. I defend the counterintuitive idea that by questioning the conditions of data production, the journalists were able to produce revelations through computation. The chapter outlines the organizational settings developed by the center's journalists to remain constructivist throughout the investigation.

Chapter 7 investigates a news project led by two journalists from the French magazine *Paris Match* between 2016 and 2019. This project, titled "The Weight of Words" ("Le poids des mots"), originally aimed to cover the French presidential campaign of 2016–2017 in a more objective way by collating all the speeches made by the main candidates in a database. In a political context marked by the rise of candidates outside the traditional parties, the web application made available to citizens throughout the campaign as well as the dozens of articles published in the magazine contributed to a better understanding of a changing political landscape. Since *Paris Match* worked closely with a research laboratory specializing in the quantitative analysis of political discourse, this project offered an opportunity to explore how journalists should work with scientists. The data journalists had to be cognizant of avoiding two pitfalls: using science merely as a facade of objectivity and, conversely, aligning their practices too closely with those of scientists—for example, by not paying attention to the time constraints they faced as news professionals or spending too much time on methodological issues that interested only the scientific community. This chapter

INTRODUCTION: TRYING TO BE NONJUDGMENTAL

shows that by establishing a symmetrical relationship with scientists, finding trade-offs between scientific standards and journalistic constraints, and building a data infrastructure focused on newsworthiness, the *Paris Match* journalists established practices particularly well suited to the challenges that data journalism raises in the relationship between journalists and scientists.

Chapter 8 focuses on the Homicide Report, a homicide map/database/blog launched by the *Los Angeles Times* in 2010 that exemplifies data journalists' turn to data and algorithms to raise citizens' awareness of a problem and mobilize them to address it. By covering all homicides through data, this news platform broke with the established journalistic practice of prioritizing coverage of homicides affecting only white middle- and upper-class people. The *Los Angeles Times* team eventually succeeded in developing publics around the problem of urban violence. I argue that this achievement is contingent on a twofold shift: first, journalists must show a certain humility by relinquishing part of their gatekeeping prerogative, which remains a central tenet of their professional identity; and, second, they must also adopt a set of practices aimed at fostering and channeling the development of publics—that is, creating spaces for discussion, defining rules to allow for a wide range of people to engage with and debate issues, and producing editorial content based on the data at stake.

The conclusion outlines an ethics of reflexivity that would be better suited to the emerging division of labor in journalism. As journalists become increasingly dependent on new actors, they have to rely on new ethical rules to ensure that their computational efforts remain aligned with the missions they have set for themselves as professionals.

PART I

TWO PATHS TO DATA JOURNALISM

1
REVEALING INJUSTICE WITH COMPUTERS, 1967–1995

Sitting at his desk in the *Atlanta Journal-Constitution*'s newsroom, Bill Dedman stares at us with resolute eyes. As one looks at this photograph (figure 1.1), one senses that Dedman was proud of the device sitting on his desk. Personal computers were still quite rare in U.S. newsrooms when this picture was taken in 1988. More significant than the novelty of having a computer, Dedman had just published the results of an investigation that would not have been possible without computing technology. Based on the collection and statistical processing of data, his investigation revealed racial discrimination in mortgage lending by Atlanta banks.[1] One can only assume that Bill's pride did not vanish after the picture was taken: his series was awarded a Pulitzer Prize for investigative reporting the following year.

In this chapter, I retrace the first of two paths that led to the contemporary journalistic practices known as "data journalism." From Philip Meyer's pioneering investigation on Detroit rioters in 1967 to the advent of the web in the mid-1990s, reporters such as Bill Dedman began collecting and processing data with computers to reveal injustices in the United States. First under the label *precision journalism* and later under the label *computer-assisted*

TWO PATHS TO DATA JOURNALISM

FIGURE 1.1 Bill Dedman, a computer-assisted reporter, at his desk.
Source: Photograph courtesy of the *Atlanta Journal-Constitution*.

reporting, these U.S. reporters introduced social science techniques into journalism. A few decades before the web appeared, they took advantage of both computer technology and the growing availability of digitized information to enhance the way journalism contributed to democracy.

A few journalism scholars[2] and social scientists[3] have studied this history. In his book *Apostles of Certainty* (2018), Chris Anderson analyzes how these practices started developing in the United States from the early twentieth century at the crossroads of social science and investigative reporting.[4] Anderson rightly identifies these emerging practices as an effort to reestablish the notion of journalistic objectivity that had been called into question during the 1960s. How U.S. reporters took up emerging computer technology while staying true to their professional values has not yet been investigated, though. Using computers for journalistic purposes was in no way straightforward at the time. Computers were cumbersome and difficult to operate in news organizations; public records were hard to obtain in a computerized format; and social science expertise did not easily bend to the constraints of journalistic work. In this chapter, I consider the material, epistemic, and organizational obstacles U.S. reporters faced beginning in the late 1960s in trying to uncover injustice through data analysis and how they managed to overcome these obstacles.

My argument is that through their struggle to adjust these data news practices to the core values of the profession, a group of U.S. investigative reporters paved the way for contemporary data journalism practices. Between the late 1960s and the mid-1990s, they forged a professional identity and established material and organizational rules that allowed for the use of data analysis to uncover injustices. Although this collective experiment occurred well before journalism was transformed by online technology, it defined a distinct way of aligning computers with the core values of the profession—a way still followed today by many news organizations throughout the world.

INVESTIGATING INJUSTICE BY NUMBERS

In the late 1960s, a handful of young U.S. reporters began collecting data and processing them with computers for their reporting, and their stories made a lot of noise within the profession. With text, tables, and occasionally charts, they uncovered injustices within U.S. society by capturing social issues with numbers: in 1967, Philip Meyer showed that Detroit rioters were neither the most disadvantaged nor the least educated men in the city but rather young college graduates frustrated with not advancing as quickly as their white peers.[5] Processing crime statistics, David Burnham demonstrated that, contrary to popular belief, Black men were by far the primary victims of urban violence in New York.[6] Analyzing court records, Donald Barlett and James Steele established that the Philadelphia judicial system was discriminating against racial minorities.[7]

TWO PATHS TO DATA JOURNALISM

These data-driven investigations became more common in the late 1980s, though they were still on the outer fringes of mainstream journalism. Labeled "computer-assisted reporting" at the time, these practices targeted a broader set of organizational and institutional issues—police misconduct,[8] wrongdoings by civil servants,[9] unequal treatment of citizens by federal agencies,[10] customer discrimination by businesses, and so on. They often challenged common perceptions, such as Stephen Doig's investigation for the *Miami Herald* on damage in the wake of Hurricane Andrew in 1992, which revealed through statistical analysis that the hurricane destroyed so many houses not because of the strength of the wind but rather because of noncompliance with construction standards.[11] Several of these investigations went on to win awards, including the Pulitzer.

How can we explain the development of these journalistic practices in the United States during this period? Beginning in the late 1950s, government agencies started keeping electronic records and maintaining databases on an increasingly diverse range of topics.[12] Journalists were gradually able to access some of these records under the Freedom of Information Act (FOIA). Passed in 1966 and subsequently supplemented, this legal framework guaranteed citizens access to government documents—albeit not necessarily digitally. By the 1980s, news organizations could more easily collect documents in a computer-readable format. With the spread of personal computers within news organizations from the mid-1980s to the mid-1990s, journalists could now better analyze these records and data.

Two other trends were also at play in the rise of these journalistic practices. The first was the type of investigative reporting that emerged in the United States in the 1960s. As several historians have shown, these investigative practices were informed by a very particular mode of production of journalistic knowledge.[13] Investigative reporting required considerable material and cognitive resources to collect and analyze huge amounts of documents. Thus, as James Aucoin puts it, investigative reporters developed the skills necessary for "organizing, correlating, and evaluating massive amounts of information" and for "conceptualizing stories at a systemic level, concentrating on patterns of abuse, illegalities, and corruption rather than on a few wrongdoers."[14] These two challenges—organizing vast amounts of documents and finding patterns across them—created a need for statistical analysis in the investigative process and gave both opportunities and credibility to young reporters interested in computer-assisted journalism and quantitative social science.

More fundamentally, these journalistic practices were also shaped by the growing influence of social science in postwar America. In the 1960s, the work of social scientists aroused great interest within the American government because they embraced more quantitative methods of inquiry and focused on various social problems.[15] A significant proportion of U.S. institutions viewed political science in particular as a means to improve public decision making in an increasingly complex society. During this time, a growing number of reporters began to train in social science and familiarize themselves with a systemic approach to social issues.[16] With the use of statistical evidence, their main intention was to demonstrate more widespread issues that could not be explained by the supposed morality of a few individuals.

In the next section, I look at how one of these pioneers sought to convince his peers that computers and quantitative social science were key to restoring journalistic objectivity.

RESTORING JOURNALISTIC OBJECTIVITY

In the 1970s, Philip Meyer was instrumental to the recognition of these news practices within the profession. He was among the very first reporters to publish major investigations based on computer and statistical analysis, to engage in the design of digital infrastructure, and to build strong relationships with social scientists. Most importantly, he tried to convince his peers that such endeavors would allow the journalism profession as a whole to address some of the major epistemological problems it faced. Philip Meyer not only was the first to defend these ideas in the 1970s but also probably the most visible in the profession. To this day, he is considered the pioneer of data journalism, as demonstrated by the creation of the Philip

Meyer Journalism Award in the mid-2000s to give greater visibility to journalistic uses of social science research methods.

Born in 1930, Meyer became a reporter for the *Miami Herald* in the late 1950s. With a background in political science, he started to practice investigative journalism and revealed several corruption scandals in Florida and Washington. The year 1966 marked a turning point in his career. He obtained a Nieman Fellowship at Harvard, where he became familiar with quantitative social science and first used a computer to perform statistical calculations. On several occasions, he presented this experience as an epiphany: "As a graduate student, I had avoided quantitative methods because of the drudgery. But here was a machine that could do the heavy lifting. As long as I understood what went into the black box and what came out, I could apply statistics to interesting questions. It would not give me X-ray vision like Clark Kent, but it did seem like a kind of superpower."[17] In the following years, he worked hard to convince his peers of the value of this "superpower." Speaking at many professional conferences and publishing a book for students and reporters, *Precision Journalism: A Reporter's Introduction to Social Science Methods* (1973),[18] he argued that the combination of social science and computers could strengthen the profession as a whole. Drawing on the strong criticisms that had been leveled at U.S. journalism in the 1960s, he made the case that the profession was facing a major epistemological problem.

According to him, journalists were able neither to evaluate government nor to provide objective accounts of major social issues. A first source of concern was that public officials were increasingly using statistics to justify their actions to the public. Meyer argued that reporters were in no position to know when they were being manipulated: "Such sources of spurious findings as regression toward the mean, testing effect and the use of testimonials may be helpful to public officials who do not wish to risk subjecting their programs to honest evaluation. But we cannot afford to let them go unrecognized and uncriticized. We must know enough about evaluation research and its pitfalls to judge when we and our readers are being led astray."[19] A second source of concern related to the political turmoil of the 1960s. According to Meyer, news organizations could not determine the influence that political leaders had on U.S. society: "Media coverage of both the civil rights movement and the anti-Vietnam War movement suffered from the same problem. Journalists were drawn to the most outrageous and extreme spokespersons of those movements, and it was never clear who or how many they represented."[20] Given the situation, Meyer called for journalists to engage in intensive fact-finding efforts. As he put it in the first pages of *Precision Journalism* in 1973,

> Instead of starting from a base of personal conviction, ideology, or conventional wisdom we can start with intensive and systematic fact-finding efforts. Such a suggestion may seem to be a plea for a reactionary return to the old ideal of objectivity, but it has this difference: instead of reporting competing viewpoints for what they are worth, we could make an effort to determine just what they are worth. It is not necessary to turn our backs on interpretation. It is necessary to reduce the size of the leap from fact to interpretation, and to find a more solid base of fact from which to leap.[21]

His solution to this epistemological crisis was for journalism to become "social science in a hurry." Thanks to computers, he argued, social scientists were fulfilling the missions that reporters claimed to be theirs: "finding facts, inferring causes, pointing to ways to correct social problems, and evaluating the efforts of such correction."[22] By adopting social science methods, reporters would be in a position to make more robust claims and ultimately to play a more important role in U.S. society. Meyer argued that reporters were well equipped to engage in these practices on a regular basis: "Social scientists speak wistfully of the need for 'fire-engine' research to bring quantitative measurement to bear on fast-breaking events. We journalists, with our fast reaction time and experience at focusing large-scale resources on small but crucial events, are the more likely firemen."[23] Meyer's proposal caught the interest of many journalism students and several managers in the news industry. Moreover, his practice of in-house polls spread to some U.S. newspapers.[24] Yet most U.S. reporters never identified with the idea of becoming "social scientists in a hurry." Meyer gave up his career as a reporter in 1980 to become a journalism professor at the University of Chapel Hill, and, as we shall see, his relative failure in sustaining his vision of journalism can be explained by the numerous obstacles faced by journalists who wanted to investigate with computers in the early 1980s.

OVERWHELMING OBSTACLES

During the 1970s and 1980s, many U.S. journalists were seduced by the idea of investigating social problems with numbers. As soon as they tried to put this into practice, however, they were faced with a wide range of material, cognitive, legal, and organizational obstacles. First, accessing a computer was no easy feat at the time. Until the mid-1980s, not only were the only computers available in news organizations voluminous and cumbersome—they were referred to as "mainframe computers" as opposed to "personal computers"—but they were also often located in the newspaper's management department. Moreover, using them to perform statistical analysis was especially problematic because the available software had been designed for business and accounting purposes. In those years, journalists had to choose: either they found a way to use management software for journalistic purposes, or they had to use a computer at a research center or university. As Elliot Jaspin—who launched into this type of investigation in the early 1980s—pointed out later, this material constraint put off most reporters: "When I started doing computer-assisted reporting at the *Providence Journal*, I was doing it on a mainframe. It was successful, and I was invited to conferences to explain what I was doing. So I get up there, and I go through it, and people got really excited about it. And they said, 'How could I do it?' And I said, 'First you have to use a mainframe,' and people go, 'No way!'"[25] Accessing the data was another issue. Until the early 1980s, collecting digitally stored information was very rare for news organizations. The reporters I mentioned at the start of this chapter were collecting paper records, which they had either produced (such as the opinion polls conducted by Meyer) or obtained from courts and administrations. Once they had gotten hold of these paper documents, they had to extract relevant information and turn it into computer-readable punch cards. Needless to say, such material practices were at odds with the usual constraints of the news-making process.

By the early 1980s, it had become more common for news organizations to obtain public records in an electronic format both because agencies were managing larger amounts of information in computer databases and because computer records were legally established as falling within the scope of the FOIA.[26] Nevertheless, it was still very challenging for journalists to access information in a computer-readable format. The first reason for this was technological: most administrations stored their records on magnetic tapes, which could not be read on a personal computer—the connection was technologically impossible at the time. Most reporters thus could not take advantage of the growing availability of personal computers and electronic records. The second reason was legal: significant limitations were introduced that made it difficult for news organizations to collect public records in an electronic format.[27] A couple of court decisions established that agencies were not required to supply records in an electronic format—only to provide information "in a reasonably accessible form,"[28] such as on paper or microfilm—and that citizens could not force governments to perform computer analysis for the citizens' own benefit.[29] As a result, news organizations were often provided with flawed or inoperable computer records.

Assuming a reporter had collected computer-readable data and found a way to process it, another major difficulty stood in her way: How should she make sense of the data? And, most importantly, how should she turn it into a news product? This cognitive obstacle was difficult to overcome in those years, and a great number of reporters never managed to publish investigations of the kind with real journalistic value. Clarence Jones, one of the first reporters to have carried out this type of investigative story, offered a powerful account of the difficulties he faced in the late 1960s. At that time, he was counting court decisions for the *Miami Herald* with the aim of revealing discrimination in the judicial system. But the more calculations and analyses he performed with the computer, the less he could draw coherent arguments from the data. This problem almost caused him to give up on his investigation, and when it was ultimately published, it did not receive any public or professional attention. Interviewed several decades later, he reached the following conclusion: "The most important thing I learned is that a computer can only count. If we aren't smart enough to tell it what to count, all we get is garbage."[30] In those years, statistical analysis raised other cognitive concerns among U.S. journalists. Some actors within the profession worried that the growing use of statistics would prevent reporters from grasping the human dimension of social problems. As one journalism professor wrote in the early 1970s, "There is danger that one may think of social problems in terms of means and medians and standard deviations rather than involving human beings about whom journalists must write."[31] Although Meyer's intention was not to overlook the human dimension of news, some in the profession feared that readers would find little interest in news products filled with numbers and technical terms.

Finally, the last obstacle was organizational. The investigations carried out before the 1990s were consistently based on an extensive network of human and nonhuman actors.[32] This was particularly striking at the start of the period. When Meyer investigated the motivations of Detroit rioters in 1967, he relied heavily on his familiarity with scholarship on the subject.[33] He began by adopting the research protocol developed in 1965 by sociologists who had studied the Watts riots (which they eventually published in 1969).[34] He then formed a team with a political scientist, a statistician, and a psychologist from the University of Michigan Institute for Social Research. Once the team members had obtained the list of Detroit residents from city hall, it defined a sample of residents and hired people to administer the survey. After collecting the four hundred forms distributed and converting the data in them into punch cards, they were granted access to a computer at the University of Michigan and were assisted by a programmer. In parallel, the *Detroit Free Press* editors successfully obtained funding from private donors. This example puts into perspective the number of actors who had to be involved to carry out a computer-assisted investigation, especially within a limited timeframe. Compared to traditional investigations, data journalism required a much larger network of actors—which was impossible for the vast majority of news organizations at the time.

With the rise of personal computers in newsrooms, the size of the networks supporting these investigations decreased over the 1980s, but they remained significant. When investigating racial discrimination by Atlanta banks at the end of that decade, Bill Dedman had no choice but to rely on research and statistical methods developed by scholars from three different universities.[35]

We can see just how discouraging all these constraints must have been for U.S. reporters who might have been convinced by Philip Meyer's arguments. Those who were genuinely concerned about journalism's epistemological crisis simply could not engage in these investigative practices: doing so would have required them to ignore their professional obligation to take into account the human and material resources of their news organization and to provide readers with intelligible and appealing news products in a timely way.[36]

In this chapter, I make the case that a coalition of so-called computer-assisted reporters had already overcome some of these obstacles by the time the web was developed in the mid-1990s. By building infrastructure, forging a new professional identity, and laying down rules for conducting such investigations, they had defined a unique way to align computers with professional standards. They thus paved the way for contemporary data journalism.

BUILDING INFRASTRUCTURE

By the late 1980s, a coalition of investigative journalists formed around the label *computer-assisted reporting*. It grew from a few dozen members to several hundred by the mid-1990s. Just like their counterparts in the 1970s, they intended to foster investigative practices based on computerized statistical analysis. They shared the conviction that such practices offered the opportunity to better fulfill journalistic missions by increasing the journalistic contribution to public debate. Although they used social science techniques, their primary concern was not to bridge the gap between journalism and social science. Technology was their primary concern as they collectively looked for ways to overcome the various obstacles described earlier, primarily by creating infrastructure—understood here as sociotechnical settings developed outside of news organization.[37]

Elliot Jaspin was a major protagonist of this collective initiative. He had made his debut as an investigative reporter in the mid-1970s, developing skills in the qualitative analysis of public records that earned him a Pulitzer Prize in 1979. A couple of years later at the *Providence Journal*, he started carrying out investigations based on electronic records. Like Meyer, he saw computers as affording greater objectivity. Being able to analyze huge amounts of public documents, he claimed, would make reporters less dependent on internal sources within government administrations.

Jaspin first tackled the difficulty of how to read magnetic tapes on a personal computer. In 1989, with the help of a programmer he designed a computer device and a software program to eliminate this problem. That same year he began selling personal computers equipped with a system called NineTrack Express. For between $9,000 and $12,000,[38] a reporter could analyze electronic government records with commercially available data-management software.

Also in 1989, Jaspin founded what we now know as the National Institute for Computer-Assisted Reporting (NICAR). Hosted at the University of Missouri, this institute was initially designed to train students and reporters across the United States. At the time, Jaspin also envisaged that any reporter could send his or her database to the institute for analysis using the University of Missouri's mainframe computers.[39] Although this part of the project never materialized, NICAR contributed to the development of two types of infrastructure. First, it began systematically to record a growing set of practical solutions for all the sociotechnical difficulties mentioned in the previous section—how to get data from governments, how to analyze electronic records using computers and statistical software, and so on.

Second, it started to provide news organizations with a catalog of available databases and to sell some databases that had been cleaned, checked, and prepared for analysis.

At the same time, another journalist was also developing similar infrastructure. David Burnham had been one of the first U.S. reporters to use statistical data in his investigative reporting. Famous for his investigations into corruption within the New York Police Department in early 1970s, Burnham was also highly critical of the role played by journalists in the United States. Since the early 1970s, he had constantly argued that bureaucracies were becoming too powerful in the country, to the detriment of citizens.[40] He believed that journalists, those "high priced stenographers," as he called them,[41] were in no position to counter the growth of bureaucratic power. Just as Jaspin was launching NICAR, Burnham partnered with Susan Long, a social scientist, to build the Transactional Records Access Clearing House (TRAC) platform, hosted by Syracuse University. The pair made systematic FOIA requests to collect a great number of databases from federal agencies (including the IRS and the FBI) and started to sell their databases to news organizations to allow journalists to have greater access to government statistics.[42] Meanwhile, NICAR played an important role in creating a community of practice. When Jaspin created the institute, his goal was to train students and reporters to investigate through data processing and analysis. His first students were investigative reporters experienced in analyzing printed documents.[43] Under the supervision first of Jaspin and later of the nonprofit Investigative Reporters and Editors, the teaching focused not on statistics as such but rather on a series of practical problems related to data collection, processing, and analysis. As Jaspin explained later, using computers and databases for journalistic purposes required significant training:

> It takes quite a lot of time and dedication to learn how to use the computer, to understand how the information is stored electronically, how to query that information using database software, how to get it from an agency, and there's a lot of technical questions there. So it's not like

picking up the phone and punching in some numbers. This requires some training, work, and some background and also some imagination in terms of saying, "OK, we have one database here; other databases exist out there, and how can we match those up in some reasonable kind of way to produce a result that nobody has ever seen before?"[44]

By the early 1990s, NICAR provided assistance to all reporters involved in this type of investigation. A mutual-assistance network of members and trainers was set up. Institute members regularly stressed that reporters could ask questions and discuss any problems they encountered, an offer regularly reiterated in internal documents: "Most important, however, is to remember that there are a bunch of extremely helpful people throughout the country who are willing to take the time on the phone to save you from going into, or spending too much time in, one of these tarpits," one NICAR tipsheet informed its readers.[45] Most significantly, the institute was at the forefront of a collective effort to formalize practical knowledge. When a reporter found a practical solution to one of the problems listed in the previous section, and if the NICAR community validated this solution, it was then formalized in the form of a tipsheet or in a newsletter. As a result, computer-assisted reporters were gradually able to overcome the many obstacles they faced. By late 1995, nearly five hundred tipsheets were available for reporters who had paid a fee or attended the training courses. One of these tipsheets, written in 1994, explained how a reporter should contact government agencies to obtain data (figure 1.2). Drawing on the experience of many journalists, the document presented a series of efficient replies a reporter could give a government employee who apologized for not being able to produce a requested data set.

Other tipsheets aimed to solve problems surrounding data preparation and cleaning. One in 1992 explained to reporters what they could do when dealing with poor-quality data (figure 1.3). The introduction was very practical: "You find out that a small state agency has collected information on thousands of businesses and keeps that information on a diskette.... [Y]ou discover that the agency's file is, unsurprisingly, fraught with problems, including garbage characters." The tipsheet then outlined the various tasks that the reporter needed to carry out to have a database tailored to his investigation.

We don't know how to do that.
- Let me show you how
- Don't you know how to do your job?
- Then who does know how to do it?
- I'd like to meet the programmer that set it up.
- I'd like to talk with your boss.

Take your equipment there and dump it yourself.

It's too late in the day to do that.
- What time to you open tomorrow?
- It shouldn't take that long.
- What are you going to do, and how long will it take?
- Might the data center be able to do it then?

Give yourself plenty of lead-time for data requests. Be clear about what you're needing, there may already be a report.

FIGURE 1.2 "The Top 38 List of Excuses Government Agencies Give for Not Being Able to Fulfill Your Data Request."

Source: NICAR Tipsheet No. 204 (1994), archived at https://www.ire.org/resources/.

Tech tips

By Brant Houston
The Hartford Courant

SUBJECT: Cleaning up data from a file on diskette so you can run a match in XDB.

PROBLEM: You find out that a small state agency has collected information on thousands of businesses and keeps that information on a diskette. You want to merge that information with your own separate database of a couple of hundred business names.

Before you can worry about spelling differences in the names, you discover that the agency's file is, unsurprisingly, fraught with problems, including garbage characters. And after you import it into a database, you discover an even sneakier problem.

FIGURE 1.3 "Cleaning Up Data from a File on Diskette."

Source: NICAR Tipsheet No. 67 (1992), archived at https://www.ire.org/resources/.

Through this process of formalization and dissemination of practical knowledge, NICAR greatly helped to reconcile these emerging investigative practices with professional standards. As an infrastructure, NICAR provided computer-assisted reporters with a set of practical rules that were constantly adjusted to the ongoing stream of technological, legal, and political developments. A community of practice thus developed from the late 1980s.

Infrastructure, however, was not the only means this coalition used to align these investigative practices with professional standards. A professional identity was also forged, the computer-assisted reporter, who at the time played a significant role in the alignment.

A NEW PROFESSIONAL IDENTITY

Until the early 1990s, most journalists who engaged in these news-production practices identified primarily as investigative reporters. But a growing number of them, especially the youngest, claimed to be "computer-assisted reporters" for two reasons. First, several data-driven investigations published in the early 1990s were highly regarded by the profession, and self-proclaimed computer-assisted reporters viewed this newly won recognition as an opportunity to stand out in a highly competitive labor market. Second, young reporters often embraced this label as a personal commitment. Computer-assisted reporters did not see themselves as regular journalists but as "disciples" who intended to "evangelize" their colleagues.[46] Accounts from the time suggest that these journalists were animated by a "kind of religious zeal."[47]

In the first half of the 1990s, reporters involved in NICAR carved out a new identity within the profession. In their view, computer-assisted reporters were not only journalists with computer or statistical skills but also reporters with a mission to disseminate these investigative practices within their news organization. As we can see in box 1.1, a computer-assisted reporter had to "preach, pitch and pray."

The computer-assisted reporter was also associated with a particular psychology and personality type. More colloquially, this journalist was often described as a "nerd": a young man who may have lacked social skills and was interested in all kinds of technology. He was identifiable by the fact that he "had used pocket protectors and slide rules in high school."[48]

BOX 1.1 "Selling the Benefits of CAR"

PREACH, PITCH & PRAY:
SELLING THE BENEFITS OF CAR [Computer-Assisted Reporting]
C.A.R. TREK, OCT. 8: 4:40–5:50 P.M.
ROSE CIOTTA, CAR COORDINATOR
BUFFALO NEWS

SELLING THE BOSS ON A CAR PROGRAM:

1) *DO MISSIONARY WORK*—Take every opportunity to memo or tell your immediate editor and higher level editors what other newspapers/television stations are doing with computers.

2) *BE PERSISTENT*—Keep the drum beat going on in a professional but persistent way. Even when you think they will never get it send another memo. . . .

7) *PREACH*—Take every opportunity to tell staffers about the wonders of CAR so you can enlist supporters. This is no time to go it alone. . . .

9) *BE POLITICALLY SMART*—Analyze who in higher management would support computer assisted reporting and include him or her in your missionary circle. Chances are that person will be tapped to head up the effort or be involved. . . .

13) *OFF THE FRONT PAGE*—If your goal is building a newsroom program with you as the driving force, be ready to support others. But, also take care to insist on public credit once you've produced or helped produce a story or series. Expect to do a lot of helping or teaching that gets no public recognition. It's a delicate balance. . . .

15) *TEACH, TEACH, TEACH*—No matter what you do, you will become known as the newsroom nerd. Be low key and humble. Adults don't need to be reminded how little they know about computers. If the boss doesn't know PCs, keep him/her informed. Offer to show him/her how you do what you do. . . .

Source: Extract from NICAR Tipsheet No. 282 (1994).

However rightly or wrongly, this psychological orientation was valued as a sign that the individual could easily learn to program. George Landau, a journalist, recounts being interviewed by Elliot Jaspin, whose newspaper's managers had asked him to hire a computer-assisted reporter:

> In the interview, Jaspin asked most of the questions. . . . I sweated and tried to sound knowledgeable about relational database theory, but it was clear to everyone that I didn't know what I was talking about. Near the end of the ordeal, Jaspin asked me if I played computer games. Uh-oh, I thought, he's making chitchat, which means I'm done for. I said no, not much, although I did enjoy those text-based adventure games, the ones where you have to type your way out of a densely plotted labyrinth. I mentioned "Leather Goddesses of Phobos," . . . When he later told me I had the job, [Richard] Weil explained that "Leather Goddesses" had been the clincher. Jaspin had read somewhere that people who enjoyed those text-based mazes were supposed to be good at programming and problem-solving.[49]

A particular state of mind was also associated with this kind of reporter. Computer-assisted reporters were expected to demonstrate a "database state of mind"—that is, an ability to view information in a structured way and to apply logical relationships to that information. Because they were often the only ones in the editorial team with these skills, they had to be able to translate their colleagues' questions and problems into a series of logical operations to be performed on data.

Undoubtedly, this conception of the computer-assisted reporter was deeply gendered: it implicitly associated this journalistic practice with a specific form of masculinity, one that was rather introverted and involved a penchant for video games. As Fred Turner has shown in relation to the history of the internet, young, educated, middle-class white men took center stage here and apparently didn't see the poor representation of women and minorities as a problem.[50] This gender imbalance was not attributable to a disregard for gender discrimination—in fact, analyzing gender and race discrimination through data was central to their journalistic practice—but to the fact that the worlds of investigative journalism and computer enthusiasts were overwhelmingly male and white at the time. It is therefore unsurprising that only a small number of computer-assisted reporters were women. Several young women who came from the world of journalism did nevertheless join the movement at an early stage and became highly recognized. Perhaps most notably, Sarah Cohen specialized in computer-assisted reporting in the late 1980s at the *Washington Post* and was awarded the Pulitzer Prize in 2002. A few women I interviewed, although not achieving the same notoriety, also joined the movement in the early 1990s and succeeded in having their skills recognized and in making a place for themselves in the profession.[51]

In the first half of the 1990s, a new journalistic identity emerged in U.S. newsrooms and was associated not only with a specific role within news organizations but also with a certain mindset and personality type. The emergence of this identity contributed significantly to aligning these emerging news-production practices with the standards of the profession.

A POLITICS OF COMPUTATION

Before the internet became central to news production, the coalition of reporters gathered around NICAR established a set of consistent rules to ensure that these material and technological practices would strengthen journalism's contribution to democracy. In other words, they wanted to increase the chance that data-based investigations would contribute to public debate, generate citizen awareness, and result in public action. These rules were disseminated mostly through textbooks,[52] internal NICAR documents, and awards for outstanding investigations. They constituted what I call a "politics of computation": a coherent framework for identifying material and technological practices that would increase journalists' ability to get issues recognized by their audience and addressed by the authorities. Developed by a handful of virtuoso reporters and influenced by social science, this politics was never widely adopted in U.S. journalism.

Nevertheless, because it was established at a time when pressure from the computer industry was less intense than it is today, it exemplified a distinct way of adjusting computing technology to the fundamental values of the profession.

As we shall see, this politics comprised norms relating to four distinct aspects of an investigation: (1) the role of technology in the generation of story ideas; (2) attention to the conditions of data production; (3) the data-handling process; and (4) the relationship with readers.

The first standard addressed the role of computer technology in the generation of story ideas. It required that under no circumstances should data be the starting point for an investigation. Reporters were advised always to start from a question or assumption that the computer processing of data could then confirm or deny. Here was the advice given in 1993 by Penny Loeb, a reporter for *New York Newsday* at the time, to NICAR members: "Don't just go get a computer tape and expect a great story. You need a tip that there is a problem that computerized data can confirm. Or you may have seen a problem occur repeatedly, such as sentencing discrimination. The computer can quantify the scope."[53] Constantly repeated in seminars, tipsheets, and even textbooks, this standard was justified by the constraints of the news-making process. Only if the reporter knew exactly what she was trying to reveal would the news organization be able to plan the time and resources needed for the investigation. It was therefore not an option for a reporter to launch into data analysis in the hope of gradually discovering the arguments that would constitute the core of a story. This rule can be found in one textbook from the late 1990s, which explained how some reporters were able to complete their investigation: "They had followed what some of my colleagues call the 'golden rule of CAR [computer-assisted reporting]': don't let the data drive the story. In other words, we had the idea and a germ of a story before we even got the database."[54] This warning can be argued to have been a way of keeping technology at a distance in the news-production process. Like any investigative journalist,[55] computer-assisted reporters were expected to drive the initiative when conducting an investigation. This first standard also aligned with how scientists traditionally build knowledge, proceeding by hypothetical-deductive reasoning.

The second standard required reporters to maintain a skeptical attitude toward data, as they would regarding any type of information. They should never consider the data as reflecting an indisputable reality. When a database came from an external source, the reporter should expect it to contain errors. It was the reporter's responsibility, as emphasized, to verify the accuracy of the information the database contained: "Because accuracy is one of the fundamentals of news reporting, the value must also be applied to databases. Inaccurate data lead to inaccurate analysis and, perhaps, improper conclusions et generalizations in news stories. The more effort spent in cleaning data, the better the information used in the story."[56] It was even explained that the databases provided by government administration offered weak guarantees of accuracy and thus were "inherently dirty":

> There is a "dirty" nature to many public databases. Dirty databases can contain keypunching mistakes. Other errors originate from machine sources, such as misread pencil marking in optically scanned data forms. More subtle errors can occur as well. These include measurement errors and data coding inconsistencies. . . . [J]ournalists should consider at least three factors involving any database: Where did the database come from? What was the original purpose of the database? How is the database being used (it could be different from the original purpose)?[57]

Such an attitude toward data can be described as fundamentally "constructivist" because it approaches data as the product of human activity. This implies not only that the data may contain errors but also that they may have been designed for uses that preclude them from being repurposed by the reporter. Again, this constructivist approach was firmly rooted in the epistemology of investigative journalism,[58] and in textbooks it was illustrated by many discussions on data cleaning, checking, and cross-referencing.

The third standard related to the data-handling process, more specifically to the calculations that could be legitimately performed. Reporters were told that they should seek to identify trends in the data but under no circumstances draw conclusions from individual data. In the early 1990s,

Philip Meyer was very critical of those he called "computer cowboys," reporters who published stories based on limited information gleaned from a database.⁵⁹ Similarly, textbooks on the subject warned against the use of a very small data sample during an investigation. The true value of the data, they argued, lay in their aggregation. Not only could individual data be false, but the investigation would also be more politically effective if it identified general trends. This was the advice David Burnham gave reporters:

> When corruption is found in an agency, the top man—and this goes for the small town police chief as well as the president of the United States—always responds with the tedious assertion that this is only an "occasional rotten apple in the barrel." . . . In fact, the moral collapse of an individual detective, or FBI agent or cabinet secretary—the alleged rotten apple in the barrel—frequently is a sign of a rotten barrel. . . . The rotten barrel story almost always is of greater consequence that the rotten apple story.⁶⁰

According to this coalition of reporters, the search for greater political effectiveness in a journalistic report was contingent on the detection of general trends in the data. They valued the methods offered by quantitative social science as legitimate tools to demonstrate the scope and causes of a problem—as illustrated by Stephen Doig's Pulitzer Prize–winning investigation in 1992, which revealed the human causes of Hurricane Andrew's damage by using statistical regression.⁶¹ Yet there was a certain reluctance among investigative journalists to take the results of statistical analyses at face value. Textbooks and trainers stressed the importance of checking "on the ground" whether the people concerned also perceived what the reporters' statistical analysis had brought to light.

Finally, a last standard was set out with the aim of regulating the type of news products that could be delivered to readers. This coalition of reporters targeted an audience composed mostly of civic-oriented readers who would supposedly be convinced by quantified arguments. Nevertheless, computer-assisted reporters did not want their publications to be filled with incomprehensible numbers and formulas. As Jaspin used to say, computer-assisted pieces should not look like an "accounting textbook." And to prevent that from happening, the news product had to include human testimonies: "I remember advising reporters that the computer-assisted reporting piece of this, if you're thinking about a house, building a house ... the computer analysis is the foundation, it is the basement. And built above that is how it affects people, about the stories of people and what it meant to them. And if you miss that, well, the story that you produce is going to be I would not say unreadable, but it's going to be kind of a very difficult slop."[62] As a consequence, those investigations often looked like regular news stories with graphs or tables. Under no circumstances should the reporter have to impress the readers with numbers and statistics.

These standards were not just a set of best practices promoted by computer-assisted reporters. On a deeper level, they constituted a politics of computation in the sense that they sought to increase journalists' ability to get public problems recognized and addressed by governments. Fundamentally, these reporters considered that the way in which data were collected, analyzed, and presented over the course of an investigation had an impact on their relationship with their audience and governments. In their view, nonobservance of any one of these standards would weaken journalists' capacity to influence public choices. It must be said, however, that this view was never actually verified. In particular, it is unclear to what extent readers found data-based investigations more credible than traditional ones.

* * *

As this chapter has shown, computational practices developed in news making long before "Big Data" or "open data" were ever mentioned. In this respect, my analysis adds to the work of several scholars who have shown that the impetus for these practices came from within the journalistic profession.[63] Deeply concerned about the epistemological crisis their profession faced, an elite group of U.S. reporters claimed that computer technology and quantitative social science offered a way to better fulfill the core missions of journalism. But what this chapter demonstrates in a unique way is that these journalists did not just want to adopt new "rituals of

TWO PATHS TO DATA JOURNALISM

objectivity"[64] so as to persuade officials, competitors, and readers of their reports' objectivity. By engaging in material and technological practices, and by seeking to resolve the major difficulties they faced, they invented an original way to align technology with the core values of the profession. This alignment resulted in a "politics of computation" that kept technology at a distance by treating data in the same way as other sources of information and by promoting human judgment in news making.

Until the late 2000s, this path was almost entirely unknown to French journalism. A few French reporters had collected data and analyzed them with computers, but they had done so individually and without setting up any organizational infrastructure or creating a set of standards. One reason for this near absence of computer-assisted reporting was the weakness of investigative journalism in France before the 1980s.[65] Thus, investigative reporters were in no position to organize in order to take advantage of computers and government records, which were much harder to get in France, as we will see in chapter 4. These particularities did not encourage them to adopt early computational investigative practices.

On the American side of the Atlantic, computer-assisted reporters cleared a conservative path toward data journalism—although in doing so they revealed injustices affecting U.S. society. They promoted the preservation of journalistic standards in a context of technological change. In chapters 3 to 5, I show that both the rise of the web and the crisis of the news industry have made this path difficult to follow since the mid-2000s by deeply renewing journalistic expectations of technology.

In the next chapter, I consider a second path to contemporary data journalism practices in both in the United States and France: the rise of journalistic rankings for health and education in the 1980s and 1990s. Although less prestigious than the investigations analyzed in this chapter, these news practices also helped define how journalists could take advantage of data and computational tools to increase their contribution to democracy.

2
RANKINGS; OR, THE UNINTENDED CONSEQUENCES OF COMPUTATION, 1988–2000

One of the most unfortunate things to happen in American higher education": this is how in 1992 the dean of Emory University in Atlanta described the college rankings published by U.S. magazines.[1] A few years later a French court ordered a magazine to pay €80,000 in damages to two dozen surgeons practicing in poorly ranked hospitals.[2] On both sides of the Atlantic, journalists came under heavy criticism when they started to calculate the performance of universities, schools, and hospitals and to publish it in the form of rankings. As in the case of the investigative reporters studied in the previous chapter, these journalists' computational efforts were informed by a democratization movement that had existed in France and the United States since the 1960s. Their initial purpose was indeed to offer readers an objective assessment of the quality of service provided by these institutions and thus to challenge the self-image that these institutions usually conveyed. Whereas universities, schools, and hospitals claimed to provide the best service to all citizens, calculations enabled journalists to show citizens that the quality of the service provided could vary greatly over time and space.

Journalists had been publishing rankings for a long time, especially in the United States. From the 1970s, several U.S. and French magazines even ranked universities and high schools by asking experts about their reputation and publishing what was called "reputational rankings." However, starting in the late 1980s journalists from both countries began to assess the performance of education and health institutions by taking advantage of the growing amount of available data on how these institutions operated. As a set of policies often labeled "New Public Management" were gradually adopted in both countries,[3] journalists were able to process these institutions' performance statistically not only to reveal which institutions offered a better service but also to influence education and health policies. These rankings immediately sparked keen interest among readers, making them extremely profitable for news organizations.

Today, it has become quite common for news organizations to calculate the performance of schools, hospitals, and other institutions by leveraging data from government or public agencies. This form of journalistic calculation has expanded considerably. The ProPublica website, for example, features a tool that visually represents the performance of each surgeon in each hospital for a specific procedure (e.g., knee-replacement surgery).[4] Similarly, several French news outlets rank *députés* (members of parliament, MPs) according to their activities in the National Assembly (e.g., committee attendance, number of amendments submitted).[5] However, few data journalists would identify as heirs of the "ranker journalist" movement. They generally prefer the glorious heritage of the investigative reporters studied in the first chapter of this book because rankings have been so widely criticized and even disregarded within the profession despite their commercial success. Even scholars have largely overlooked this journalistic practice, focusing instead on the effects of rankings on consumer choices and institutional change.[6] However, in this chapter I argue that these "ranker journalists" provided a valuable lesson for today's data journalists: the use of computation in journalism in no way guarantees a greater contribution to democracy, and it is therefore of paramount importance for journalists to consider the consequences of their own computational practices.

Ranker journalists were the first to experience the fundamental problem facing data journalism today: the unintended consequences of computation. Although they used statistical calculations to make institutions more transparent and to allow citizens to make better-informed choices, they were criticized for exacerbating injustices between institutions and for being a vehicle of neoliberal policies in education and health. This chapter shows how these American and French pioneers attempted to adjust their computational practices in light of these consequences. They were challenged to find not only calculation methods that could be seen as fair by a wide range of actors but also a way to avoid becoming an instrument of public policy. Although generally ignored, this second path to data journalism highlights the fact that the ethics of journalism must be attentive to the consequences of computation.

A MOVEMENT WITHIN U.S. AND FRENCH JOURNALISM

How did the same journalistic practice emerge on both sides of the Atlantic over the same period? A simple explanation is that the statistical evaluation of universities and hospitals first appeared in American journalism and then spread to European countries.[7] It is easy to see that the first rankings of this type, published by *U.S. News & World Report*—"America's Best Colleges" in 1988 and "America's Best Hospitals" in 1992—had a major influence on French news organizations. When the editors of *Science & Avenir* set up a team of journalists in 1995 to rank the best hospitals in France, they explicitly took the U.S. magazine as a model.[8] However, this explanation overlooks the common dynamics that affected French and American journalism at the time and drove such rapid development of similar computational practices in both countries. These dynamics were both endogenous and exogenous to U.S. and French journalism. On the one hand, the rise of journalistic rankings was part of a more general movement that emerged in the 1960s among French and American journalists to increase public scrutiny over institutions. On the other hand, these computational practices can be explained by a set of social and political changes that made it possible and legitimate to calculate the performance of institutions. Let us first examine the professional dynamics underpinning the almost simultaneous adoption of these practices in France and the United States.

In both countries, the journalists who started to compute the performance of universities and hospitals in the 1980s exemplified a change of attitude in the profession toward such institutions that had started in the late 1960s.[9] Although they were young reporters who specialized in education or health, they had not been trained primarily in those fields; rather, they often had a background in social science or journalism. Because they were more sensitive than their older colleagues to the demands for equality that had been voiced since the 1960s, they were highly critical of the opacity of the institutions they covered as journalists. In France, the first reputational ranking of universities was published in 1976 by *Le Monde de l'Éducation*. Like most education reporters in France at the time,[10] the two editors who produced this ranking had been involved in the education-reform movement since 1968. In their view, rankings afforded an opportunity to put an end to the "reigning hypocrisy of good conscience and academic conformity."[11] Reputational rankings in particular made it possible to challenge higher-education leaders' discourse about themselves as having an "independent," "rigorous" and "objective view."

In the United States, the journalists behind "America's Best Colleges" at *U.S. News & World Report* had similar backgrounds. They had studied longer than their older colleagues, were sympathetic to the ideals of equality that had been voiced in the 1960s, and had specialized in education reporting. Alvin P. Sanoff, for example, joined the magazine in 1977 and was the editor of "America's Best Colleges" from 1992 to 1998. Initially trained in sociology and journalism, he had been an education reporter for the *Baltimore Sun*, where he had covered the riots in 1968 and published many stories on racial discrimination in universities.[12] He and his colleagues at *U.S. News* maintained that ranking colleges offered a way to achieve greater equality in higher education. In the 1980s and 1990s, the editors behind "America's Best Colleges" regularly emphasized the need to shake up the "custodians of the academic world": "The custodians of the academic world can pretend that nibbling at the edges of reform constitutes fundamental change. But in the era of the K–16 experience, $27,500-a-year tuition, shrinking government subsidies and college graduates who cannot read bus schedules, a nibble here and a nibble there simply won't do. Either America's colleges and universities will embrace change as eagerly as they have clung to the status quo, or many of them will risk being relegated to the institutional ranks of the unaffordable, the irrelevant and, ultimately, the altogether defunct."[13]

On the other side of the Atlantic, journalistic interest in computing the quality of institutions in the early 1990s was also driven by a critical stance regarding those in charge of education and health systems. As the sociologist Frederic Pierru has argued, this stance more often than not translated, for example, into a denunciation of the injustice done to poor people who had no alternative to low-quality hospitals. This view was expressed in colorful terms by one of the reporters behind the first hospital rankings published in *Science & Avenir*:

> The woman in Pithiviers who is having surgery . . . [s]o a woman who is poor . . . , she dies on the table at 32, it's stupid. It's stupid, especially since she's the third one, and then you start to panic because the agency director says, "That's enough, I'm fed up." Hold on a second, these are poor people. But all these assholes [the administrative officials], they don't go to [the deceased's] husbands. We [the reporters] used to see them. When you see their kid, you think to yourself: he's half orphan. Great. It's never the rich.[14]

The interest in rankings was expressed differently in the two countries, with French journalists more often adopting a rhetoric of scandal.[15] Thus, the first French hospital rankings published in the 1990s were presented as a "list of hospitals to avoid" (1992) and a "hospital blacklist" (1997). However, in both countries this interest stemmed from a movement within the profession to challenge the opacity of institutions. For these journalists, rankings afforded an opportunity to weigh in on institutional reforms in higher education and the health-care system. Although the profitability of such rankings immediately aroused the interest of media corporations, the journalists saw them first and foremost as a vehicle to increase the transparency of institutions.

THE LEGACY OF CONSUMER JOURNALISM

In both countries, the journalists who engaged in these computational practices were able to harness the legacy of consumer journalism. This form of journalism, introduced on the fringes of U.S. journalism in the 1920s before spreading to Europe after World War II,[16] gained professional recognition in both countries in the 1960s. As a result, in the 1980s it became more legitimate for French and American reporters to seek to defend consumers by providing them with more objective information than they could get from advertising or public relations. More importantly, consumer journalism provided an avenue for assessing the quality of institutions that would be legitimate from a journalistic point of view. This assessment involved setting up evaluation procedures and constituting the news organization as a "calculation center."

As Norman I. Silber has shown, the tests published by *Consumer Reports* in the 1930s focused first on everyday products (razors, soaps, etc.) and then on more complex industrial products (cars, household appliances, etc.).[17] After 1945, the magazine developed its own measurement and calculation capabilities, building laboratories and forging partnerships with research centers. Relying on laboratories both internal and external to the organization, the implementation of such procedures allowed *Consumer Reports* to act in two ways. First, it published editorials calling on public authorities to take action. Second, it provided readers with consumer assessments in the form of articles as well as ratings and rankings. Starting in the 1950s, car evaluations published by *Consumer Reports* became increasingly popular among American consumers.[18]

The way in which *Consumer Reports* evaluated new cars released on the U.S. market from the late 1950s reflected this search for "mechanical objectivity." As Silber has analyzed, the magazine created both standardized and impersonal internal evaluation procedures on which it based its editorial products: each car was bought new; it was then measured and photographed; it was washed and tested for leaks; its functionality was tested; its lights, wheel alignment, and meter accuracy were checked; it was driven on a range of roads for two thousand miles; its performance was checked again; its performance and fuel consumption were tested on a circuit; its climbing and braking ability were measured; and, finally, its fuel consumption was tested in town and over long distances.

This form of journalism gradually gained recognition in American and European journalism. *Consumer Reports* played a central role in several major product controversies in the 1960s—particularly surrounding the effects of tobacco and automobile safety—and by the early1980s reached more than two million subscribers. On the other side of the Atlantic, the consumer press also developed in the late 1960s and was likewise supported by government agencies. As a result, established news organizations in both countries opened their columns to consumer issues in the 1960s. Although this recognition undoubtedly benefited the journalists who began to calculate institutional performance in the 1980s, it would not have been enough to sustain the practice. They also had to benefit from a new environment that required institutions to be more transparent.

AN ENVIRONMENT CONDUCIVE TO INSTITUTIONAL TRANSPARENCY

In the 1980s, large swaths of the U.S. and French populations were paying increasing attention to their education and health-care choices. Although this increased attention materialized very differently in the two countries, it led individuals in both places to compare a greater number of institutions based on their quality of service. American and French journalists therefore met a growing social demand as they set out to evaluate schools, universities, and hospitals.

In the United States, the higher-education market in particular experienced unprecedented growth. Colleges witnessed a sharp increase in enrollment, from six million students in 1965 to more than twelve million in 1980.[19] For most American families, access to undergraduate education had become a right, with the number of colleges increasing dramatically as a result. Competition between U.S. universities reached new heights, and they began using marketing techniques to attract students (advertising, telephone marketing, etc.). As the *U.S. News* editor Alvin Sanoff explained two decades after the launch of "America's Best Colleges," "A generation of parents who were college-educated brought both pragmatism and status-seeking to the college search process."[20]

In the 1980s, France was in a very different position. The system guaranteed free education and health care for all but in theory left no room for individual choice. An education market had nevertheless gradually emerged as larger sections of the French population accessed lower and higher secondary education. Conscious of the inequality in the education system, they began to form strategies for choosing schools and identifying their value.[21] A growing proportion of families then turned to private education or implemented different strategies to choose their children's schools. At the same time, schools themselves gradually started to select students, which compounded differences between these institutions.[22]

Although the education and health markets were far less developed in France than in the United States, citizens in both countries began paying increasing attention to their choices in these domains. As they sought to make their own choices, they realized that they had very little objective information on which to base them because price was not an indicator of institutional quality. Whether the price was zero or near zero, as in the case of education and health care in France, or very high, as in the case of U.S. colleges and hospitals, it said absolutely nothing about the quality of the service provided.[23] It should thus be no surprise that journalistic rankings were immediately met with public interest.

Beyond consumer demand, a set of policy reforms made it both conceivable and practically achievable for American and French journalists to compute the quality of institutions. Under the banner of New Public Management, these reforms put institutions under growing pressure to make their performance visible through accounting procedures used in the private sector.[24] Gradually introduced in both countries, the reforms decisively contributed in three ways to the emergence of these computational practices in journalism in the late 1980s: by giving journalists the opportunity to access data on how institutions operated; by providing journalists with a cognitive framework for assessing the quality of institutions; and, finally, by promoting accountability as a political principle that added legitimacy to these journalistic practices.

Because universities, schools, and hospitals were increasingly required by law to systematically release a range of data about their activities, news organizations were spared the burden of collecting the data by their own means. In the 1980s, the U.S. government was concerned about rising education and health-care costs, so universities were forced to produce and report graduation rates and other statistics on their performance—their finances, their treatment of minorities, the air quality of their location, and so on.[25] For instance, the Student Right-to-Know and Campus Security Act passed by the U.S. Congress in 1990 required all universities to report their graduation rates; if they failed to do so, they would be excluded from federal student financial aid programs. The American health-care system was in a fairly similar position at the time as the considerable rise in spending in the 1980s led a group of reformers, experts, and consumers to call for the implementation of new regulations.[26] Public agencies were subsequently formed that required hospitals to release a set of statistical indicators on the nature, costs, and effects of medical treatments administered to patients.

The situation in France was hardly different. Between the mid-1980s and mid-1990s, the Ministry of Health introduced the Information System Medicalization Program to monitor health organizations. Hospitals were gradually required to provide a wide range of information on medical activity (costs, duration of care, etc.).[27] French high schools were subject to the same requirement from the early 1990s, when the Ministry of Education made it compulsory for them to report each year on their students' pass rates, baccalaureate graduation rates, and students' social backgrounds.[28]

French and American journalists also benefited from the development of a cognitive framework that made it possible to compare the functioning of different organizations, irrespective of their particularities. Despite variations between the two countries, the model that gradually prevailed in the 1980s was based on the concept of universities and hospitals as "production systems"—in other words, as standard organizations producing outputs from inputs. From this perspective, any organization, whether dedicated to training students or to healing patients, had to draw on its own human, material, and economic resources to deliver outputs, whether graduates or healed patients. Along with this perspective came measurement tools and calculation models to ensure comparability across many organizations. When doing their own calculations, journalists could therefore rely on a cognitive framework that provided them with instruments to calculate the quality of institutions.

Finally, by establishing accountability as a major political principle, these reforms strengthened journalists' legitimacy to publish institutional rankings. This principle entailed not only that institutions should be held accountable by requiring them to compile and submit to government agencies a set of statistical indicators on their activities but also and more importantly that these indicators should be made widely available. Disseminating quantitative results to all stakeholders of an organization was supposed to guarantee effective evaluations. Owing to their public nature, statistical indicators were expected to encourage organizations to improve their own performance. It thus became less and less legitimate for organizations to keep their evaluations secret. This political principle was not uniformly imposed in France and the United States; for example, in 1999 the French Parliament adopted a law that deprived journalists of access to French hospitals' official performance database. Nevertheless, this principle provided a solid case for journalists: for an institution to improve, the public had to have access to the indicators measuring its quality.

PROFESSIONAL MISTRUST

Although it became quite common for magazines and newspapers to publish rankings based on performance calculations, most French and American journalists nevertheless remained highly suspicious of this practice. Consumer journalism in the United States flourished in the 1960s and 1970s, but it subsequently went through a period of decline brought on by deregulation policies and pressure from advertisers.[29] Furthermore, educational or hospital rankings were not immediately associated with consumer journalism, which did not take the form of rankings but rather consisted of investigations into specific industrial products or processes. Even at *U.S. News*, most of the journalists who did not do consumer reporting judged the rankings initiative harshly. Here is how Robert Morse, the man who designed the calculation methodology for "America's Best Colleges" in the late 1980s, recalled his colleagues' criticisms:

> At that time at [*U.S. News*], the rankings were like being in Siberia in terms of how the real journalists thought of them. . . . They believed it was creating the information, that it should not be the role of journalism at that point. We should just cover events or analyze current events versus being the news. Journalism shouldn't be the news itself. I mean it's different if you're covering the government release of the GDP or the price index or a merger at Wall Street; you're still covering an event even though it was numbers. But making your own judgment about weights and so creating a metric or a scale or a ranking and rating institutions against one another, it was not highly thought of. It was thought of very lowly.[30]

For most journalists, producing rankings conflicted with the dominant standard of objectivity—being objective meant covering events or numbers provided by institutions but certainly not producing one's own event through calculations. This criticism echoed those leveled at Philip Meyer and computer-assisted reporters in the 1970s and 1980s (as we saw in chapter 1) and at the pioneers of fact-checking in the 1980s.[31] There was a major difference, however, for the latter computer-assisted journalistic practices had appeared in prestigious U.S. newspapers and had been driven by journalists who were highly regarded within the profession. By contrast, many rankers did not come from the heart of the profession and did not work for the most prestigious news organizations. Unlike computer-assisted reporters, they never organized themselves into a professional segment—either in the United States or in France. The title "ranker journalist" never emerged as a label for journalists who made rankings on a variety of topics. Until the late 1990s, this practice remained the preserve of journalists who specialized in education and health and who were later joined by individuals who had not been trained in journalism. Over the past two decades, the majority of U.S. magazines that have published rankings have chosen not to develop their own in-house computing capacities but rather to rely on outside consultants or analysts. As a result, most American journalists have remained highly critical of using these computational practices in journalism.

Moreover, the significant commercial success of educational and hospital rankings did not help these practices to gain legitimacy within the profession. In France, the profitability of rankings made them all the more suspect in the eyes of most journalists because they were closely tied to commercial considerations. Thus, journalists who calculated institutional performance were often accused of being driven by marketing concerns. As Pierre Falga, a French journalist who started making rankings for several news magazines in the 1990s, explained more recently: "The rankings are still subject to debate in newsrooms. It's always a sensitive topic. There are always journalists who say it's not right to rank. It's still a journalistic subgenre that is disdained. It's rarely said up front, it's recognized as a commercial asset, but that won't earn you more respect."[32]

COMPUTING UNDER A FLOOD OF CRITICISM

The toughest criticisms of rankings journalism, however, have come from outside the profession. In both countries, the journalistic claim to measure the performance of institutions objectively has been deeply and forcefully challenged—not only by academics and physicians protesting against what they view as a direct attack on their professions but also by bureaucrats, public officials, journalists, and social scientists. In order to understand the nature of these criticisms and how they have changed the conditions under which journalistic computation is carried out, I studied the most established and controversial ranking in the United States: "America's Best Colleges" by *U.S. News & World Report*. In the late 1990s, each issue in which the rankings appeared sold more than two million copies,[33] and two out of three parents with a child who graduated from high school considered it "really helpful" for choosing a college.[34] Yet each new edition sparked heated debate on campuses, in the press, and within the academic community.

In 1987, *U.S. News* editors set up a team to produce an annual issue called "America's Best Colleges." Initially, it was only a reputational ranking: reporters sent a questionnaire to all college presidents asking them to rank the ten schools they thought offered the best education. The response was fierce, with twenty colleges presidents going to *U.S. News*'s editorial office and asking for the magazine to drop the query. To shield themselves from criticism, the editors decided to increase the magazine's computing capabilities by hiring a statistician, Robert Morse. Morse recalled that the first task was to develop a methodology that incorporated objective elements to measure college performance: "We realized we had to be more sophisticated because we were measuring characteristics of higher education institutions. . . . We had to understand what data would be available, that could be collected, that was credible. From that, we decided not to have an aspirational methodology, we had an aspirational methodology that we could succeed at."[35]

Morse's account supports Theodore Porter's argument that a profession often uses quantification techniques to protect itself from outside criticism.[36] Here, the method adopted was similar to the statistical indicators used by agencies at the time to evaluate educational organizations. A college's performance was calculated as a weighted average of several variables: its reputation; its ability to recruit the best students; the quality of its faculty; its financial resources; and, finally, its graduation rate (box 2.1).

BOX 2.1 The Statistical Model Behind
"America's Best Colleges" (1988)

College performance = reputational survey + student selectivity + faculty quality + institutional resources + student retention

VARIABLE DESCRIPTION

Reputational survey = 1,000 college officials (asked to pick the ten schools in their academic category that performed best in providing an undergraduate education)

Student selectivity = 1 (acceptance rates)
+ 2 (the "yield," or the percentage of those accepted who actually enrolled)
+ 3 (average standardized-test scores of a college's entering class)
+ 4 (high-school class-rank data: for national universities and national liberal-arts colleges, class standing was measured by the percentage of freshmen finishing in the top 10 percent of their high-school classes).

Faculty quality = 1 (the ratio of full-time students to full-time faculty)
+ 2 (the percentage of full-time faculty with PhDs)
+ 3 (the percentage of faculty employed on a part-time basis)
+ 4 (the average salary, including all fringe benefits, for tenured full professors).

Institutional resources = Total of the college's educational and general expenditures, divided by its total enrollment.

Student retention = The average percentage of students from the 1982–1984 freshman classes who graduated within five years of the date they enrolled.[37]

In the early years, the colleges provided most of the data in response to a questionnaire issued by *U.S. News*, but later the data were obtained from government agencies. But whatever the source, journalists soon realized that a dedicated team and a formula were not enough to produce the ranking. According to Morse, dedicated infrastructure quickly became necessary: "Pretty soon, I realized, if we wanted to make a long-term company product—which it was—we had to take it off the people's desktop computers, and we built an Oracle database. We started doing the programing in Oracle [software]. It was on the company's computers. I mean the data was stored, so it was not just on somebody's hard drive."[38]

Year after year, the data from questionnaires were thus stored in a single database, to which each journalist had access. The mathematical formula was translated into a computer program that allowed journalists to calculate a "performance score" for every college. The program returned a list of colleges that were ranked according to their score, with the top-ranked college receiving a score of one hundred points (figure 2.1).

The creation of a calculation center within the newsroom was therefore driven by the editors' desire to defend themselves from criticism. However, it did not stop the flood of criticism between the late 1980s and the late 1990s.

BEWARE OF THE CONSEQUENCES OF COMPUTATION

A first set of criticisms concerned the very principle of measuring the quality of an institution: quality depended on such a variety of elements that journalists could only be unduly reductive by focusing on a few variables. As the president of the American Council of Education put it, "I think that arriving at five criteria for determining institutional quality oversimplifies a very complex problem." The council asked *U.S. News* to cease and desist. "We've asked them in letters and we've met with them and the answer comes back in so many words that this issue sells magazines."[39]

BEST NATIONAL UNIVERSITIES

These are the leaders among the 204 schools that are research-oriented

Rank. Name	Overall score	Academ. reputation	Student selectivity	Faculty resources	Finan. resources	Grad. rate rank	Alumni satisfact.	Avg. Midpt SAT/ACT score	SAT/ACT 25-75 percen.	Freshmen in top 10% of HS class	Accept. ance rate	Faculty with doctorate	Student/ faculty ratio	Educ. program per student	Graduation rate	Alumni giving rate
1. Harvard University (MA)	100.0	1	1	3	6	1	29	1385	1290-1480	90%	16%	98%	12/1	$36,291	97%	27%
2. Princeton University (NJ)	99.6	1	4	5	10	3	5	1355	1260-1450	90%	16%	97%	8/1	$27,779	95%	44%
3. Yale University (CT)	99.4	5	3	7	4	3	6	1345	1250-1440	95%	22%	95%	11/1	$39,110	95%	42%
4. Mass. Inst. of Tech.	99.1	1	6	4	7	10	12	1375	1290-1460	94%	33%	100%	10/1	$32,825	90%	34%
5. Calif. Inst. of Technology	98.7	7	2	1	1	27	14	1415	1350-1480	98%	28%	100%	6/1	$60,623	82%	33%
6. Stanford University (CA)	97.6	1	5	6	5	8	77	1345	1250-1440	91%	22%	99%	14/1	$35,854	92%	18%
7. Duke University (NC)	97.5	7	9	8	13	7	2	1315	1220-1410	88%	27%	97%	13/1	$26,498	93%	47%
8. Dartmouth College (NH)	96.2	16	10	12	11	2	1	1320	1230-1410	85%	26%	99%	9/1	$29,556	95%	54%
9. University of Chicago (IL)	95.2	7	26	2	8	23	11	1300	1190-1410	71%	44%	100%	6/1	$36,937	85%	35%
10. Cornell University (NY)	94.9	7	12	11	20	16	31	1275	1170-1380	84%	32%	98%	13/1	$20,923	88%	26%
11. Columbia University (NY)	94.8	7	13	9	9	10	85	1300	1200-1400	78%	30%	98%	11/1	$31,029	90%	17%
12. Brown University (RI)	94.0	16	8	18	28	5	10	1300	1190-1410	87%	24%	100%	13/1	$19,570	94%	36%
13. Northwestern University (IL)	93.4	16	16	10	15	17	4	1240	1140-1340	85%	42%	100%	11/1	$25,385	88%	23%
14. Rice University (TX)	93.3	23	7	17	22	17	7	1364	1257-1471	86%	19%	100%	9/1	$21,266	88%	41%
15. Johns Hopkins University (MD)	92.2	7	24	37	2	17	23	1315	1230-1400	72%	43%	95%	9/1	$55,101	88%	30%
16. University of Pennsylvania	90.3	14	14	50	21	14	8	1290	1190-1390	83%	40%	98%	11/1	$22,337	89%	39%
17. Georgetown University (DC)	89.4	31	21	20	25	10	38	1230	1130-1330	68%	29%	90%	13/1	$19,486	90%	24%
18. Washington University (MO)	88.7	26	37	23	3	28	25	1220	1120-1320	65%	65%	99%	10/1	$45,946	80%	28%
19. Univ. of Calif. at Berkeley	88.6	5	11	13	44	36	165	1235	1100-1370	95%	43%	98%	19/1	$13,901	77%	9%
20. Vanderbilt University (TN)	88.4	26	36	14	17	31	32	1195	1090-1300	64%	56%	98%	11/1	$23,051	79%	26%
21. University of Virginia	87.0	16	17	47	57	9	22	1220	1110-1330	74%	35%	92%	13/1	$12,934	91%	30%
22. Univ. of Calif. at Los Angeles	86.9	16	15	27	26	46	133	1160	1020-1300	93%	42%	99%	19/1	$19,738	72%	12%
23. University of Michigan	86.7	7	38	32	38	25	58	1185	1070-1300	64%	69%	98%	16/1	$14,882	83%	20%
24. Carnegie Mellon University (PA)	86.5	25	40	22	18	47	21	1240	1130-1350	58%	59%	92%	9/1	$22,903	72%	30%
25. Emory University (GA)	86.1	36	32	29	16	26	39	1205	1110-1300	71%	58%	96%	13/1	$26,151	83%	23%
25. University of Notre Dame (IN)	86.1	36	20	34	55	6	3	1265	1160-1370	78%	49%	95%	13/1	$13,193	93%	46%

FIGURE 2.1 "America's Best Colleges," rankings for 1994.

Source: *U.S. News & World Report*, October 4, 1993.

College presidents sought to sever the link between journalists' calculations and the "quality" of their institutions. The two were completely different, they argued, for higher education in the United States was so rich and diverse that it could be put into numbers only at the cost of an intolerable reduction. A "college education cannot and should not be quantified like household appliances," said the vice president of Associated Students of Stanford University in 1996.[40] Moreover, among the wide range of elements that made up the quality of an institution, many could not be expressed in quantitative terms: the atmosphere on campus, the working environment, the support of the faculty, the helpfulness of administrative staff, the solidarity among students, and so on: journalists dismissed all of these elements because they could not be quantified. Accordingly, several actors in academia encouraged future students to pay attention to these elements that contributed to the quality of a college but could not be expressed in numbers: "Visit the campus, whether it's in your own backyard or 500 miles away. Talk to students, faculty, and staff. Eat in the cafeteria, sit in on a class, watch an athletic practice. Listen to your inner self and be true to what you hear. Is this college a place where you will be challenged to be all that you are capable of becoming? If it is, it just may be the best college for you—no matter where it ranks in the *U.S. News and World Report* special issue."[41]

A second line of criticism denounced the political nature of the calculation. The statistical model on which the *U.S. News* ranking was based, critics argued, was anything but neutral. On the contrary, it was "politicized" insofar as it served the interests of particular actors within academia. More specifically, the model was blamed for systematically favoring the richest and most prestigious universities by including too many variables related to colleges' resources and too few variables concerning educational outcomes. As a result of this imbalance, the statistical model used to rank "America's best colleges" was criticized for "militating" against public universities: "Eighty percent of the nation's college students enroll in public colleges and universities. Despite this, across all *U.S. News* categories, national as well as regional, public colleges and universities are missing from the top tier. The status- and resource-driven nature of the *U.S. News* model—its focus on continuous undergraduate enrollment, high graduation rates, high spending per student, and high alumni giving rates—militates against public universities."[42]

For the most part, the actors voicing this criticism in the 1990s were researchers and managers from the least-privileged institutions. They argued that the weighting of the calculation merely reflected the prejudices of journalists, for whom the best colleges apparently had to be the most prestigious.[43] They called for a model that was fairer to institutions that performed well despite their limited resources.

Critics in the 1990s also identified another reason why the *U.S. News* journalists' rankings calculation was not neutral: it was based on data produced by college managers. As each institution sought to obtain the best possible ranking, the data it sent to the magazine were intended primarily to defend the institution's own interests. In 1995, the *Wall Street Journal* revealed that many colleges were manipulating the data they sent to the magazine. In an article widely commented on, a reporter compared the data that about one hundred colleges sent to *U.S. News* with the data they sent to auditing firms, which were subject to stricter requirements because lying to an auditing firm is subject to federal prosecution: he estimated that 25 percent of the data sent to the magazine were more or less falsified. He detailed some of the tricks used by colleges to improve their statistics: "[The] dean of admission at Rensselaer Polytechnic Institute in Troy, N.Y. [explains]: 'Suppose you had 5,000 applications and suppose in the first round you accepted 2,500 of those. Then you had a waiting list.' 'So when the question comes up, how many did you accept, you can in good conscience say you accepted 2,500. That's true.' The school, however, would later accept another '400 or 500' students off the waiting list but continue to count them as rejects, he says."[44] In the mid-1990s, this criticism of false neutrality in journalistic computation was echoed far beyond the circles of university officials.

A last line of criticism highlighted the unintended effects of "America's Best Colleges." Within the education sector, a range of actors explained that journalists' calculations profoundly affected how universities worked. Counselors attested to how the rankings influenced students by diverting them from the colleges they felt were best suited to them: "As a former college counselor at one of our nation's most prestigious independent schools, I always cringed when the 'best colleges' edition surfaced. Within days, the students that I had counseled for months would suddenly arrive with a new college list in hand. Gone would be the colleges we had carefully researched and come to see as a nice fit."[45]

Researchers noted the growing importance of the *U.S. News* ranking in college management. They explained that the whole organization of colleges had been affected by the redirection of resources to the variables included in the *U.S. News* statistical model. According to education researchers, focusing on the model's variables had a number of perverse effects: "Thirty-five percent of the faculty resources component is [sic] determined by the average salaries of full and tenured professors. Yet a school that increases faculty salaries or recalculates how it reports their benefits to *U.S. News* will not necessarily improve the quality of instruction, but it will improve the school's rank. The *U.S. News* ranking also provides incentives for overinvestment in research. Spending more money on research directly rewards schools through the financial resources component."[46]

In the late 1990s, several scholars pointed out the self-reinforcing effect of *U.S. News* college rankings. Differences in rankings were bound to increase over time as resources and the best students moved to the top-ranked colleges. In 1999, the economists James Monks and Ronald G. Ehrenberg showed that the statistical effect of an institution moving down one place in the rankings was a 0.5 percent increase in its student acceptance rate; in other words, lower-ranked institutions became less selective in order to fill their classes.[47] College officials and researchers highlighted how very small differences in rankings led to increasingly large differences in the quality of institutions. In the following decade, the sociologists Wendy Espeland and Michael Sauder labeled this correlation a "self-fulfilling prophecy."[48]

American and French "ranker journalists" were fiercely confronted with the unintended consequences of their calculations in the 1990s, to a degree that data journalists today have not experienced.[49] Although they claimed to use statistical calculations to reduce the opacity of institutions and enable citizens to make better-informed choices, they were blamed for exacerbating injustices between institutions and for being a vehicle of neoliberal policies in education and health. Still focusing on the case of "America's Best Colleges," let us now consider how these journalists adjusted their computational practices in light of these criticisms, first by finding new ways of calculating that a wide range of actors could consider fair and second by finding a way to avoid becoming instruments of public policy.

DEALING WITH THE EFFECTS OF COMPUTATION: TRANSPARENCY AND FAIRNESS

Unlike the computer-assisted reporters studied in chapter 1, the journalists discussed here were never in a position to define a consistent and original "politics of computation." Rooted in the prestigious field of investigative reporting, the former had been able to develop standards independently, free of strong commercial or political pressure. By contrast, "ranker journalists" were not only more dependent on the market—a ranking that did not sell was unlikely to be maintained—but also under constant pressure from powerful actors who had a say in what should be measured and calculated. Their marginal position in the journalistic profession did not allow them to decide for themselves what criteria should be used to determine good and bad rankings. It is nevertheless interesting to examine how *U.S. News* editors and reporters adjusted the ways they calculated the quality of institutions in response to harsh criticism. Although they did not develop a set of standards for the profession as a whole, they did start to sketch out what from a journalistic point of view might constitute a responsible way of calculating.

In the face of critics who questioned the principle of measuring institutional quality, *U.S. News* editors' response was deflective. Certainly, this was a difficult undertaking, they argued, and it would be excessive to claim to fully capture a college's quality by calculating a few variables. But the ranking was a process of continuous improvement, which was in any case more satisfactory than maintaining a situation where students and their families remained wholly in the dark about the quality of an institution. In their justifications, the editors focused the discussion on the statistical model applied and the underlying choices, which enabled them to recognize its shortcomings and to call for more constructive criticism to make improvements.[50] Disclosing the statistical model behind calculations quickly became a standard for *U.S. News* journalists. Because they claimed to assess the quality of institutions, it was not possible for them to keep their method entirely secret. As early as 1988, the "America's Best Colleges" issue detailed the variables used to evaluate college performance. From 1991, the statistical weightings were also made public. As the former *U.S. News* editor Alvin Sanoff explained, the goal was to deflect the accusation that reporters were acting "behind the curtain of secrecy": "The explanation of the methodology in the 1991 edition was the beginning of an ongoing effort to spell out clearly how the rankings are determined. The aim was—and is—to make the methodology transparent. Experts could quarrel with the methodology— and quarrel with it they did—but they could not accuse *U.S. News* of operating behind a curtain of secrecy."[51]

The need for transparency emphasized by the *U.S. News* editor here was not entirely original. It reflected a norm that was beginning to prevail in American and French journalism when these calculation-based rankings appeared. This transparency norm requires journalists to explain and justify the choices guiding their news-production practices because those choices are likely to affect the status and safety of their fellow citizens.[52] The use of calculations did not absolve news organizations from following this norm. Therefore, from the early 1990s most French and U.S. magazines added methodological details to their rankings to shield themselves from criticism and possible legal action.[53] Statistical models were rarely described in full, and raw data were never released, but journalists could not escape the imperative to disclose information on the choices informing their models.

Moreover, the *U.S. News* reporters gradually adjusted their model to make their evaluations fairer. In 1997, they introduced a new variable called "added value" to measure the rate of students graduating from each college within five years, irrespective of its financial resources and the number of students recruited. The assumption was that a college with greater resources and better students should have a higher rate of students graduating in five years. The magazine began to calculate every college's "expected rate" to establish the proportion of students who were expected to graduate within five years, given their initial level of education and the college's financial resources. The difference between the expected rate and the observed rate allowed journalists to determine the institution's "added value." As Sanoff explained, "The data show that some schools with less academically gifted students and lesser resources do as good a job of retaining and graduating students as more well-endowed institutions that enroll students with higher test scores. Again, this is not a perfect measure, but it represents an effort to address complaints from a number of institutions with lesser resources that the rankings unfairly rewarded well-endowed institutions that enrolled students with higher test scores."[54]

Journalists saw the measurement of added value as a way to earn institutional rankings greater legitimacy. It allowed them to challenge the traditional hierarchy of institutions because a rich and prestigious college would have little added value if, given the very good students it attracted, it did not succeed in making them perform better than they would have in any other college.

On the other side of the Atlantic, this practice of including added value in calculations was required by the government. From 1994, the Ministry of Education introduced this type of model to evaluate high schools, and French magazines immediately adopted it. As the sociologist Christian Baudelot explained, the objective was to "debunk the consecrated glories":

> With this method, you could debunk the consecrated glories: based on these criteria, the Lycée Louis Le Grand and the Lycée Henry IV were no longer the best high schools. By rejecting their bad pupils every year and taking the cream of the crop from other high schools, they had a very high apparent success rate, but measured in terms of the educational work accomplished, their success rate was very low. Their social selection practice was thus exposed and sanctioned. On the other hand, there

were very good schools elsewhere, less well-known or unknown schools, where quite a respectable job was being done, and which were never talked about.[55]

Although this added-value standard did not prevail in all news organizations, for most American and French journalists it appeared to provide a statistical response to the accusation of "politicized computation."

DEALING WITH THE EFFECTS OF COMPUTATION: FINDING THE RIGHT DISTANCE FROM INSTITUTIONS

Journalists producing rankings first positioned themselves as detached observers whose legitimacy derived from their ability to evaluate institutions from a distance. The use of impersonal procedures and especially of calculations was central to this approach because it allowed for a considerable distance to be maintained between the news organization and the schools, universities, and hospitals being evaluated. Close and sustained contact with actors from higher education or health-care systems seemed both unnecessary and potentially harmful. And yet as seen with "America's Best Colleges," critics highlighted how the use of calculation was no guarantee of impartiality both because most colleges' executives used tricks to manipulate the data sent to the magazine and because journalists had to choose a statistical model and their choice could implicitly favor the interests of a few institutional actors. As a result, it became less justifiable for journalists to claim to be measuring college performance from afar. Conversely, they could not get too close to institutions, or they would no longer be able to claim to defend the public interest. They therefore had to find the right distance from institutions: neither too close nor too far.

In the early 1990s, *U.S. News* reporters and editors established regular contact with higher-education actors by attending conferences, meeting with experts, and even organizing their own symposia on educational evaluation. They also sought to integrate education professionals into the magazine by setting up "advisory committees" with admissions officers, guidance counsellors, and people in charge of producing statistics from universities. From the editors' point of view, the purpose of fostering a closer relationship with institutions was twofold. First, they saw it as a way to adjust their evaluation method. Because there were many debates around evaluation in higher education, and because public authorities constantly requested the release of new data, *U.S. News* reporters found it necessary to remain close to the actors in the academic world. As Robert Morse acknowledged in 2015, "We are not experts. In essence, we're picking people's brains. We're always talking to experts in the field or attending conferences to find out what new data can be available."[56]

Second, in the search for greater proximity the editors and reporters endeavored to channel criticism without giving the impression that they were trying to escape it. They therefore paid close attention to the criticisms and requests that they regularly received. As a result, even those who were the most critical of rankings recognized the magazine's openness: "*U.S. News*, in turn, has been extremely responsive to these concerns," wrote one expert in educational policy. "Not only has the magazine opened its doors to visitors, but its editors regularly attend national higher education meetings and sometimes host their own in Washington, DC. Without question, this willingness to listen and to make changes has positioned *U.S. News* as the leading arbiter of college quality in the United States today."[57] Paradoxically, calculating the quality of institutions while remaining at a considerable distance from them proved impossible for *U.S. News*. The same went for those who produced the rankings that emerged in Europe in that period.[58] As journalists could not remain at a distance from the institutions they evaluated, they instead sought to be accepted as a part of this institutional world.

Furthermore, because the poor quality of the data sent to *U.S. News* by colleges was a sword of Damocles hanging over the rankers' heads, the magazine's journalists joined forces with a range of actors and organizations to strengthen their claim to measure college performance. Federal agencies and administrations in charge of evaluating universities provided them with data, thus helping them to establish an asymmetry between the magazine and colleges: "At the beginning," Morse explained, "we became powerful not because of the freedom of information but because we would rank schools even if they wouldn't submit the data. We would come up with a way of using existing government data or other data, and it would be our choice whether we would rank this school and not the school's choice. So they could not get out of the ranking by not participating."[59]

When in 1995 the *Wall Street Journal* revealed the manipulations underlying the data received and used by the magazine,[60] the metrological assumption suddenly appeared to be weakened. But *U.S. News* journalists managed to maintain their position by strengthening their relationships with the public agencies that evaluated U.S. universities and with the professionals who produced the data within colleges.[61] Not only did they collect more data from the federal government and more systematically cross-check it with the data reported by colleges, but they also began to develop data standards with stakeholders in the American academic community. According to Morse, "We had to create our own definitions. This was at the very beginning. But over time, [as] we developed with other people the common data sets, we realized we needed common standardization. So we worked with other publishers and higher educators to develop a common data set so [as] to standardize educational data definitions."[62] Thanks to these alliances, the *U.S. News* journalists managed to maintain asymmetry with colleges. As a result, a large part of the academic community has reluctantly been forced to accept the journalists' metrological pretensions.

The case of *U.S. News* thus shows that the calculation of institutional performance has had the effect of making these journalists full-fledged players in the world of higher education. Measuring performance did not imply staying away from institutions but rather building alliances within this world. However, such proximity to institutional actors has put news organizations at risk of becoming too dependent on the institutions being ranked, and this risk has become all the greater because ranker journalists never mobilized within the profession to gain recognition and autonomy. Apart from *U.S. News* and a few other American news outlets, which continue to have in-house capacities to crunch the data, most U.S. media outlets have chosen to rely on outside firms or consultants to produce rankings. As a result, these media ranking practices have largely ceased to be journalistic practices as such both because media groups have sought to make these editorial products more profitable, removing them from concerns relating to educational reform, and because journalists have remained uncomfortable with these calculation practices. French magazines seem to have kept the practice more internalized, but suspicion has remained high regarding the calculation methods used, and media organizations have been accused of aligning themselves with the methods used by the government.[63] This collective inability to maintain a distance from institutions may explain why data journalists today have little appreciation for the legacy of French or American ranker journalists.

* * *

This chapter has revealed that alongside the pioneering work by American computer-assisted reporters to reconcile professional ethics and computational practices, humbler French and U.S. "ranker journalists" have written another history of contemporary data journalism. Although now widely overlooked, their experience showed what it meant before the web for journalists to face the consequences of computation. However, it cannot be said that this experience should serve as a model for contemporary data journalists. Rather, it should serve as a reminder that computation alone cannot guarantee more transparent institutions and better-informed citizens. As journalists engage in computational practices, even ones driven by a commitment to democratization, they remain accountable for the undesirable effects of their calculations.

With these historical lessons in mind, I now turn to the rise of data journalism in France and the United States since the late 2000s. In the context of intense transformation of journalism, the ethical problems that computer-assisted reporters and rankers faced earlier only grew larger as a result of greater access to data and calculations.

PART II

A CHALLENGE FOR JOURNALISM

3
REBOOTING JOURNALISM

A strange expression has emerged among journalists advocating the use of data and algorithms in journalism since the late 2000s: in response to the major crisis affecting the news industry, they have called for "rebooting journalism."[1] This stance conveys remarkable faith in technology, in sharp contrast not only with most journalists' understanding of their own professional identity but also with the approach of the journalists discussed in the previous chapters. Whereas computer-assisted reporters before the web had forged a politics of computation concerned with keeping technology at a distance and adjusting it to the core values of the profession, "data journalists" have pushed for the exact opposite: to rebuild the values, practices, and organization of journalism *through* technology. The second part of this book shows that this technology-driven approach to journalism has challenged the profession as a whole, highlighting the need for a renewed ethics of journalism. This chapter illustrates how this approach to technology has crystallized around a professional segment of data journalists, which emerged internationally in close connection with the developments that defined the web from the mid-2000s. Chapter 4 discusses the unequal importance that the profession has given these practices in France and the United States, challenging the narrative of two distinct "cultures of objectivity." Finally, chapter 5 explores the controversy surrounding data journalists' epistemological propositions and the reactions to those propositions from the profession as a whole.

The expression *data journalism* was coined in England at the end of 2008 by the editors of the *Guardian*. Although French journalists had no words to name these news practices at the time, several similar expressions were already circulating in the United States, including established expressions such as *precision journalism* (1970s) and *computer-assisted reporting* (1990s) as well as more recent ones such as *database journalism* (early 2000s) and *hacker journalism* (late 2000s). Around the world, thousands of journalists gradually embraced the term *data journalism* and the claim that integrating data practices and computational skills in newsrooms and properly recognizing them as fully-fledged journalism would enable the whole profession to better fulfill its missions: to make governments more transparent, shed light on social issues, and help citizens make better-informed decisions. As we saw in the previous chapters, this claim was nothing new in and of itself. What was unprecedented, however, was both the level of expectation placed on technology and the international scale of the trend, as evidenced by the number of translations of the term *data journalism* (*journalisme de données*, *Datenjournalismus*, *periodismo de datos*, *журналистике данных*, 数据新闻, etc.) and the vast network of technical and cognitive resources that has developed for this practice throughout the world.[2]

Data journalism has not developed equally in France and the United States. In the United States, we can estimate that at least two thousand people identified with this segment as of 2020,[3] be they individuals hired as a "data journalist" or with related titles such as "data reporter" or "data editor" or more regular journalists who use these skills in their daily work. In France, the segment is much smaller, involving only a couple hundred people.[4] Although small in number, these French enthusiasts have nevertheless taken the plunge, and major French media companies have created data journalist positions. In the next chapter, I look at the differences surrounding professional groups' integration of this segment across the two countries. For now, however, the key question is: How has this professional segment been able to form in such a short period of time not only in the United States, where data journalism practices have a fairly long history, but also in France, where they long remained uncommon and marginal?

Like other technology-oriented areas of journalism that have emerged over the past decade, such as mobile journalism, robot journalism, and ambient journalism, data journalism raises a challenge for the study of journalism as a profession. The emphasis on technology is at odds with how the profession took shape in the United States and France. Since the late nineteenth century, the journalism profession has built its identity on mastering general skills, such as writing and news gathering, over the technical skills specific to each medium. As Henrik Örnebring notes, although the emergence of new media in the twentieth century required new skills from journalists—for example, with radio journalists having to use their voice as a professional tool—it was unnecessary for most journalists to demonstrate any knowledge of printing, radio, or TV broadcasting technology.[5] In the construction of professional identities in both countries, specialization in subject areas or "beats" has clearly prevailed over technological specialization.[6] How then can we explain that some journalists see data and algorithms as essential to the reconstruction of the profession?

Building on Anselm Strauss's theory of professions,[7] I consider journalism as a constantly evolving entity within which multiple coalitions develop and thrive in opposition to others, often by relying on a specific technology. From this perspective, data journalism has emerged as a "segment"—that is, a coalition that draws on technology to challenge the missions and practices of the whole profession.[8] To shed light on the dynamics that have guided the constitution of this segment in the United States and France, I interviewed seventy-five people who were involved in this process on both sides of the Atlantic.[9] This chapter demonstrates precisely that the rise of this segment in different national contexts is closely linked to a series of developments affecting the web since the mid-2000s. In a context where journalism has seen its social role and working conditions profoundly weakened, these web developments have allowed a group of journalists to promote an alternative vision of the relationship between journalism and technology that has attracted a growing number of individuals looking both to change journalism and to secure a place for themselves in a very competitive job market.

INCREASINGLY BLURRED LINES BETWEEN "PIPELINE" AND "CONTENT"

Until the late 2000s, it was generally clear to most journalists that their role was to produce editorial "content" and that the role of people in information technology was to provide the "pipeline"—that is, the infrastructure that would allow for this content to be formatted and delivered to audiences. Although some journalists and news organizations started exploring innovative ways of producing news by using web technology as early as the 1990s,[10] the vast majority of French and American journalists long viewed the web as a channel for disseminating news that was designed primarily for another medium.[11] However, this division of labor between journalists and information technologists has gradually been challenged by the developments shaping the web since the mid-2000s. The efforts of major web companies, open-source communities, and open-data activists have enabled computer people to claim a more active role in the production of editorial content.

Since the mid-2000s, the web has evolved by integrating infrastructures that facilitate the production of a range of information services drawing on data, be they data produced by companies or administrations or other organizations. These services, called "web applications," have taken many different forms, including interactive maps and searchable databases, and have been developed in a wide variety of sectors (weather, transportation, health, finance, commerce, etc.). The economic and human resources required to produce these applications have decreased with the development of such infrastructure as application programming interfaces (APIs), data-mining techniques, web frameworks, cloud computing, data-visualization techniques, and so on. Accordingly, a growing number of people have been in a position to produce editorial content for the web.

APIs were first introduced in 2005 by Amazon and Google, which saw an economic interest in disseminating some of their own data. By allowing businesses and people to exploit these data to create new services, these companies aimed to extend their influence over the web. With APIs, any organization could thus make a data stream available on the web in a sufficiently standard format for developers to be able to exploit it to design new services. As companies and organizations distributed their data via APIs, it became cheaper to produce applications that would provide information to users about a variety of topics. For instance, the Google Maps API, launched in 2005, provides access to mapping data, which has enabled a large number of programmers, often self-taught, to quickly produce maps on a wide range of topics—from crime and transportation to public services.

"Web-development frameworks," designed within open-source communities, are another type of infrastructure that considerably reduced the time and resources required to produce web applications. The best-known frameworks, Ruby on Rails and Django, appeared in the mid-2000s: they allowed for certain development tasks to be automated and made it easier to connect with APIs. Together with other infrastructure, these frameworks helped to grow the population of data application producers by making the process accessible to computer enthusiasts and self-taught developers. Moreover, they enabled web developers to build applications within days or even hours instead of weeks. This web infrastructure allowed a greater number of people with a background in web programming to challenge the way they were perceived by most journalists. Far from just building pipeline, they could now produce editorial content from data.

The vast majority of French and American journalists still unequivocally do not see these web applications as journalistic content. Nevertheless, the developments that have shaped the web have made it more difficult for them to claim that programmers can contribute to journalism only by building pipeline to format and deliver news content. With the rise of the open-data movement in particular, the established division of labor between journalists and web workers has become blurrier. By promoting data infrastructure as political technology, open-data activists have claimed stake to certain missions that journalists have traditionally seen as their prerogative in the profession.

THE CIVIC POTENTIAL OF DATA

Until the late 2000s, only journalists and social or political scientists were concerned with accessing government records. However, such access has gradually become a major cause among web activists, computer enthusiasts, and workers in the computer industry. Mobilizing on an international scale, they have sought to see data infrastructure recognized as political technology on the grounds that such technology can afford greater citizen participation in public affairs, increased government transparency, and better communication between different levels of government.[12] By claiming to fulfill some of the missions traditionally assigned to journalists and by developing online information frameworks for citizens, open-data activists have in fact also strengthened web activists' and workers' claim to contribute to public debate through data-oriented technology.

In the United States, this mobilization has stemmed from two distinct movements. The first, known as the "open-government movement," dates back to the postwar era and involved a large number of civil society actors advocating government transparency.[13] It led to the Freedom of Information Act of 1966, which guaranteed citizen access to government records, subsequently providing a foundation for the push for government accountability. The second movement, known as the "open-data movement," pertains mainly to the scientific domain. As early as the 1980s, it established the conditions for broad access to scientific data.[14] The two movements have gradually converged since the mid-1990s and more decisively under the impetus of the Obama administration, which in 2008 launched an open-government directive requiring federal agencies to publish at least three major databases in an open format on the new portal Data.gov.

In France, no social movement ever developed around citizen access to government records. Nevertheless, open-data advocacy found an echo among the actors advocating internet freedom in the late 2000s, when two laws were passed to regulate copyright on the internet.[15] A movement subsequently formed among proponents of the political virtues of the internet and the free flow of information.[16] These individuals, originally involved in open-source software, grew interested in institutional politics as they challenged these new copyright laws. It was in this specific context that some of them joined the international movement that began to form around open data in the late 2000s. The impetus here came not so much from the United States as from Great Britain, which has seen the rise of a particularly vigorous movement for open data since the start of the 2010s. The campaign launched in 2006 by the *Guardian* against British government agencies commercializing the data they produce by means of taxpayer funds, thus making taxpayers pay twice for those data, particularly resonated with French web activists fighting for internet freedom a few years later.[17]

Through this international movement, activists have developed an original perspective on how more open-government data could contribute to better democracy. Guided by some of the ideals rooted in the history of the internet, this approach emphasizes the benefits of a free flow of information and the need to remain wary of public authorities.[18] Activists have come to define a set of sociotechnical conditions that data must respect in order to be "open" and to contribute to the greater accountability of those in power: not only should government records be available in digital form and freely accessible to the greatest number of people, but they should also be comprehensive, constantly updated, and granular.[19] Access to granular data—that is, nonaggregated data—is particularly important for these activists, as Daniel X. O'Neil, a Chicago-based activist, explains: "Aggregate is a way to lie obviously. So [the information] has to be granular—i.e., incident level, right?—in order to be even remotely useful."[20] This approach to government data, which I further discuss in chapter 5, departs from journalists' traditional approach embraced by computer-assisted reporters in the 1990s. For the latter, the aggregation of data guaranteed not only that they were of high quality but also that the journalist would be able to interpret them. For open-data activists, on the contrary, data should be

A CHALLENGE FOR JOURNALISM

aggregated as little as possible so that there will be no manipulation by public authorities.

Far from simply calling for public data to be made available, these activists have also engaged in the production of websites or applications designed to increase government accountability and involve citizens in public affairs. Both in the United States and in France, they have begun collecting data from local and state governments on a variety of subjects (public spending, legislative votes, business licenses, roadworks, law enforcement, etc.) and processing them to make the actions of those in power visible through tables, charts, maps, and search engines. They have engaged in these technological practices as a means to fix some of the flaws of democracy, such as the influence of money in politics or unequal service to citizens. French activists, although in smaller numbers than in the United States, have devoted considerable energy to obtaining data and designing websites. For example, the nonprofit organization Regards citoyens was launched in 2009 by a handful of open-software activists with a view to making French democratic institutions more visible. They built data infrastructure that retrieves information about the in-government activities of members of the French National Assembly and presents that information through interactive charts and tables on a dedicated website. Through this website, we can thus learn that during the year 2016 the MP Jean-David Ciot participated in thirty-nine committees, spoke in Parliament twenty-eight times, and drafted one bill, ranking among the 40 percent least-active members of Parliament (figure 3.1).

Neither in the United States nor in France, however, has the rise of these activist practices directly weakened the journalistic profession. First, open-data activists have experienced major difficulties in reaching the general public because most of the websites they produce have attracted only a small number of users.[21] Second, as the sociologist Andrew Abbott has pointed out, the computer professions tend to be poorly organized and constantly restructured.[22] Nevertheless, this international movement has given data-driven technological practices a set of political meanings that strongly resonate with the journalistic profession—in particular by increasing government accountability and by fostering citizen participation in public

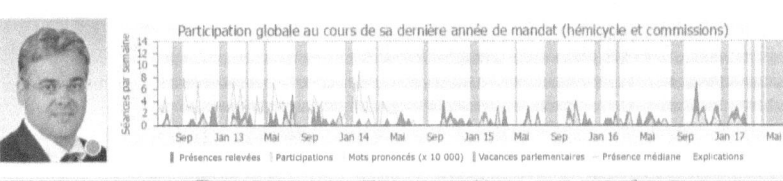

FIGURE 3.1 The government activity of a French MP exposed through data, 2016.
Source: Screenshot from the NosDéputés.fr website at http://www.NosDéputés.fr.

affairs. Building on this movement, some journalists in both countries have come to promote data technology—though in different ways—as a means to reinvent journalism, which has been severely weakened over the past couple of decades.

ADVOCATING FOR AN ALTERNATE DIVISION OF LABOR

In the United States, several journalists gained visibility within the profession in the mid-2000s by advocating an alternate division of labor between journalists and programmers. Having initially trained at journalism schools but also being trained in computer-assisted-reporting, Aron Pilhofer, Adrian Holovaty, Ben Welsh, and Matt Waite distinguished themselves from their peers by becoming personally involved in the developments of the web that I have just described. With the support of journalism institutions such as major U.S. newspapers and foundations, they articulated a critique of the way journalism integrates technology. In substance, they argued that the division between journalists who produce editorial content and programmers who build the infrastructure to gather, format the data behind this content and to disseminate that content was no longer appropriate. In their view, recognizing data and computational practices as having a place in journalism would enable the profession to better fulfill its missions. By arguing that news organizations should set up dedicated units staffed with people equally familiar with both journalism and code, they have played a decisive role in the formation of data journalism as a segment of American journalism.

Adrian Holovaty's early career is emblematic of the rise within U.S. journalism of figures with one foot in journalism and the other in web programming. After graduating in journalism from the University of Missouri in 2001, he was hired as a journalist and web developer first at the *Atlanta Journal-Constitution* and then at the *Lawrence Journal-World*, two newspapers known for their innovative use of technology. In 2005, he gained notoriety in open-source communities by designing Django, a web-development framework that made it possible to design web applications within a timeframe that fit the journalistic pace of news production. That same year he became one of the first programmers to build a "mash-up," a web application connecting two different sources of data, in this case Google Maps data and data provided by the Chicago Police Department. The result was a website called ChicagoCrime.org, which provided users with a map of all crimes committed in their neighborhood. This project earned him journalistic recognition, as evidenced by the media coverage of ChicagoCrimes.org ("one of the 'best ideas' of 2005," according to the *New York Times*),[23] the prizes he was awarded by journalism schools, and the job offers he received from major news organizations. Within a matter of months, he was hired as an "editor of editorial innovations" at the *Washington Post*, where he led the redesign of the newspaper's website and created several data-driven applications that attracted a national audience.[24] In 2007, Holovaty obtained funding from the Knight Foundation to build EveryBlock.com, a website that collects data from major U.S. cities to provide residents with local information about crime, shops, roadworks, and real estate transactions. EveryBlock.com, with ties to the open-data movement, has gained a certain recognition within American journalism, as its acquisition by NBC News in 2009 attests. After promoting "journalism via computer programming," Holovaty left journalism in 2012.

Holovaty's career trajectory reveals the connection that has gradually developed between journalism, open-source communities, and the open-data movement. Throughout the 2000s, he proposed innovative editorial formats strongly rooted in these communities, becoming a translator of the web's infrastructural transformations in U.S. journalism. More importantly, Holovaty's early career highlights journalism institutions' strong support for this translation effort. Not only was he recruited to prestigious positions by major newspapers and funded by major foundations, but he also quickly attracted the interest of journalism schools and media companies. Clearly, many players in U.S. journalism see technology as the solution to the major crisis facing journalism. For example, as Seth Lewis has shown, the Knight Foundation changed its standards in the mid-2000s, prioritizing funding for journalistic projects that integrate software development and computer-generated data.[25] The attention given to Holovaty and his fellow "programmer-journalists" was therefore a product of the expectations that many journalistic institutions began to place on technology.

In discussions with their colleagues, these programmer-journalists criticized journalism in two different ways, pointing to both the profession's struggle to fulfill its democratic mission and the lack of efficiency in the news-production process. The first criticism is informed by both long-standing criticisms of journalism in American society and criticism from within the profession: journalism is too dependent on institutional sources; it values opinions too much at the expense of facts; it is not transparent enough about how information is produced; and it does not allow enough citizens to make informed decisions. The novelty here lies not in the nature of these criticisms but rather in the epistemological propositions made by these programmer-journalists and data journalists more broadly (which I discuss in detail in chapter 5). These propositions, building on the transformations of the web and the open-data movement, make the case that integrating specific data and computational practices into the core of journalistic labor could alleviate the listed problems.

The second criticism voiced by programmer-journalists is related to the industry as a whole. Adrian Holovaty played an important role here when in 2006 he pointed to a "fundamental way newspaper sites need to change."

A CHALLENGE FOR JOURNALISM

He argued that newspapers are facing an industrial problem in that they spend significant resources on collecting information that is no longer usable by either readers or the newspaper once it is published in articles. It would be more efficient, he claimed, to think of what journalists collect on a day-to-day basis as "structured information," information that can be cut and sliced in an automated way by computers:

> For example, say a newspaper has written a story about a local fire. Being able to read that story on a cell phone is fine and dandy. Hooray, technology! But what I *really* want to be able to do is explore the raw facts of that story, one by one, with layers of attribution, and an infrastructure for comparing the details of the fire—date, time, place, victims, fire station number, distance from fire department, names and years experience of firemen on the scene, time it took for firemen to arrive—with the details of previous fires. And subsequent fires, whenever they happen.[26]

According to Holovaty, looking at journalistic information as a set of "structured data" would benefit news organizations because they would be able to reuse information collected in the past to easily offer new editorial products. Holovaty thus translated a set of theories discussed in the world of the web that propose to consider the web no longer simply as a medium to access documents but as sets of data that can be processed automatically.[27] News organization would avoid missed opportunities by storing their own already published information in databases: "But the goal for me, a data person focused more on the long term, is to store information in the most valuable format possible. . . . [I]t's a problem of *lost opportunity*. If all of your information is stored in the same 'news article' bucket, you can't easily pull out just the crimes and plot them on a map of the city. You can't easily grab the events to create an event calendar."[28] This push for a greater rationalization of news production did not originate within data journalism. As Eric Klinenberg has shown, already in the late 1990s the rise of the web offered media companies the opportunity to reprocess information initially tailored for particular media.[29] However, the programmer-journalists sparked interest, particularly among their fellow journalists, by highlighting the rationalization opportunities surrounding data practices. By positioning themselves as journalists, they escaped any suspicion of trying to rationalize journalism by breaching the standards of the profession.

The idea that tasks such as maintaining a database and designing scripts to collect, connect, or visualize data should be considered journalistic has, however, been met with skepticism within the profession. In response to his colleagues' reservations, Holovaty has urged them to "care less about what is or is not 'journalism' and [to] care more about the important information that is useful to people and helps them understand the world."[30]

A NEW SEGMENT OF AMERICAN JOURNALISM

From the late 2000s, a professional coalition gradually emerged within U.S. journalism around the designation *data journalism*. This development was linked to the creation of independent and sometimes nonprofit media that have a strong focus on data, such as ProPublica, but it was also driven by more established news organizations, which began hiring people from various backgrounds to handle a wide range of data practices within the newsroom. For newspapers such as the *Chicago Tribune*, the *New York Times*, and the *Washington Post*, the main goal here was not to increase traffic or commercial revenue in the short run. Rather, as my study of the *Chicago Tribune* and Cindy Royal's study of the *New York Times* illustrate,[31] it was to foster new forms of cooperation between traditional journalists and programmers by reducing the spatial and professional distance between them. The expected benefits revolved around the rationalization of news production, even if brand building was also important for these prestigious newspapers, which were keen to be seen as contributing to innovation.

The data journalism teams within major newspapers' newsrooms included individuals with a background in web development or open-government advocacy. At the *Chicago Tribune*, for example, a "news applications team" was created in the spring of 2009 to bridge the gap between the newspaper's editorial staff and the information technology department by helping investigative reporters dig through piles of data and build web applications. With no previous experience in journalism, the team's members had come from web development and programming. The team leader, Brian Boyer, had previously worked as a consultant and software architect in marketing, banking, and the medical industry before obtaining a grant from the Knight Foundation dedicated to training developers in journalism. At the *Chicago Tribune*, he hired three colleagues in the open-data community in Chicago. One of them, Joe Germuska, had long worked as a web developer in advertising, devoting his spare time to coding open-source software. Highly involved in open-data activism, he founded the organization Open Government Chicago in 2009 while looking for a job in state government. He subsequently met Brian and was asked to join the applications team at the *Tribune* as a news-application developer. For these individuals, journalism thus appears to have been a way of aligning their professional life with their attachment to the civic potential of technology.[32]

Other individuals without any previous professional experience in web development or any commitment to open-source communities gradually joined this team and others. They were young graduates from journalism schools who were recruited to work alongside the more technology-oriented professionals. Some of them had trained in web programming and acted as intermediaries between traditional journalists and web developers. This was the case of Tasneem Raja, who a few years after graduating in journalism from the University of Berkeley became an interactive editor at *Mother Jones*, where she was in charge of "translating back and forth between the technology team and the editorial team" and of "creat[ing] projects that were better than what [each team] could do alone."[33] Others were recruited by established news organizations as "data reporters" in charge of verifying and enriching databases built as part of an investigative project. Traditional journalistic skills remain crucial in these roles because they are required for interviewing sources, gathering documents, and carrying out relatively simple statistical processing. This expansion to include people with no professional experience in web programming has undoubtedly contributed to the success of data journalism in U.S. journalism since the early 2010s. Far more than earlier forms of computer-assisted reporting, data journalism has made it possible to integrate a great variety of profiles and skills.

Despite their diverse profiles and skills, workers who identify with data journalism in the United States have developed a certain solidarity, reflected in discussions and resource sharing that transcend the boundaries of media organizations. As several professionals I interviewed in Chicago and San Francisco explained, it is common for them to share code with one another or even to discuss how they organize work in newsrooms. For example, when Tasneem Raja was put in charge of setting up a news-application team in a newly created news organization in San Francisco in 2009, she contacted the people in charge of the most reputable data teams in the country:

> I just kind of cold-called Brian Boyer over at the *Tribune*, and I talked to Scott Kline at ProPublica and somebody at the *LA Times*. I just reached out to them, and I said, "Hi, I'm from the *Bay Citizen*. You don't know me, but I know you and your work, and I really want to do what you guys are doing in your markets in the Bay Area." . . . I said, "I got the resources; I just don't know how. How do you do this?" So they were amazing, and they really talked me through their workflows and how they managed their teams . . . and just how long it takes and what you need to worry about.[34]

Above all, this solidarity is exemplified by a set of cognitive and technical resources, such as coding libraries and tutorials made widely accessible in keeping with the principles of open-source communities. The growth of this segment in the United Stated is producing what Michel Callon calls "hybrid communities"—that is, collectives that extend beyond organizations, comprise humans and nonhumans, and include laymen, professionals, users, and experts from different areas.[35]

A SIMILAR SEGMENT IN FRANCE

A similar segment emerged around data journalism in France after 2010, bringing together people from different backgrounds around the idea that journalistic recognition of data and computational practices would enable the profession to better fulfill its missions. Apart from the fact that this segment has remained much smaller in France than in the United States, major news organizations have also played a very different role in its emergence. It was not until 2012 that major French newspapers such as *Le Monde* and *Libération* hired data journalists to work in their newsrooms. As a result, unlike in the United States, in France the new segment first appeared at the margins of the professional group.

The introduction of data journalism in France around 2010 was not the direct product of American influence—computer-assisted reporting was totally unknown to French journalists at the time, as were the American programmer-journalists of the late 2000s. Rather, it was British influence, more precisely the *Guardian*, that first introduced the term *data journalism* to France at the end of 2008. The impetus came from a small organization called Objet web non identifié, or OWNI (Unidentified Web Object), created in 2009 by a young entrepreneur involved in the movement for internet freedom. This organization was far removed from the profession at the time: its founder had no experience in journalism; it was not a news website but "a laboratory for experimenting with new ways of creating added value in the field of information," and it was a nonprofit media organization affiliated with a commercial company that produced websites and web applications for clients. However, at the initiative of Nicolas Kayser-Bril, a young journalist versed in web development, the organization imported the term *data journalism* from the *Guardian* and made it the core of its activity by hiring young developers involved in the open-data movement. Over the three years of its existence, OWNI contributed to legitimizing these practices within French journalism in two ways. First, it captured the interest of many journalists, particularly by building a web application in 2010 at the request of Julian Assange with the purpose of leaking four hundred thousand confidential documents on the war in Iraq. The Warlog Irak application, which received an award from the Online News Association in the United States,[36] thus gave significant visibility to data journalism within the profession in France. Second, OWNI legitimized data journalism practices by designing web applications for French media organizations that allowed dozens of individuals from a programming background to engage in journalism and work for major mainstream news organizations.

When OWNI went bankrupt in 2012, a space opened up in the French media ecosystem where people with a background in web development could engage in editorial production. Journalists and developers in that space have set up a work organization that challenges the established division between content-creating journalists and pipeline-building programmers, as explained by Pierre Romera, who was hired at OWNI after studying computer engineering: "When we started working on the Warlog project, we all sat down together, journalists and developers, and we all came up with ideas. It was the first time that I, as a developer, was given a seat at the table, and that's when we started working together. And after that, it was almost systematic."[37] At OWNI, the promotion of data journalism therefore went hand in hand with less division of labor between journalists and developers. It also involved paying constant attention to all the data collection, processing, and visualization tools made available on the web by British and U.S. journalists or by open-source activists more broadly. This organization of work, however, has taken much longer to emerge within the most recognized French news organizations than in news organizations on the other side of the Atlantic.

Starting in 2012, several news outlets in France opened data journalist positions with the aim of producing innovative web content and exploring new journalistic formats. *Le Monde* initiated the process by hiring a data journalist from OWNI to produce a richer analysis of the 2012 French presidential campaign in line with the newspaper's significant fact-checking efforts surrounding that campaign. This data journalist, positioned at the heart of the newsroom, was to interact with the more traditional journalists and familiarize them with data-collection and analysis processes. In the following years, national and regional newspapers (*Libération*, *Le Figaro*,

Le Parisien, etc.), magazines (*Paris Match*), television networks (France Television), news agencies (Agence France Presse), and various news websites hired data journalists, sometimes setting up data teams in charge of producing editorial content. In most organizations, data journalists work across a variety of topics (politics, economics, society, sports, etc.). In contrast with the United States, however, most French news organizations show little division of data labor. Data journalists thus appear to be generalist workers, who interact primarily with traditional journalists.

Although some forerunners in this segment in France had a background in web development, the segment eventually became predominantly populated with men initially trained in journalism. A questionnaire I sent to news organizations in late 2019[38] thus shows an overrepresentation of men among French data journalists: 70 percent, compared to 52 percent in the global profession as a whole.[39] It also suggests that about 60 percent of them trained in journalism, surprisingly in line with all French journalists who entered the profession in the 2000s.[40] The segment therefore comprises primarily individuals who were first trained in journalism and for whom data journalism offered a way into a competitive job market. To a lesser extent, it also includes individuals with backgrounds in computer science and graphic design as well as in science and marketing. For some of these professionals, who until now could contribute to the production of information but could not claim to be journalists, the data journalism segment thus provides an opportunity to cross a professional boundary.

As the segment has opened up to a wider array of professional profiles, the range of skills and practices that fall under the scope of data journalism has also broadened, as scholars in several countries have noted.[41] Responses to the survey I sent out indicate that French journalists who identify with this segment are mostly in charge of data-collection practices (mostly via scraping and APIs), the verification and enrichment of original databases, statistical processing using spreadsheet software (rather than R programming language or SPSS software), and the use of software to publish graphs and maps (rather than in web-application development). As the segment has grown, the scope of the tasks involved has expanded well beyond web-development practices to include practices with less demanding but still uncommon requirements, such as operating a spreadsheet or using visualization software.

Thus, in both France and the United States the data journalism segment comprises mainly young individuals trained in journalism, who see data journalism as an opportunity within a context of crisis and who are motivated by certain shared dynamics in both countries.

COPING WITH THE CRISIS

In both the United States and France, young journalists joining the data journalism segment see these technology-oriented practices as a solution to the problem of navigating the current crisis of journalism: they view them as a way both to find a place for themselves in a highly competitive job market and to enable the journalism of today to better align with the ideals of the profession.[42] The newspaper crisis in both countries has been demonstrated by a shortage of jobs, the intensification of work, and the decline of trust in newspapers.[43] Although it has materialized in different ways in the two countries, it has weighed heavily on newcomers to the profession since the mid-2000s and has led them to embrace the challenge of data journalism.

In my interviews with data journalists in both countries,[44] these individuals identified a broad set of data and programming skills that they felt provided them with a better chance of entering or remaining in the profession. On both sides of the Atlantic, the crisis has considerably exacerbated the challenge of getting any job in journalism, let alone an interesting one. For this reason, young journalists have either seized the opportunity to put forward skills that they acquired alongside their journalism training or consciously decided to train in technologies that they expect will broaden their opportunities to enter the profession. Jules Bonnard, a data journalist at Agence France Presse and a teacher at a journalism school, exemplifies the first type of situation. Born in 1991, as a teenager he developed a passion for computers and web programming, but without linking this interest in any way to his plan for a career in journalism. It was by talking to a professor at his journalism school that he discovered that his skills could have professional value: "It was one of my professors at Science Po Grenoble who told me that journalism and programming could go together. I went to see him and asked him what I needed to do to become a journalist: 'Do I have to learn languages? Do I have to do internships?' He replied by asking me what I could do. I told him that I'd been coding since I was a little kid. He told me about OWNI, data journalism, and all that. I didn't know anything about it. But I quickly realized that there were things I could do. It instantly clicked."[45] Young American journalists share similar stories, although they seemed from early on to have a greater awareness of the potential profitability of computer skills. Many of them graduated from journalism schools and found it difficult to get a job as a reporter for a major newspaper. Michael Corey, for example, now a news developer at the *Minneapolis Star Tribune*, was forced to take a job as a web producer for a website, a job in which he received little journalistic recognition. As he began to take an interest in web development, he discovered the work of Adrian Holovaty, who offered him a career model:

> I have to say the first person I knew of that was like a journo-programmer role model would probably be Adrian [Holovaty] just—and I only sort of knew who he was, but ChicagoCrime was super cool. . . . ChicagoCrime's coming out . . . kind of led to the People Mass API coming out, and that was like, "Sweet, this is exactly what I want to do . . . I want to build something on top of this." And so I think that's about the earliest thing that I knew of that was like a sort of model for future career kind of stuff.[46]

The majority of the journalists I interviewed did not initially have data and programming skills. They explained that they had chosen to develop some of these skills in order to compete in a highly competitive job market. They hoped to gain a comparative advantage that would allow them not only to find work but also to avoid "dirty work," such as news editing and other news-production practices governed by audience metrics. Agustin

Armendariz, a data reporter at the *New York Times* until 2019, explained that he deliberately chose to develop his skills in statistics and web programming so that he could pursue a career in journalism and contribute to "big stories": "I wanted to do my own reporting. If I wanted to have an impact on the big stories, then the only way I could really contribute to that was through data. I mean, I'm not going to be as good of a writer as all these other people or even sometimes as good of a reporter, but because I can bring this other piece to it, I can still contribute and make a valuable contribution potentially."[47]

Young French journalists have developed similar strategies. Damien Brunon, for example, did not have any specific data skills when he graduated from journalism school in 2013. He chose to do an internship at a data journalism agency in Berlin, and during this internship he became aware of the profitability of these skills. Learning how to use a spreadsheet, identify data sources, and verify them has helped him get competitive jobs:

> All those people who hired me in one way or another did so because I had "data" skills. Professionally, this opened doors that I would not have opened as easily. After journalism school, I got a job at Europe 1. During the job interview, I understood they were interested in a data journalist profile. I've been told: "Obviously you have skills that nobody else has; that's weighing in the balance." The following year, I left Europe 1 for France TV Info. They were looking for someone with a data profile, and they were given my name.[48]

Data journalism thus appears to be a profitable career path in a context where there is no real prospect of finding a job if "you don't speak three languages and are not very well connected," to quote Nicolas Kayser-Bril, the journalist who imported to France the term *data journalism* from Great Britain.[49] It also offers a way, according to many, to avoid the tedious tasks that are often assigned to web journalists. In France, awareness of the material realities of web journalism work has been particularly pronounced within the profession: since the late 2000s, web journalists have often been referred to as "les OS de l'info," "the blue-collar news workers," indicating that they are exposed to poorer working conditions.[50]

Journalists from both countries explain that at the same time and almost inextricably data also offer a way to reconnect with the ideals of journalism, either by promoting the practice of investigation, which is more autonomous from the authorities, or by sharing voluminous and complex information in a more accessible way. For several journalists I interviewed, data provide an opportunity to practice investigative reporting at a time when it is weakened or marginalized. As the American press is seeing a sharp reduction in the resources allocated to investigation, data are considered a means to reduce the costs of investigation.[51] For journalists specializing in science, medicine, or sports, data also provide an opportunity to enhance the value of investigation in these areas. Peter Aldhous, for example, has worked as a science journalist since the 1990s, serving as editor at *Nature* and the *New Scientist*. In the late 2000s, as he gradually distanced himself from the explanatory perspective that dominates the scientific press, data journalism seemed a way to promote investigation in science journalism:

> Over the years, I got more interested in not just passively reporting on what's going on in science but bringing back in the analytical skills that hopefully I have as a former scientist, making that part of what I do and being not just an explainer but a journalist reporting on science, and part of that is being a watchdog, doing more investigative work into issues including scientific fraud and misconduct, which is one topic I've written quite a lot about. . . . That led me into doing more and more data journalism.[52]

The data journalism segment thus provided Peter with the opportunity not only to criticize the dominant practice of science journalism, which he considers too dependent on researchers, but also to reconnect with his own former experience as a researcher. Most of the French data journalists I interviewed share this mindset that data journalism makes it possible to reevaluate investigation in journalism. Jules Bonnard, for example, saw it as an opportunity to counterbalance the weight of reportage in students' training: "My students love to investigate with data. Often, they have done reportage, magazine work, good things, but not really investigative work. . . . In journalism schools, the emphasis is on gathering facts, but often with a view to doing reportage with them. In reportage, you convey the mood, you capture an emotion, and you describe the course of events, whereas in an investigation you try to put facts together to draw new conclusions."[53]

According to these journalists, the reevaluation of investigation supported by data journalism should provide answers to some of the criticisms leveled at the profession as a whole, primarily regarding the lack of distance between journalists and institutions. In France, where investigative journalism only really started to develop in the 1980s, data journalism has been embraced as a way to adopt a more critical perspective of political authorities. Jules Bonnard's account of one of his first investigations illustrates this effort to establish distance from elected officials:

> Back then, I worked at the AFP [Agence France Presse] office in Créteil, covering all the schools in the area. Every time, the same scenario unfolded: at 5:00 a.m., we would be informed that a school had burned down, we would rush out on the road, we would find a car with a bit of smoke, and the mayor would come to tell us that this was happening everywhere. But nobody had any numbers! So I started compiling them. Within five years, I had twelve fires in city buildings. They said three or four, but I had twelve.[54]

We can thus see that young journalists entering the data journalism segment in both countries are seeking to reconcile a personal goal (finding a job, avoiding dirty work, gaining recognition) with a desire to reconnect with the ideals of the profession. These individuals' attraction to a set of technology-oriented journalistic practices is therefore rooted in the crisis of journalism.

* * *

A CHALLENGE FOR JOURNALISM

This chapter has shown that in France and in the United States the emergence of data journalism, a professional segment marked by high expectations placed on technology, is rooted in a set of transformations that have shaped the web over the past two decades. Paradoxically, even as the web has contributed to destabilizing and weakening the news industry, it has concomitantly given rise to the antidote as a variety of actors, primarily young journalists struggling in a business in crisis, have come to see data-oriented technology as an opportunity to reboot journalism. However, the effectiveness of this antidote raises many questions.

The rise of data journalism breaks with the journalistic practices that developed before the web, such as computer-assisted reporting in the United States and the making of rankings in the two countries, which already linked computer data processing to the promise of democratization. As we saw in the first chapter of this book, the computer-assisted reporting movement sought to put technology at the service of the journalistic standards shared within the profession by developing a "politics of computation" inspired by social science. With data journalism, however, practitioners have come to rely on knowledge and technology that are both farther removed from journalism and associated with much stronger political imaginaries. The social sciences in particular have been supplanted by other knowledge dominated by engineering and forms of statistical modeling foreign to the social sciences. Journalists' traditional representation of themselves as professionals in charge of collecting, analyzing, and presenting information has thus become problematic as web professionals and activists seem to be able to handle these tasks more effectively. As we will see in chapter 5, the technology-driven practices promoted by data journalists have been controversial within the profession, so that tensions surrounding professional ethics have arisen in the practice of data journalism.

But before we address these questions, let us take a closer look at the differences in the data journalism segments in France and the United States. In France, data journalism not only developed later and to a lesser extent than in the United States but also received much less support and visibility from professional institutions because it emerged at the margins of the profession. A particularly tempting explanation would be that these differences are fundamentally due to distinct "cultures of objectivity" within French and U.S. journalism, but this is precisely the narrative that I challenge in the next chapter.

4
A TALE OF TWO CULTURES?

The differences identified in the previous chapters are unsurprising if we consider the history of American and French journalism. The fact that data journalism has developed both later and less profoundly in France and has remained far less visible there seems largely consistent with how journalism has unfolded in the two countries since the early twentieth century. Whereas U.S. journalists forged an independent professional culture centered on standards of objectivity and factuality, French journalists long gave less importance to facts and placed greater emphasis on the expression of opinions or ideologies.[1] If French journalists are indeed less accustomed than their American counterparts to separating their work from the partisan environment in which they are immersed, then it is not surprising that engagement in news practices striving for greater objectivity has remained relatively limited in France.

Yet there is something amiss in this representation of two distinctive professional cultures. French journalism has undergone a series of significant transformations since the 1980s that challenge its long-standing image as opinion-based journalism with little concern for facts. First of all, strong anti-institutional sentiment began to flourish in French journalism in the 1970s, resulting not only in new practices such as hospital and educational rankings in the following decade, as explored in chapter 2, but also in the growth of investigative reporting. By engaging in intensive fact-finding practices, French investigative reporters have pushed the standards of objectivity to the limit, disqualifying political journalism in its traditional form.[2] For the public and for new entrants in the profession, these fact-oriented practices have thus come to embody the very image of the good journalist fighting for truth, justice, and democracy.[3] Furthermore, commercial pressures have intensified sharply since the 1980s as the revenues of French news organizations have become increasingly dependent on sales and advertising. With commercial considerations gaining influence over news practices, French journalists have been encouraged to distance their work from their personal opinions. These transformations, which have been further compounded by the rise of online journalism, therefore seriously challenge the image of French journalists as unconcerned with objectivity as a professional ideal.

To consider the unequal importance of data journalism in France and the United States as the product of allegedly distinct attitudes to objectivity within each country's professional group would therefore be to fall into the essentialist trap of culturalism. Such an approach particularly fails to grasp why, despite these differences, data journalism has found its way into French journalism, as we saw in chapter 3. In this chapter, I make the case for an alternative perspective on the cultural differences underlying the development of data journalism in both countries. Drawing on pragmatic sociology's approach to cultural comparisons between France and the United States,[4] I identify the cultural specificities that promote or limit the practice of data journalism in the two countries. Specifically, I consider the set of cultural arrangements in each country that make the practice of data journalism *desirable*, *feasible*, and *accountable*. This practice is desirable if journalists can identify a benefit from it to themselves and their organization, whether formulated in civic or commercial terms. It is feasible not only if data collection is practically and materially possible but also if the data come with quality guarantees and can be connected to journalistic interests.

Finally, it is accountable if journalists are able to share their practices within the professional group in order to make them intelligible.

This chapter shows that the elements that in each cultural context contribute to data journalism's desirability, feasibility, and accountability cannot be reduced to a set of shared values within the professional group or to the multitude of computational techniques available on the web. Rather, they revolve around three key factors that clearly distinguish France from the United States: (1) the way governments and administrations provide access to data; (2) the presence of citizen observatories (i.e., nonprofit organizations that sponsor research, scrutinize those in power, and contribute to public discussion through the collection and dissemination of data); and (3) the presence of actors within the profession who translate computational technologies to make them intelligible for their colleagues by associating the technologies with professional identities and convincing their colleagues of the technologies' professional value. These factors explain the more limited adoption of data journalism practices in France far better than the claim of French journalists' disinterest in the ideal of objectivity. Finally, my analysis suggests that although these data journalistic practices are developing in many countries around the world, they remain predicated largely on cultural specificities that have long flourished primarily in the United States.

DO FRENCH JOURNALISTS LACK A TASTE FOR OBJECTIVITY?

Whereas in the early twentieth century U.S. journalists forged an independent professional culture centered around the separation of facts and values, French journalists long gave less importance to such a separation. Most researchers agree that in the United States specific news-production and discursive practices emerged between the 1830s and 1920s to gather facts and maintain distance from opinions.[5] Over the same period, not only did French newspapers handle smaller volumes of information, but French journalists were also accustomed to interpreting this information according to the political doctrine of their newspaper. Presented in a far more literary format, the news thus placed little emphasis on facts. When journalism gradually established itself as a profession in the early twentieth century, objectivity therefore prevailed as a fundamental norm in the United States but not in France.

Until the first half of the twentieth century, French journalists' lesser interest in objectivity as an ideal was arguably first and foremost a product of their relationship to politics. French journalists had long been subject to significant pressure from political forces. Censorship was enforced for much longer in France than in the United States, until the law of 1881 establishing freedom of the press, and the greater number and diversity of political parties made it more difficult for French journalists than for their American counterparts to escape political pressure.[6] Second, French newspapers' economic model has long failed to foster their independence from political forces. While U.S. newspapers were quick to derive significant revenue from sales and advertising, French newspapers long had to rely on government and party financing. For example, *Le Petit Parisien*, which was the most popular and profitable newspaper in the late nineteenth century, earned only 13 percent of its revenue from advertising between 1879 and 1914, whereas advertising accounted for 60 percent of American newspapers' revenue during the same period.[7] This economic configuration made it difficult for French journalists to distance themselves from political forces, especially because there was less competition between media outlets. As Herbert Gans puts it, "As long as journalists are involved in competition and must deal with heterogeneous sources and audiences, the constant expression of conscious values and opinions would surely enrage some sources, viewers, and readers all of the time."[8]

Moreover, from the nineteenth century on, the history of French journalism is marked by strong reliance on literature, a pattern not found on the other side of the Atlantic. Not only did many prominent authors write for newspapers, but for many journalists there was no greater achievement than to gain recognition as a writer.[9] This connection led to French journalists attributing high value to literary techniques, which in turn involved disregarding the focus on facts favored by American journalism. For example, at the turn of the twentieth century, when French newspapers adopted the news-reporting format applied in the United States, they systematically added literary effects to it.[10]

This historically lesser concern for objectivity was crystallized by occasional use of the expression *objectivité à l'Américaine* (American-style objectivity) among French journalists in a somewhat derogatory way.[11] Finally, it can also be explained by the ecology of relations between French journalists, public-relations professionals, and the government. Unlike their American counterparts, early twentieth-century French journalists did not see the ideal of objectivity as a way to distinguish themselves from the public-relations professionals and propagandists, two groups that influenced American public life in the 1920s.[12] Most importantly, because the state bureaucracy enjoyed far greater prestige in France than in the United States, there was less of a need for French journalists to build an ideology at the service of the public. As a result, the context in which French journalists found themselves at the beginning of the twentieth century encouraged them neither to brandish objectivity as an ideal nor to develop fact-oriented news-production and discursive practices.

Some of these peculiarities largely subsisted throughout the twentieth century and still persist today. In particular, the appeal of literature and the value given to literary techniques have remained characteristic of French journalism, even if a significant segment of American journalism has explored literary techniques since the 1960s to critique journalistic objectivity.[13] Studying how French and U.S. online journalists interpret audience metrics, Angèle Christin found that French journalists and editors' relationship to literature remained different.[14] Similarly, French journalists still seem to be more inclined to mix facts and opinions in their articles than are their American counterparts, as Rodney Benson illustrates in his study of immigration news.[15]

French journalism has, however, undergone major changes since the 1980s, which have largely minimized differences in its perception of objectivity as a professional ideal. First, as mentioned earlier, investigative journalism has become a legitimate genre in France as national news organizations have embraced it. This legitimation has been driven both by the judiciary's growing independence from political power, which has provided French journalists with new sources, and by stronger competition between news outlets.[16] Although investigative reporting has been limited by legal restrictions, particularly surrounding the protection of privacy,[17] it has nevertheless become emblematic of the profession in the eyes of the general public. More importantly, this trend has led to a profound challenge to the traditional practice of political journalism as being too close to power.[18] In parallel, the growing economic constraints affecting news production have undermined the importance of ideology in French journalism. From the 1980s, the increase in the number of news outlets, the growing weight of advertising in the financing of news organizations, and the concentration of media outlets led to a significant decline in partisan journalism. These developments also contributed to the reevaluation of objectivity as a professional ideal in French journalism.

Cyril Lemieux and John Schmalzbauer illustrated this change in French journalism in a study they carried out in the early 2000s. Interviewing journalists in the two countries, they challenged the idea that American journalists would be more attached to keeping their personal opinions out of their work than their French counterparts.[19] In both countries, they found, most journalists in mainstream media share a similar commitment to keeping the expression of their opinions and their editorial work separate. The authors concluded that the two countries have become more similar, with French journalists increasingly being constrained by market imperatives, while U.S. journalists are coming to question objectivity as a cardinal professional value. In both countries, there is a clear distinction between journalists working for mainstream media and those working for opinion media, with the latter being quick to reject what they depict as "naive factualism."

For all these reasons, it would be deceptive to attribute differences in the development of data journalism in the United States and France to distinct cultures of objectivity in the profession on either side of the Atlantic. Not only are these cultures probably far more similar today than they were in the first half of the twentieth century—at least in mainstream media—but, more profoundly, such an explanation also tends to essentialize differences between the two countries. As we saw in the previous chapter, it appears that part of the profession in both places is embracing data journalism as a way to strengthen the claim to objectivity in journalism. We therefore need to find another way of conceptualizing the cultural differences between France and the United States, a way that is informed by more than just the values emphasized by the professional group in each country.

DESIRABILITY, FEASIBILITY, AND ACCOUNTABILITY

To capture the cultural differences between the two countries while steering clear of the essentialist trap of culturalism, I propose to view data journalism as encouraged or hindered by a set of cultural arrangements that are observable at a given time and in a particular context, both inside and outside the professional group. Building on pragmatic sociology's approach to cultural comparisons,[20] I focus not on the values to which the professional groups in both countries explicitly ascribe but rather on the material, legal, and normative elements on which journalists can draw to assess the value of technological practices in journalism. More specifically, I consider which of these elements affect the desirability, feasibility, and accountability of data journalism practices. I thus find that French journalists generally assign less importance to these practices than their American counterparts do primarily because these three elements are either lacking or do not carry the same weight among them.

First, the practice of data journalism must be desirable for journalists: they must see it as a benefit to themselves or their organization. This benefit can be formulated in civic terms as revealing injustices, scrutinizing governments, or providing a decision-making tool for citizens or in commercial terms as providing personalized information, streamlining the news-production process, or even enjoying a more innovative brand image than competitors. However, that is not to say that journalists can necessarily identify the benefits of these technological practices in and of themselves: they are not rational individuals as defined by economic theory, able to assess

A CHALLENGE FOR JOURNALISM

the objective value of these technological practices by their own means. Drawing on actor-network theory,[21] I consider that the value actors see in data journalism does not preexist them but rather stems from the mobilization of an "actor-network" that seeks to convince them that it is in their own interest to adopt these technological practices. To be more precise, the vibrant community of computer-assisted reporters in the United States, which I explored in chapter 1, raised interest in these technological practices among the American profession as a whole. On the contrary, in France no similar segment formed until the early 2010s, and so the conditions for journalists there to consider data journalism as a desirable practice were not created.

Second, data journalism must be seen as materially feasible within news organizations: it must be possible to collect the data with relatively limited human and economic resources as well as adequate quality guarantees and to articulate them with established journalistic interests. This factor relates to the organizational constraints surrounding news production: like any document needed to produce news, data have to be collected and processed within a limited timeframe and with restricted resources.[22] From this perspective, the feasibility of these practices appears to be far more problematic for French journalists given the more limited range of data available to them and the more restricted access to government data. As we shall see, this variation in feasibility is due to the different organization of the state in the two countries and the different way in which public policies structure the dissemination of data. It can also be explained by the weakness of the ecosystem of citizen observatories in France versus the strong ecosystem on the other side of the Atlantic, which contributes not only to verifying and enriching data but also to articulating data sets with the issues receiving public attention.

Finally, like any organized activity, data journalism practices must be made intelligible inside and outside the profession. In Harold Garfinkel's words, they must be made accountable—that is, "detectable, countable, recordable, reportable, tell-a-story-aboutable, analyzable."[23] This constraint is particularly strong because of both the numerous technical and methodological difficulties involved in data journalism and the fact that computational techniques are foreign to most journalists in both countries. Thus, the individuals who implement these techniques should not be the only ones able to report on, narrate, and analyze them. And although in many countries, as we saw in the previous chapter, the emergence of the data journalism segment is supported by a network of individuals who share their practices with one another, the intelligibility of these practices must also be built into national professional groups. However, the conditions for achieving this collective intelligibility appear to be more precarious in France than in the United States, particularly due to the absence of a tradition similar to computer-assisted reporting and to weaker ties with universities.

By looking beyond the values that professional groups set for themselves, this pragmatist perspective on cultural differences between France and the United States sheds light on both why data journalism practices are less widespread and less visible in France and why they have nevertheless developed there in the past decade.

ACCESSING GOVERNMENT DATA IN FRANCE

One of the factors directly affecting the feasibility of data journalism is access to government data, either as digitized records or as statistical data. At least until the past decade, access to government data was far more restricted in France than in the United States, where public access to government records emerged long before the international movement for open data described in chapter 3. In the latter country, access was introduced as part of a series of legislative reforms adopted after 1945 that were aimed at increasing citizen and press scrutiny of those in power and led to the adoption of the FOIA in 1966.[24] The FOIA legal framework allowed citizens to turn to the courts to request access to public records, first in printed form and then later in digital form. Alongside this movement, in the early 1990s many federal agencies as well as a few states (e.g., Florida, California, Washington) and cities (e.g., Seattle and Chicago) began to release some of their statistics on various topics (economics, demographics, crime, taxes, education, health, etc.) via CD-ROMs, commercial online networks, and the web.[25] Admittedly, the conditions under which U.S. journalists had access to government data at the time have been widely criticized, both because administrations resisted requests for access and because the data made accessible did not meet the standards of completeness, quality, timeliness, or granularity promoted by open-data activists today.[26] The fact remains, however, that by the late 1990s American journalists had access to a variety of government databases that were unparalleled anywhere else in the world, including France.[27]

It has long been very difficult for French journalists to access government data such as archives and statistics. When investigative journalism emerged in France in the 1980s, it therefore relied mostly on documents leaked by legal professionals or government employees.[28] However, a law was passed in 1978 that recognized the right of citizens to access administrative documents, thus forcing the administration to disclose documents to any citizen requesting them.[29] Both the scope of the documents covered by the law (written documents, audio or visual recordings, computer files) and the range of administrations concerned (not only state bureaucracy, local authorities, and public agencies but also companies with a public-service mandate) were rather wide. Nevertheless, this legal framework differs from the FOIA in two ways. First, French journalists cannot go to court to obtain access to public documents but have to go through an administrative agency, the Commission for the Access to Administrative Records (CADA), which allows more leeway for administrations not to disclose their data.[30] Second, the grounds for refusal provided by the law are more extensive in France, with much greater emphasis on the protection of privacy, including that of public employees.[31] Moreover, until the mid-2000s French administrations rarely shared their archives or statistical data. For example, whereas the U.S. Census Bureau started publishing statistics on the web in 1994, it was not until 2003 that the French National Institute of Statistics and Economic Studies began disseminating data on its website, launched in 1997. What is more, this decision was mainly a

A TALE OF TWO CULTURES?

product of the institute's efforts to comply with a European Union directive encouraging the dissemination of public information.[32] Although the situation has significantly improved in the past decade, with central and local governments sharing more databases in open and usable formats,[33] the long-standing difficulty of access to government data in France explains in part why French journalistic practices based on digital data have long been more precarious than in the United States. As the CADA director recently pointed out, "A culture of secrecy continues to permeate the administration."[34]

This is due primarily to the highly centralized nature of the French state and the far greater autonomy that the French bureaucracy has enjoyed compared to its U.S. counterpart. As Theodore Porter has explained, the French administration was long able to avoid having to share statistics because its autonomy was far less challenged than that of the U.S. administration. Comparing state engineers in the two countries before World War II, he shows that although French engineers had extensive mathematical skills, they never felt the need to produce reliable statistics, to communicate them, or to justify their decisions through quantified procedures. They were thus able to make their own decisions away from the scrutiny of elected officials and the public and by relying solely on their own cultivated judgment. By contrast, members of the U.S. Army Corps of Engineers faced such suspicion and mistrust that they had to produce and disseminate statistical indicators.[35] To some extent, the far greater autonomy given to the French bureaucracy remained throughout the twentieth century, though New Public Management reforms were adopted in the 1990s. Public institutions have been forced to produce a large volume of statistics to justify their efficiency, but most of these data have often been made available only to the French central government, not to the general public. As a result, the intense production of statistics has remained less accessible for citizens and journalists, at least until the past decade.

The case of crime data reflects the distinct role that public policy assigns to statistics in the two countries. Whereas in the United States several authorities produce their own crime statistics (the FBI as well as state and city police departments), which they often disseminate on both wide and street-level scales, in France these statistics are produced centrally by the Ministry of the Interior, which disseminates them in an aggregated form. As a result, it is not possible, for example, for a French journalist to access crime data on the level of a street or district of Paris because of the centralized structure of the French state: city governments do not have control over the activities of the national police. While the central government is accountable for changes in crime statistics, this accountability is never at the city or neighborhood level but most often on the county or country level. These ways of releasing crime statistics also reflect major differences in urban policy. In the United States, disseminating crime statistics is one of a number of tools enabling police officers to interact with residents and find solutions to the problems they identify. In the early 1990s, for example, cities such as Chicago reformed the police by implementing an information system to collect data from the city's police officers, which enabled them to produce and release maps of crimes committed in a given area of a city. As Jacques Donzelot, Catherine Mével, and Anne Wyvekens put it, allowing residents to consult an online map of crimes committed in a specific area of Chicago was intended to "get people back on the move, getting them to build a community." In France, on the contrary, a police officer is seen as a state representative and in no way as a service provider for the population. These authors write that "in France, the force of the State requires that citizens agree to renounce producing force themselves"; thus, it is easy to understand why the dissemination of crime data is treated with utmost caution in France.[36] As an urban policy, sharing granular crime statistics is seen as risky: there is a fear that if every citizen has access to all the statistics presenting crimes at a neighborhood level, the most advantaged inhabitants would leave their neighborhood, further degrading the area.

The long-standing difficulty of access to French government data thus reflects the more centralized nature of the state and the greater autonomy given to the administration. However, it is also the product of very different policy approaches in the two countries, with data sharing taking on very different meanings on either side of the Atlantic.

A TALE OF TWO CULTURES?

AN ECOSYSTEM OF CITIZEN OBSERVATORIES

In France, in addition to the greater difficulty of accessing government data, the absence of an ecosystem of political or citizen observatories similar to the ones that have flourished in the United States since the 1970s has also hindered the development of data journalism practices in France. As Michael Schudson has shown, these nonprofit organizations have come to constitute a democratization movement within American society, sponsoring research, scrutinizing those in power, and contributing to public discussion through the collection and dissemination of information.[37] Specifically, these organizations have contributed to the development of data journalism in the United States by both building information infrastructure and articulating the objects of public debate with digital data and quantification tools. Long before the web, many of these observatories built information infrastructure by collecting, verifying, and enriching large volumes of government documents in order to better inform journalists and citizens on major issues such as political financing, government policies, and the environment. For example, the Center for Responsive Politics, founded in 1983 to monitor the impact of money on politics, launched opensecrets .org in 1996. For this organization, the web appeared to be an appropriate channel for disseminating statistics to the public. Likewise, Environment Defense, an organization created in the late 1960s, launched Score-Card.org in 1998 to enable every citizen to check the level of pollution in any area of the United States. By entering their zip code, users could access a database showing toxic substances, the companies that emit them, and their location in the United States. Long before the rise of the open-data movement, these observatories played an intermediary role in public debate, reprocessing a large body of data from governments, first in the form of reports and then as digital data, and producing information tools for the public. For journalists, some of whom were involved in these observatories,[38] the infrastructure of observatories provided quality data that could be integrated into news production without requiring the expenditure of major resources because the data had already been verified and enriched. Moreover, by becoming objects of public debate, the observatories accustomed the public to thinking about major issues such as public policy and the environment through statistical indicators, more or less interactive maps, and search engines. The unique ecosystem of citizen observatories in the United States has thus contributed to the practice of data journalism, influencing its desirability and feasibility for journalists and news organizations.

By contrast, the absence of a similar ecosystem in France has long contributed to making these data journalistic practices less desirable and less feasible. The lack of nonprofit organizations focused on holding government accountable through the dissemination of information and statistics has long been apparent outside the United States. In France, it can be attributed to the weight of political parties and unions in discussions on public affairs as well as to the French state's monopoly on social science research, which developed after World War II.[39] Nevertheless, new forms of collective action began to appear in France in the 1970s, seeking to build expertise that would be independent from and opposed to government bodies.[40] This trend echoes the emergence over the same period of anti-institutional sentiment among some French journalists, who engaged in the production of journalistic rankings in the 1980s, as discussed in chapter 2. These nongovernmental organizations, associations, and observatories, identified as "new social movements,"[41] have engaged in knowledge-production practices around major issues such as health and the environment, sometimes targeting a wider public. This goal has constituted a major break with the social movements traditionally focused on gaining political power or defending particular interests. Yet these practices have resulted in very little development of data infrastructure or production and dissemination of statistics in part because in France, unlike in the United States, expertise is largely monopolized by the state, leaving social movements with limited access to material and cognitive resources.[42] As a result, an ecosystem of citizen observatories equivalent to the one created in the United States has not developed in France, which has made it more difficult for data journalism practices to flourish in the latter.

Although the gap between the two countries has narrowed significantly in the past decade, with a growing number of French activist organizations engaged in the production and dissemination of data about political, health, and environmental issues, the fact remains that French journalists cannot rely on an ecosystem of citizen observatories offering a wide range of collected, enriched, and interpreted data. As a result, for these journalists, a greater number of issues are difficult to address using digital data and statistical processing.

MISSING TRANSLATORS

Another development within the profession was instrumental in making data journalism practices both desirable and accountable for U.S. journalists: the computer-assisted reporting movement, which, as we saw in chapter 1, emerged within American journalism in the late 1980s and grew into a vibrant community in the 1990s.[43] Comparing the two countries highlights the decisive role these reporters played in the early adoption of data journalism by American news organizations. Although computer-assisted reporters appeared on the scene before the web, they served as "translators" in U.S. journalism, not only promoting the value of database and computational techniques for journalism among their peers but also establishing themselves as spokespersons for these technologies in the profession.[44] This translation effort led to the professional recognition of statistical and computer skills and to the creation of spaces within the professional group for sharing experiences with and socializing technology. The absence of such translators in France explains in part why these practices long remained scarce and invisible in the country until the rise of data journalism there around 2010.

As discussed in chapter 1, computer-assisted reporting emerged as a movement within American journalism aiming to promote databases and computational techniques as tools for journalism. By setting up training courses and organizing opportunities for sharing and capitalizing on experiences with computation, the movement promoted the idea that this set of technological practices would allow journalism to better and more efficiently fulfill its missions. In the early 1990s, computer-assisted reporters were able to establish themselves as spokespersons for computational technologies within the profession, finding themselves on the front line when the web appeared. This position led them to promote the idea that the computational possibilities afforded by the web would enable the profession both to achieve greater autonomy from government and to streamline the news-production process. These reporters therefore advocated for investigations that would exploit data from the web, such as the investigation published in 1998 by reporters from the *St. Paul Pioneer Press* who used the online database of congressional campaign contributions to reveal the tobacco industry's considerable influence on Minnesota legislators.[45] Even if proponents of computer-assisted reporting stressed the need for caution in handling online databases in conjunction with the "politics of computation" they were developing,[46] they saw this type of reporting as a way for journalists to distance themselves from governments by turning the newsroom into a calculation center. Moreover, from the mid-1990s the journalists involved in the computer-assisted reporting movement saw opportunities to streamline the news-production process through the web. Georges Landau, who was in charge of streamlining news production at the *St. Louis Post-Dispatch*, echoed the arguments of the data journalists mentioned in the previous chapter as he recalled the following:

> Big ideas began to percolate at the 1996 conference of Investigative Reporters and Editors in Providence, R.I. Night after night, beer after beer, it became obvious that lots of U.S. CAR [computer-assisted reporting] nerds were wrestling with the same challenges—how to use the tools of the Internet (web browsers and the network itself) to share knowledge within our newsrooms. . . . On my return from Providence, the big picture revealed itself in full: I saw the newsroom as a funnel through which huge amounts of a community's information flowed every

day like crude oil. A typical newsroom was nothing but an antiquated, inefficient knowledge refinery. Reporters were technologically ill-equipped for this flood of raw information, in which ever-larger quantities were arriving in digital form. Clearly, outfitting those journalists with modern information-management tools had become an urgent, competitive necessity for the news industry.[47]

Landau's take, however, differs from the claims made by data journalists in the following decade, even though many of the U.S. precursors of data journalism were trained in computer-assisted reporting. Most notably, computer-assisted reporters did not call for overhauling the division of labor between journalists and web programmers, nor did they consider that coding skills should be recognized as full-fledged journalistic skills. Nevertheless, Georges Landau's account shows that by the mid-1990s these reporters were already positioning themselves as spokespersons for the integration of web computing capabilities in American newspapers. In contrast, French journalists could not develop the desire to engage in these practices or get the opportunity to discuss them within the profession.

Moreover, the computer-assisted reporting movement enabled U.S. journalists with computational skills to gain recognition and even a certain professional prestige. Because the movement originated within investigative journalism, it afforded a prestigious identity to individuals who shared a strong interest in computational and quantitative techniques. Darnell Little's career trajectory is a testament to how the movement led to the journalistic recognition of computational skills.[48] Born in 1966 to a modest Illinois family, Darnell became passionate about journalism in high school but opted for a career in engineering for financial reasons. After six years as a software developer at AT&T, he took the leap into journalism, graduating with a master's degree in journalism from Northwestern University in 1995. Hired the following year as a web reporter at the *Chicago Tribune*, Darnell soon realized that his computer skills allowed him to be involved in projects that attracted attention. Influenced by a fellow investigative journalist, he became interested in computer-assisted reporting in 1997, seeing it as an opportunity to practice a prestigious form of journalism while leveraging his computer skills. Although made redundant in 1999 when the internet bubble burst, he was hired back at the *Tribune* in 2002 as a computer-assisted reporter. For seven years, he worked at the heart of the newsroom and contributed to numerous investigations on racial discrimination based on statistical data, which earned him several professional awards. Finally, he joined the Medill School of Journalism as a professor in 2009, becoming an active member of the computer-assisted reporting community.

In France, by contrast, there was no similar movement in the profession to support the recognition of journalists with computational skills. Until the rise of data journalism in 2010, these individuals worked for newspapers or magazines but had no opportunity to connect with one another or claim a shared professional identity. Pierre Falga's career path illustrates this difficulty in having statistical skills recognized within the profession.[49] Born a few years before Darnell Little, Pierre Falga entered the Lille School of Journalism in 1985, one of the most prestigious journalism schools in France, where he was the only student in his year to have trained in statistics and to want to do political journalism using statistics. Throughout the 1990s, he analyzed electoral, economic, and sociodemographic data for newspapers and news magazines and developed a taste for spreadsheets and a familiarity with government statistics. On several occasions, Pierre carried out political journalism projects—for example, building a database of French elected officials who had been prosecuted—yet he failed to gain recognition as a full-fledged political journalist. He eventually took on a better-recognized identity as a producer of rankings, which distanced him from political journalism and made him an object of suspicion to his colleagues. Only since the rise of data journalism in France has he been able to build relationships with journalists who share his interest in data.

The comparison of these two individual career paths illustrates the major role that the computer-assisted reporting movement played in the recognition of computational skills in American journalism. It is no coincidence that the precursors of data journalism, such as Adrian Holovaty and Ben Welsh, were first trained within that community in the mid-2000s.

A TALE OF TWO CULTURES?

THE DECLINE OF CULTURAL EXCEPTION

For all the reasons discussed in this chapter, the journalistic practices explored in this book thus appear to be historically embedded in the cultural context of the United States. In this respect, Theodore Porter's analysis remains essential, demonstrating that the long and deep mistrust of government and bureaucracy in the United States created an environment conducive to the advent of quantification practices in public life. Since the early twentieth century, there has been a far greater need to rely on impersonal procedures in this country than in France and in Europe in general, where this need has never been as pronounced. By contrast, as discussed throughout this chapter, for a long time France displayed a number of particularities that made it rather inhospitable to journalistic practices involving the collection and processing of digital data. The considerable autonomy of the French bureaucracy and its ability to monopolize expertise, the highly centralized nature of the French state, and the absence of translators between computing and reporting within the journalistic profession made such practices at once less desirable, more impractical, and less accountable.

The recent rise of data journalism in France and in many other countries, however, shows that these journalistic practices have been gradually spreading beyond the U.S. cultural context. Although computer-assisted reporters failed to export their practices outside the United States in the late 1990s,[50] thousands of journalists around the world have embraced such practices in the past decade. As mentioned in the previous chapter, it was not a drive to imitate American computer-assisted reporters or programmer-journalists that prompted the sudden rise of data journalism in France around 2010. At the time, the *Guardian* was the main and only reference for the first French data journalists. The growth of these practices in France was subsequently enabled by the establishment of a global community of data journalists, supported by the sharing of cognitive and technical resources (coding libraries, tutorials, etc.) and the creation of a European network.[51] Although American data journalists have undoubtedly contributed to enriching these resources, the spread of these journalistic practices in France cannot be described as imitation of an American model.

The perspective offered in this chapter enables us to make sense of this trend. By focusing on a set of cultural arrangements that encourage or hinder the desirability, feasibility, and accountability of data journalism practices, my theoretical approach steers clear of the essentialist pitfalls of culturalism and above all accounts for the dynamics at play in contemporary journalism in different places. Specifically, it does not consider the rise of data journalism in France as the result of the spread of an American approach to journalistic objectivity in countries where more partisan approaches to journalism long dominated. Rather, my approach suggests that the dynamics identified in the previous chapter, which are closely linked to the rise of the web, have contributed to the advent of these journalistic practices outside the United States. The international open-data movement has been instrumental in this respect, as has the support it has received within European and French institutions, which have increased the amount of government data available to journalists. The crisis of the news industry has also played a decisive role, leading some entrants to the profession to embrace computational technology as a way both to renew journalism and to find a place for themselves in a highly competitive job market.

I now turn to the substance of the epistemological proposals made by data journalists in both countries that have fueled controversy within the profession. By advocating the use of computational technology to contribute to greater objectivity, these journalists have indeed destabilized the ethics of journalism.

5

THE TENSIONS FACING DATA JOURNALISM

> *This is data journalism, capital-D. . . . It's not just numbers, but numbers are a big part of this. We think that's a weakness of conventional journalism, that you have beautiful English language skills and fewer math skills, and we hope to rectify that balance a little bit.*
>
> —NATE SILVER ON THE LAUNCH OF FIVETHIRTYEIGHT, 2014

In the spring of 2014, Nate Silver presented his New York City–based website FiveThirtyEight. With a background in economics, this thirty-six-year-old made a name for himself by developing statistical models first to predict baseball players' performances and then to predict election results for the *New York Times*. Silver's ambition was to renew the objectivity standards of the profession as a whole by covering a variety of news topics with a quantitative approach. Reproaching editorialists with the harboring of prejudice, he called for journalism to give greater importance to facts by making use of data and statistical analysis. Judging by the growth of FiveThirtyEight's staff and traffic as well as the interest it has generated in the media industry, this initiative seems to have been quite successful.[1]

Yet this website has also received much criticism, including within the journalistic profession. Several articles published on Silver's website have been accused of indulging in naive empiricism and of providing biased analyses. Even to the many reporters who were originally seduced by Silver's critique of journalism, FiveThirtyEight has on several occasions appeared to violate some of the core standards of the profession. Critics argue that journalists cannot approach reality just through equations: they need to understand the context of a subject. Moreover, critics claim, mere data analysis does not always protect journalists from their own opinions. Thus, although Silver has sought to achieve greater objectivity within journalism, he has been criticized for achieving the opposite.

This chapter examines the epistemological claims made by U.S. and French data journalists regarding their ambition to "reboot journalism" and how these claims have fueled controversy within journalism. As the debates have been far more intense in the United States than in France, I focus on U.S. journalism to analyze these controversies. Data journalists have urged fellow journalists to make several shifts with a view to increasing their collective autonomy and their contribution to democracy. Each of these shifts builds on standards widely shared within the profession—making governments more accountable; keeping reporters' personal opinions out of their work; being more transparent about news production; and providing more services to readers. However, as we saw in chapter 3, these shifts involve strong reliance on technology and knowledge drawn from outside journalism—from web development, statistical modeling, data science, and so on. Thus, as soon as data journalists started producing news informed by these shifts, other fellow journalists began sounding the alarm. The shifts, they argued, were going too far either because they had an effect opposite to what was initially intended or because they appeared to conflict with other standards that were equally important to the profession.

My aim is not to vindicate either side in this debate. Rather, it is to add to recent research by documenting and analyzing the ethical, epistemological, and organizational tensions surrounding the practical applications of data journalism.[2] Drawing on the sociology of disputing processes,[3] I approach the debate as a critical moment in which actors call into question established beliefs and invent new ways to regulate their relationships.

I argue that an arena has formed within the profession to discuss and evaluate the epistemological challenges raised by data journalists. On the one hand, data journalists have imported techniques and ways of knowing from outside journalism with the aim of better accomplishing the ideals of the profession. On the other hand, members of the profession have reacted with skepticism and concerns about the potential drawbacks of incorporating these techniques and ways of knowing into journalism. They have cautioned data journalists against jeopardizing the profession with the production of pernicious effects or the erosion of some of the most important standards in the profession. Taken together, these challenges and warnings have benefited all journalists by giving them the opportunity to set limits on how computing technology can be used without endangering professional values.

In this chapter, I examine the four main shifts data journalists have been calling for since the early 2010s in both the United States and France: (1) increasing government accountability; (2) minimizing journalism's dependence on values; (3) making news more verifiable; and (4) enabling readers to make better-informed choices. As part of this examination, I also look at the warnings that these shifts have sparked from some U.S. journalists.

FIRST SHIFT: INCREASING GOVERNMENT ACCOUNTABILITY

Echoing widespread criticism in the profession, data journalists claim that news organizations have failed to hold elites and state actors sufficiently accountable. Like computer-assisted reporters and ranker journalists before them, they argue that the rise of digital media and the profusion of databases provide tools to tighten government accountability. This claim builds on a widely shared standard within the profession—even in France, where journalists' proximity to the political elite has long been more pronounced than in the United States.[4] But what has made this first shift so novel is that it relies on instruments forged within the open-source and open-data advocacy communities.

French and U.S. reporters have conventionally had three main ways of obtaining government data. First, they can use the freedom-of-information laws that developed in both countries in the 1960s and 1970s to reach out to an authority—a court in the United States or a regulatory agency in France—to force reluctant bureaucracies to disclose their data. However, this approach has revealed significant limitations not only because, as noted in chapter 1, governments retain legal leeway not to disclose their data but also because few journalists have actually exercised their right to obtain government data. In 2006, a study found that only 6 percent of the 6,500 FOIA requests submitted in the United States in September 2005 came from journalists.[5] In France, the situation is probably worse because the total number of requests is ten times lower.[6]

Two other avenues are available to U.S. and French journalists to obtain government data. They can take advantage of a leak inside a bureaucracy when one of its employees shares data without the consent of his or her supervisor. And if this is not possible, then the reporter has no choice but to collect data by conducting field surveys. Needless to say, neither of these two solutions is well suited to the requirements of news production.

Without rejecting these three conventional avenues,[7] data journalists have amended and supplemented them with new ways of obtaining government data by borrowing computer techniques and skills from activists, hackers, and computer enthusiasts who are committed to an ideal of transparency.[8] With internet technology, these activists seek to uncover information that is public from a legal point of view but remains secret or totally invisible—either by design, by accident, or simply by poor organization. These new ways of obtaining government data are designed to tackle specific configurations, depending on whether governments release the data intentionally or unintentionally or not at all. Table 5.1 presents the three news ways of obtaining government data (open government, scraping, and

TABLE 5.1 Old and new ways of collecting government data

	INTENTIONAL RELEASE BY GOVERNMENTS	UNINTENTIONAL RELEASE BY GOVERNMENTS	NO RELEASE BY GOVERNMENTS
Active acquisition by the reporter	Freedom-of-information laws	Scraping	Field surveys
Passive acquisition by the reporter	Open government	Data leaks	Crowdsourcing

crowdsourcing) that complement the existing ways (freedom-of-information laws, data leaks, and field surveys).

First, hackers and internet activists have transformed the practice of leaking data. The most significant initiative in this respect has been WikiLeaks, which has altered the way data leaks are solicited and mass collected, bypassing news organizations.[9] Despite raising significant concern among their fellow reporters,[10] several data journalists established ties with WikiLeaks, especially between 2010 and 2016.[11] But they have also promoted other instruments to gather data within the profession.

One such tool is connected to international open-government advocacy.[12] In the second half of the 2000s, a coalition of activists and nongovernmental organizations formed to force all governments and bureaucracies to release their data on a regular basis and in a standardized way and to respect technical standards ensuring the circulation and further use of the data.[13] Data journalists, who were often personally involved in this mobilization, argued that the adoption of such policies would benefit news organizations not only because it would minimize uncertainty about data availability but also because it would reduce the amount of human and material resources needed to access the data. Provided governments complied with the technical standards proposed by the open-government movement, the cost of data acquisition for journalists would indeed drop.

Another new avenue for obtaining government data involves a set of techniques and skills called "scraping." Scraping is the use of computer scripts to transform digital documents (web pages, texts, images) into actionable databases. When a government agency provides citizens with only fragmented information on its website, not access to the entire database, the use of a web scraper allows the journalist to reconstruct a comprehensive database by sending a large number of requests to the website. The journalist can thus bypass the agency's unwillingness to disclose the data and analyze those data to reveal inequalities or trends in the way the agency carries out its mission. Open-data activists have made extensive use of scraping since the mid-2000s, before data journalists started to consider it a way to extract data without the government's consent.[14] As explained by a journalist working for *Le Monde*, this method frees reporters from the task of interacting with the agency: "Some French physicians are free to choose their own rates, so that one can pay between €70 and €500 for a 30-minute visit at an oncologist, for instance. This data regarding rates is legally public, but the administration provides only a hard-to-navigate online database. In order to have a good view of the doctors' rates for *Le Monde*, I decided to scrape the entire database."[15]

Data collection is therefore no longer a legal and organizational issue but exclusively a technical one. Like virtuosos, some data journalists describe how they managed to overcome the technological barriers raised by bureaucracies.[16] In the words of the same French reporter,

> That's where the fun began. The front-end search form was a Flash application that redirected to an HTML result page via a POST request. . . . [I]t took us some time to figure out that the application used a third page as a "hidden" step between the search form and the result page. This page was actually used to store a cookie with values from the search form that was then accessed by the results page. It would have been hard to think of a more convoluted process, but the options of the cURL library in PHP make it easy to overcome the hurdles, once you know where they are! In the end, getting hold of the database was a 10-hour task, but it was worth it.[17]

The third new instrument for obtaining government data, crowdsourcing, applies to situations where agencies deliberately or involuntarily do not release their data. Through an open call, a reporter can ask agents or clients of an administration to provide the data an agency refuses to supply. She can also ask people to structure information in the form of data—for example, by identifying and reporting specific information across a large number of images or photographs. Through this practice, the journalist delegates a set of judgments and decisions to the participants, leveraging the virtues of collective wisdom and the power of the internet.[18] For this reason, I consider that in this case the data are acquired passively by reporters even if in practice the process often requires them to engage significantly with their audience.[19]

WARNING: ACCESSING GOVERNMENT DATA DOES NOT ALWAYS LEAD TO GREATER TRANSPARENCY

The implementation of these various techniques has been met with resistance among some U.S. journalists, however. These journalists argue that these instruments paradoxically may not contribute to improving governments' transparency. A journalist having access to the data produced by an authority does not mean that she will be able to expose the actions of that authority more clearly or give citizens a better understanding of how it exercises its powers.[20] These skeptical journalists have warned data journalists that collecting and releasing government data may not increase public scrutiny of governments both because of the issue of the quality of government data and because of how those data are conveyed to the public.

Several journalists have highlighted the constructed nature of government data. These data are often incomplete, deceptive, or informed by classifications that do not make sense to news organizations.[21] It can therefore be misleading to treat these data as a true record of bureaucratic activity and to expect administrations to become more transparent as a result. This criticism has been voiced on several occasions, often in connection with particular news projects.

In the United States, the website EveryBlock.com (now Nextdoor.com) sparked controversy for this very reason. Founded in 2007 by Adrian Holovaty, one of the pioneers of data journalism I mentioned in chapter 4, this website offered hyperlocal news in several major U.S. cities. By automatically collecting a large amount of data from local government, it enabled users to check not only for crime at the street-block level but also a vast range of data from public records (building permits, liquor license applications, etc.). In April 2009, however, a couple of *Los Angeles Times* journalists revealed that EveryBlock.com regularly reported misinformation about crimes committed in Los Angeles. Because some of the Los Angeles Police Department data were biased, the website had systematically attributed a large number of crimes to a certain neighborhood when they had in fact been committed in other parts of the city. In their article, Ben Welsh and Doug Smith found it problematic that this website had continuously published the data without checking them: "Using the LAPD data, Every-Block has consistently ranked 90012, one of downtown's ZIP Codes, the most dangerous in the city, positioning a large, foreboding orange cluster over the Civic Center with the number of crimes regularly updated.... EveryBlock, an enterprise that specializes in pulling together local data from many sources, has been praised as a model for the future of journalism, but unlike traditional publications, the site takes no responsibility for the accuracy of its aggregated data."[22] When they asked Adrian Holovaty about this issue, he refused to set up any systematic procedure for verifying data. Stating that "despite any effort we make into fixing problem data, there will always be dirty data,"[23] he claimed that a disclaimer on the website was enough. In their article, Welsh and Smith thus argued that this website, although "praised as a model," conflicted with a major professional standard: the duty to provide one's audience with accurate information.

For most U.S. reporters, shifting to such a model is not acceptable if it leads news organizations to take the accuracy of government data for granted. Under these conditions, these editorial products cannot be expected to subject government action to greater public scrutiny de facto. Because false or misleading data can be disseminated if the necessary precautions are not taken, greater transparency cannot be expected to ensue. As I argued in chapter 1, this first warning had already been issued by computer-assisted reporters in the early 1990s: data journalists had to keep in mind that the data they accessed did not always reflect an objective reality.

There is another reason why data journalists cannot expect government data to automatically enhance public scrutiny of governments or institutions. For most of the data journalists I interviewed on both sides of the Atlantic, allowing citizens to access and search data was very important. Although many U.S. journalists consider the mere dissemination of data to be appropriate sometimes, they have argued that this should not be their only role. On many occasions, they have reiterated that their role is to provide explanations and interpretations. In their view, their objection to

THE TENSIONS FACING DATA JOURNALISM

journalism as just a provider of data is not just about defending a standard that has developed in U.S. journalism over the past decades[24] but, more fundamentally, about warning that if citizens are given access only to the data without analysis or perspective, what happens inside government agencies will remain unnoticed or muddled by too much seemingly unrelated information.

Here is what a young investigative reporter from the *Chicago Tribune* told us about EveryBlock.com:

> I question the usefulness of it because data by itself, what does it tell you? Okay, you had some crimes in your neighborhood, but what does it mean? Journalists interpret, filter, do all kinds of things that I think are important. That's what we bring to bear. So data in and of itself isn't necessarily valuable, I guess. It's valuable for people that know how to use it and know how to make sense of it, but for your average person I don't think it's enough. I think it's a good thing to have, but I don't think it's enough, and I don't think we should rely just on that.[25]

This argument was widely echoed by other journalists I interviewed in the United States not only because they believe that they need to select what is newsworthy from the vast amount of information available but also because they consider that their role as journalists is to produce more general interpretations of the data in question.

This warning also extends to the skills attributed to the audience. For most of the journalists I met, it was highly unrealistic to assume that readers have the resources and skills to analyze the data, do their own calculations, or find inconsistencies. As Owen Youngman, the former head of innovation at the *Chicago Tribune*, told me, "A user wants to know, 'How good is my school this year? Did it get better than it was last year?' And a reporter will say, 'Boy, that school got a lot better, and there's no evidence why it should. I need to figure that out.' Well, you need both. You want to satisfy the needs of the people who have content questions that they want answered. But there's always things that they'll never think about that the journalists should be trained to ferret out and communicate."[26]

These are the reasons why the first shift that data journalists have been calling for, increasing government accountability, has generated strong resistance within the profession. At bottom, if journalists take the data they have obtained at face value and simply share them with their audience without proper analysis, they should not expect authorities and institutions to automatically become more transparent as a result.

SECOND SHIFT: MINIMIZING JOURNALISM'S DEPENDENCE ON VALUES

"We believe facts trump opinions": this sign adorned the windows of the *Bay Citizen*, a San Francisco–based news organization specializing in data journalism, in 2012.[27] If this sentence echoes the present situation in the United States, it in fact exemplifies a second shift that has been very popular among those who call themselves data journalists: the desire to escape ideology and to "get back to the facts." Undoubtedly, Nate Silver has been the most prominent figure questioning the role of ideology in journalism. He criticizes the op-ed columnists at the *New York Times*, *Washington Post*, and *Wall Street Journal*: "They don't permit a lot of complexity in their thinking. They pull threads together from very weak evidence and draw grand conclusions based on them. . . . It's people who have very strong ideological priors, is the fancy way to put it, that are governing their thinking. They're not really evaluating the data as it comes in, not doing a lot of [original] thinking. They're just spitting out the same column every week and using a different subject matter to do the same thing over and over."[28]

Many U.S. journalists have read Silver's tirade or followed his blog hosted by the *New York Times* between 2010 and 2014 or read his best-selling book published in 2012.[29] Although Nate Silver is largely unknown in France, this second shift, which his words and approach exemplify, builds on a standard widely shared among journalists in both countries. French reporters have long been less committed than their U.S. counterparts to the separation between the opinion page and the newsroom, but the gap has narrowed significantly, as my research and sociological research have made evident.[30]

At all stages of the news-production process, data journalists have embraced databases and algorithms to reduce the influence of values. They view technology as a way to foster objectivity in both the fact-finding stage and the analysis and interpretation stages of journalism.[31] In their approach, several data journalists have focused on "gatekeeping," or the way news organizations select newsworthy occurrences. For decades, social scientists have shown that journalists provide a distorted picture of reality by systematically prioritizing occurrences promoted by institutions or public officials.[32] Several data journalists have responded to this criticism by setting up websites that provide comprehensive news coverage. For example, the *Los Angeles Times* used to cover about 10 percent of all homicides committed in the city, so some of the newspaper's data journalists launched a news platform that offers coverage of all homicides based on data from the city's police department and coroners.[33] Each homicide is represented by a dot on a map, and clicking each dot opens a page sharing the associated story and standardized information about the homicide (its causes and circumstances, the characteristics of the deceased, etc.). According to Jill Leovy, the reporter who initiated the project, the intention was to offer "a story for every victim" and to give readers "a more realistic view of the people who are dying."[34]

Mobilizing different techniques and knowledge, several data journalists have taken an interest in other stages of the news-production process. As we saw in chapter 4, they have designed innovative ways of presenting news to provide readers with what the journalists see as a more objective account of reality. Drawing on information-design and web-development techniques, their aim has been to reduce the influence of the journalist's subjectivity on news presentation. Other actors in data journalism have focused on explanations and predictions. According to Nate Silver, this stage of the news-production process is the most problematic:

While individual facts are rigorously scrutinized and checked for accuracy in traditional newsrooms, attempts to infer causality sometimes are not, even when they are eminently falsifiable. . . . Instead, while the first two steps of the process (collecting and organizing information in the form of news stories) are thought to fall within the province of "objective" journalism, explanatory journalism is sometimes placed in the category of "opinion journalism." My disdain for opinion journalism (such as in the form of op-ed columns) is well established, but my chief problem with it is that it doesn't seem to abide by the standards of either journalistic or scientific objectivity. Sometimes it doesn't seem to abide by any standard at all.[35]

In this statement, Silver identifies a gap between conventional reporting and how explanations are produced by news organizations. Whereas reporters usually collect and organize information rigorously, opinion journalists produce explanations because they are not constrained by any empirical considerations. In his view, algorithms and statistical analysis offer a way to fix this problem. Even predictions, he asserted, can be made using statistical techniques. Specifically, he advocates leveraging predictive algorithms that can handle large amounts of information while limiting the normative assumptions informing them.[36] With these algorithms, he successfully predicted Obama's victory in the Democratic Party primaries in 2008 and in the 2008 and 2012 presidential elections—but failed to predict Trump's election in 2016.

Given most U.S. and French journalists' attachment to the separation between facts and values, this second shift has aroused great interest among them. However, it has also raised legitimate concerns within the profession.

WARNING: THE DATA DO NOT SPEAK FOR THEMSELVES

After the launch of FiveThirtyEight in 2014, a controversy broke out in the United States indicative of the way U.S. journalists have responded to the

THE TENSIONS FACING DATA JOURNALISM

call for minimizing journalism's dependence on values. Various journalists argued that it was neither possible nor desirable to separate facts and values so clearly and that claiming to get rid of values raised the risk of indulging in naive empiricism. The data do not speak for themselves, they asserted, and assuming they do will weaken journalism.

Unsurprisingly, opinion journalists were the first to react to the call for this shift. When it came to major social issues, they claimed, facts or data cannot offer objective solutions. In 2014, Leon Wieseltier, the *New Republic*'s then editor in chief, held that "many of the issues that we debate are not issues of fact but issues of value. There is no numerical answer to the question of whether men should be allowed to marry men, and the question of whether the government should help the weak, and the question of whether we should intervene against genocide. And so the intimidation by quantification practiced by Silver and the other data mullahs must be resisted. Up with the facts! Down with the cult of facts!"[37]

But the strongest criticisms interestingly came from journalists who were versed in data analysis. Although they shared Silver's ambitions, they were disappointed by data-focused articles that they found uninteresting, biased, or misleading. In their view, such results were due primarily to the fact that most news organizations used statistical methods without knowing much about the context of the issues they examined. Alberto Cairo, a data journalism consultant and teacher at the University of Miami, presented the issue this way:

> You can't really extract meaning from data using only cookie-cutter templates. No matter how great you are at analyzing stuff with the R statistics language, you'll be in trouble if you don't have a deep understanding of where the data came from, of how they were gathered, filtered, and processed, of their strengths and shortcomings.
>
> That's the reason why, in many universities, science departments teach their own statistics courses: it's not the same to use stats for sociological observations as for genetics, psychology, astronomy, or physics. The equations may be similar, but the outcomes of your analyses don't depend only on those equations. Context matters.[38]

A CHALLENGE FOR JOURNALISM

In Cairo's view, data journalists will not meet the high expectations that they have set both inside and outside the profession if they do not develop a deep understanding of the topics they cover. Without that understanding, they cannot be all-purpose professionals who use data sets and algorithms to reveal what none of their peers could see using traditional methods of journalism.

Several economic journalists also weighed in on the debate, sharing their experience in quantitative social science analysis. While applauding the rise of data journalism, Allison Schrager warned that data analysis does not protect against prejudice: "The recent boom in 'data-driven' journalism projects is exciting. It can elevate our knowledge, enliven statistics, and make us all more numerate. But I worry that data give commentary a false sense of authority since data analysis is inherently prone to bias. . . . [E]ven well-trained social scientists seek out methods that confirm their biases. Anytime you use data it is [sic] subject to bias and it can be manipulated to push a particular point of view. . . . Data analysis is more of an art than a science."[39] In her view, journalists can use data analysis simply to confirm their own prejudices. And even if a data journalist is not prejudiced, the *New York Times* columnist Paul Krugman added, she still might make implicit assumptions.[40] In any case, it seems unreasonable to believe that the data can speak for themselves.

Thus, this proposed second shift toward greater objectivity was greeted with equal skepticism and enthusiasm. It led part of the profession to set some limits. As the controversy sparked by the launch of FiveThirtyEight revealed, the line between the goal of objectivity and naive empiricism was blurry.

THIRD SHIFT: MAKING NEWS MORE VERIFIABLE

The third shift pushed by data journalists has involved urging conventional journalists to increase the transparency of news production. News

THE TENSIONS FACING DATA JOURNALISM

organizations have been asked to publish online all their databases and the algorithms they use in order to provide readers with access to all the information they have collected and organized. Because this shift was never promoted by computer-assisted reporters or by rankers, it is specific to data journalists. Although transparency has been an established norm in American journalism since the 1990s, the vision championed by data journalists draws on the ethics of open-source communities. This ethics goes further than the conventional approach to transparency within the profession: as Seth Lewis and Nikki Usher have argued, "instead of seeing news as the end product," such ethics would enable users "to see journalism as a more fluid set of interactions—a *process* to which they can meaningfully contribute."[41]

In particular, for most of the data journalists I interviewed in the United States and in France, public access to the data and calculations used in a journalistic project is absolutely crucial. This view differs quite significantly from the strategy of *U.S. News* ranker journalists, discussed in chapter 2, for whom transparency was first and foremost a way to protect themselves. Some data journalists I interviewed, such as Brian Boyer, a news-application developer for the *Chicago Tribune* at the time, even considered the provision of access a moral requirement for data journalists: "I got into a pretty good argument . . . with somebody from *USA Today* about the idea of giving away the data, and they don't do it. They might put their] website online, but they're not going to publish all the information that builds the website. And that's just greedy. That's shitty. Sorry, that's my rant."[42]

I found the same passion among many data journalists who, like Brian, turned to journalism after a career in web development. The concern with transparency is most widely shared by data journalists who used to be computer enthusiasts or open-source activists. Pierre Romera, for example, was a data journalist for a news agency based in Paris and Berlin when I interviewed him. He told me how he routinely published his code on GitHub, the software-development platform: "I have been an open-source supporter since I was a kid. That's how I learned, so this is something for which I am an advocate. In practice, today we do this actively, most of our projects at Journalism++ are open-source projects, and we publish the source code on GitHub. We sometimes involve contributors; we use a lot of open-source software."[43]

Scientific practice is often used as a model for journalism. Just as researchers allow their colleagues to access their data and verify their calculations, so, too, journalists should allow anyone to verify the soundness of the information they provide to the public. This is the argument defended by Nathaniel Kelso, who produces data visualizations for a San Francisco–based agency: "I always appreciate it when someone has put the entire database [online] because as a journalist data person, like, I want to see the data. I don't want to see just some massaged extract of the data that proves someone else's point. So it's good in terms of, like, replicable experiment, like you want as a scientist, you want someone else to be able to look at the data and come to the same conclusions, so it's really important to just to validate, like, a conclusion."[44]

According to reporters committed to data journalism, these practices of providing access would allow the profession as a whole to restore public confidence in journalism. As Simon Rogers, a former data journalist for the *Guardian*, wrote, readers would be able to scrutinize numbers or graphs produced by journalists and more generally check the way in which news is produced.[45]

This call for greater transparency in news production, although expressed in a new way, builds on a well-established standard in the profession—both in the United States and in France.[46] It is in line with several previous initiatives in journalism, including the extension of ombudsmen in news organizations and the development of news sections that explain how news is produced. It also stems from the way many journalists have used blogs and social media to render their news making more transparent.[47]

As my interviews suggest, this shift has been supported largely by the computing and programming worlds and the open-source movement, which has long fought the appropriation of knowledge by the software industry.[48] It also reflects the way in which the open-data movement has promoted the dissemination of data using scientific practice as a model. According to data journalists, news organizations should be held to the same standards as any other knowledge-producing institution that collects and organizes large volumes of information.

WARNING: DO NOT JEOPARDIZE NEWS ORGANIZATIONS' RESOURCES

In most U.S. news organizations, the promotion of this shift has not aroused any fundamental objections. In theory, most journalists consider it perfectly reasonable and even desirable to publish their data and algorithms.[49] Nevertheless, concerns have been raised about the resources required to implement this shift. To release a data set online, significant resources must be devoted to making it understandable to a large audience. After a few months at the *Chicago Tribune* as news-application developer, Brian Boyer realized the magnitude of the costs involved:

> I expected to meet reporters and have people not want to give away data. And it turns out that preconceived notion was wrong. Reporters are all about giving away all the information they possibly can. But the reason news organizations, especially the *Tribune*, don't publish as much data, like supporting data, for every story has much more to do with production cost. Like, the people who make the website, put things on the website, just don't have that much time. So only when something was extremely high value did they put something on there.[50]

These economic considerations are especially important because once the data are online, they are rarely downloaded. As a result, it seems unrealistic and unnecessary to devote significant resources to preparing these data and putting them online. As Boyer explains, the data must therefore have high journalistic value for the organization to decide to put them online.

Beyond costs, other considerations have also been raised by journalists. Sources are sometimes reluctant to consent to their data being posted online, and journalists may also fear that publication could create legal risks for the news organization if some of the data turn out to be false or to violate privacy law.

Like more traditional transparency instruments, the dissemination of data by news organizations must contend with a number of considerations, which data journalists themselves are aware of. Although journalists have widely supported making news more transparent and verifiable, implementation appears to have generated costs that are difficult to cover for most news organizations. This economic constraint has limited the spread of this practice.

FOURTH SHIFT: ENABLING READERS TO MAKE BETTER-INFORMED CHOICES

A last shift receiving wide support from data journalists—though to a lower extent in France—is encouraging journalists to create tools to help people make better-informed choices about various aspects of their lives. Without openly claiming this legacy, data journalists have followed in the footsteps of fellow journalists who have been ranking universities and hospitals since the 1980s—as discussed in chapter 2. The new data journalists have extended the scope of this approach, however, not only by comparing the quality of educational or health services but also by examining a growing set of new topics such as environmental quality, road conditions, neighborhood security, the integrity of elected officials, and so on. Taking advantage of both new data sources and algorithms, data journalists have designed a set of instruments to empower citizens and consumers in their daily lives.

For example, regarding the environment, a number of news organizations have designed online applications to allow people to compare air quality based on data collected and analyzed by state agencies or nonprofit organizations. *USA Today* was one of the first to offer such a service in 2010, comparing air quality in the vicinity of all schools in the United States based on risk-assessment models developed by the Environmental Protection Agency. More recently, other organizations such as the *New York Times* have

THE TENSIONS FACING DATA JOURNALISM

used data from a nonprofit organization to develop graphs comparing the daily level of pollution in major cities around the world (figure 5.1). Like more traditional rankings published by news magazines, these comparisons are based on measurements and statistical modeling that originated from outside the news organization. But unlike the educational and health rankings discussed in chapter 2, current applications are based not only on management theories but also on a more diverse set of disciplines—including physics and environmental science, as in the air-quality example.

These tools have aroused great interest among U.S. data journalists and in the news industry in general. The data have been seen as giving journalists the opportunity to design tools that people can use to make informed choices—be it about which neighborhood to settle in or who to vote for in an election. Daniel O'Neil, the cofounder of EveryBlock.com—a website that has been praised as the "future of journalism" and supported by the Knight Foundation—has argued that such news projects offer readers a convenient "decision-making tool" or "research tool" for daily life through simple and standardized access to data: "It could be a citizen who finds out about something and goes and looks at it, and then makes a decision about the neighborhood, about what they're going to bring back to their block

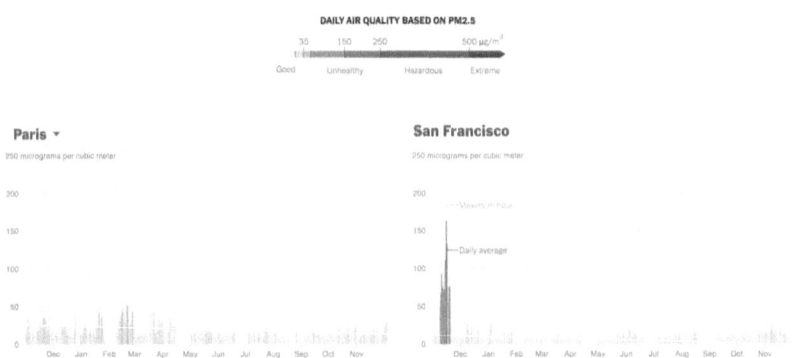

FIGURE 5.1 Comparing daily air quality in Paris and San Francisco.

Source: From Nadja Popovich et al., "See How the Worlds' Most Polluted Air Compares with Your City's," *New York Times*, December 2, 2019. Data reflect regional estimates by Berkeley Earth based on observations at ground-level monitoring stations.

club or what—you know, if I'm going to live here or not. So it's a decision-making tool and a research tool for everybody."[51]

U.S. data journalists seek not only to serve citizens or consumers but also to help local communities solve their problems. For Daniel O'Neil, the aim of EveryBlock.com, for example, is to enable Chicago residents involved in community policing to "make connections between a business and an increase in crime." For Tasneem Raja, formerly a data journalist at *Mother Jones*, the goal would be to design an application to allow San Francisco residents to report bicycle accidents and ultimately to help them fight for more safety on their streets: "That should've been super-easy for people to—after they had a bike accident, they would be like, 'I'm not going to report this to the police, but I am going to report it to the *Bay Citizen*, and here's my information,' and then that would require some PR around the project to get the word out there, like, 'Hey bikers of San Francisco, we have this app to help us keep it up-to-date.' This is about community safety and funding for street improvements and things like that."[52]

For news organizations, such tools have also appeared as a potential revenue stream. Like the more traditional rankings discussed in chapter 2, these news products are likely to be of interest to a large number of readers. In 2011, the *Texas Tribune* came into the spotlight when it announced that it had attracted most of its online traffic through the databases it offered—especially the one revealing Texas civil servants' salaries.[53]

This shift has received less attention from French data journalists than from their U.S. counterparts. As it is for U.S. reporters, serving readers is one of the traditional missions of French reporters. However, the journalistic landscape is much more centralized in France, where the mainstream media address primarily a national audience. Because data journalists there have been hired mostly by national organizations and not by local ones, their primary mission and desire have not been to engage with local communities. They have therefore not devoted the same efforts to developing tools for city or neighborhood residents and focus mainly on projects comparing phenomena on a national scale.[54] A number of these journalists even consider that the publication of such informational databases no longer constitutes true journalism, derogatorily associating it with making "city guides."

THE TENSIONS FACING DATA JOURNALISM

WARNING: DO NOT RISK CAUSING PEOPLE HARM

In December 2012, a New York state newspaper posted an interactive map showing the names and addresses of handgun permit holders in its readership area. The journalists' goal seemed legitimate at the time: against the backdrop of frequent mass shootings, they wanted to give readers an instrument to know where the guns were. Within a few weeks, the application had received more than one million page views but had also sparked outrage among people who felt they were being presented as potential criminals.[55]

Unlike more traditional journalistic rankings, innovative news products like this one usually have not given rise to major protest because they do not primarily target established institutions or professionals but rather groups of individuals or organizations that often cannot make their collective voices heard. However, as the handgun-map example indicates, several such news applications have provoked outrage in recent years, which has led members of the profession to alert their colleagues to the unanticipated harm those applications could cause people.

In this arena, U.S. journalists are concerned about privacy. As soon as personal information is posted online through an application, it becomes increasingly visible, with the potential to harm individuals. As one journalism teacher put it, data journalists cannot simply "dump data" online; they must exercise their professional judgment:

> Yes, public records *can* be obtained by anybody. . . . But when a journalist chooses to copy that information, frame it in a certain (inherently subjective) context, and then *actively* push it in front of thousands of readers and ask them to look at it, he's taken a distinct action for which he is responsible. Good data journalists will tell you that data dumps are not good journalism. Data can be wrong, misleading, harmful, embarrassing or invasive. Presenting data as a form of journalism requires that we subject the data to a journalistic process.[56]

A few prominent U.S. journalists, such as Steve Doig, have issued the same warning: using data as a news source "doesn't absolve you of the same kind of ethical considerations that you're supposed to be taking."[57] Accordingly, some U.S. journalists have set a limit, maintaining that personal information cannot be widely disseminated if doing so does not serve a journalistic purpose.

Some data journalists have been recognized by their colleagues for managing to reconcile the dissemination of personal information with respect for privacy. While working for the *St. Petersburg Times* in 2009, Matt Waite, one of the few U.S. data journalists to have been awarded the Pulitzer Prize (for PolitiFact, a fact-checking website), was asked by the editors to design an application showing pictures of people who had been arrested by the police, mostly because "mugshots" are very popular among readers/viewers. Although this application could be fed automatically from publicly available information on the web, Waite and his colleagues promptly expressed their concerns: "We immediately recognized that because we were a news organization, because we had an audience and because we thought this thing would get some traffic, that the first record in Google for somebody's name was going to be this site. And we were absolutely not comfortable with that. . . . We took multiple steps to prevent that from happening."[58]

In a context where the publication of "mugshots" by an established news organization raised serious concerns within the profession, Waite's team decided to prevent Google's search engine from indexing these web pages and to set up a function that would automatically delete each picture after a period of sixty days. Although this practice of automatic deletion has been positively reported on by a few professional organizations and journals (including Poynter and *Columbia Journalism Review*), it has not become a standard within U.S. news organizations.[59]

More speculative concern has also been raised within the profession about these tools' ability to enable citizens to address a collective problem—be it the level of crime in a neighborhood, the poor quality of air in a city, or corruption among elected representatives. Journalists have argued that such information will not necessarily lead citizens to mobilize because

THE TENSIONS FACING DATA JOURNALISM

they may be more inclined to adopt an exit strategy based on that information (e.g., by moving to another neighborhood or city).[60]

In the United States, the debate has focused mainly on applications reporting on crime—not only those designed by news organizations, such as the "mugshot" application, but also those designed outside of journalism, which have been decried as having no place in journalism. This is the case of applications claiming to assess the "risk of assault" associated with a neighborhood based on crime statistics. Although these applications were not designed by news organizations, they have been widely castigated by journalists, including data journalists such as Daniel O'Neil: "That application got a goodly amount of attention. It's a disgusting piece of software that makes terrible judgments. And it's made for white people to stay away from black people. Just basically what it's for. So that's terrible."[61]

The proliferation of crime maps has raised other concerns among U.S. journalists. One concern is that data journalists do not help readers grasp the more general aspects of a problem simply by providing a map of disparate occurrences (crimes, pollutions, accidents, etc.). As a result, citizens are not in a position to identify more systemic causes of the problem. Several journalists have thus called for applications to facilitate the transition from the individual level to a more collective level to allow readers to "zoom out" and perceive the general dimensions at stake beyond single occurrences.

One practice adopted by major news organizations to deal with this concern consists in combining a data-driven application with more conventional articles presenting the more general aspects of an issue. Brian Boyer, head of the *Chicago Tribune*'s news-applications team in 2010, explained this practice: "You read the story, your grandmother is sick, she's in a nursing home, but they can only write about—they only have a handful of anecdotes in a written piece. So you think, 'Shit, is my grandma safe?' And you go to the website, and you look it up, and you realize that she's safe or she's not safe. But it's all about telling these—being able to personalize this general story for individuals."[62]

The development of instruments to help people make informed choices has not been without its complications and trade-offs. For both news organizations and scholars, it has been challenging to know exactly how people use these data-driven applications. Site-traffic figures often do not say much about users' practices and motives. As Michael Schudson has emphasized, there are limits to the "information-based model of citizenship" on which data journalism commonly relies.[63] It would thus be fair to assume that readers do not mechanically or automatically become more engaged in public affairs when they use data-driven applications.

* * *

This chapter reveals the gap between what data journalists claim to be doing—making governments more accountable, keeping reporters' personal opinions out of their work, being more transparent about news production, and providing more services to readers—and what the practical implementation of data-driven projects entails for news organizations. Through professional journals, public statements, and informal discussions, an arena has formed within the profession where this gap has been recognized and debated. But this gap should not be seen as evidence of the rhetorical nature of data journalism. As this chapter has shown, the epistemological shifts brought about by data journalists are consistent and grounded in knowledge and techniques that are increasingly being used in other social worlds. Most importantly, they highlight the actual difficulty for journalism to reach its ideals.

Bringing this gap to light, however, has enabled the whole profession to define rules to set limits on how computing technology can be used without jeopardizing professional values. This process still has a long way to go, and there is no consensus on how data and algorithms might help journalism better contribute to democracy.

In part III, I scrutinize "data journalism in the making" to shed light on the conditions under which the use of data and algorithms can strengthen the voice of journalism. Each of the following three chapters focuses on a single data journalism project—two American and one French—that has been widely acclaimed as having made a significant contribution to democracy. The first is an investigation by the San Francisco–based Center for Investigative Reporting that revealed in 2011 that the State of California had failed to enforce earthquake-safety standards in the building and maintenance of public schools. The second project, "The Weight of Words" ("Le poids des mots"), was led by two journalists from the French magazine *Paris Match* and originally aimed to cover the French presidential campaign of 2016–2017 in a more objective way by collating all the speeches made by the main candidates in a database. Finally, the third project is a news platform built by the *Los Angeles Times* to cover all homicides in Los Angeles since 2010, not just those of white middle- and upper-class individuals.

The teams that conducted each of these projects successfully overcame some of the tensions I have just identified: making an authority more transparent by leveraging the data produced by that authority; establishing the right level of distance from academic researchers, avoiding using science as a mere facade of objectivity, and aligning too closely with scientific practices; and, finally, creating publics around the problem of urban violence, despite the usual tendency of news dissemination through data to hinder citizen engagement.

In choosing to investigate these projects, I posited that the journalists who led them had explored standards that could benefit the entire profession. I wanted to know which ways of working, cooperating inside and outside the organization, and designing and using computational practices had enabled these professionals to overcome the tensions and to outline a renewed ethics of journalism.

PART III

DATA JOURNALISM IN
THE MAKING

6

THE MAKING OF A REVELATION

Tonight, a 19-month investigation by the Center for Investigative Reporting finds the state is failing to enforce earthquake safety standards in Californian public schools. It uncovers faulty constructions as well as a troubling lack of oversight by those in charge of keeping our children safe.

—KQED (BAY AREA) TELEVISION SPECIAL, APRIL 15, 2011

In April 2011, millions of Americans learned that thousands of public schools in California were not protected against earthquake risk. Until then, most residents and public officials had assumed that the Field Act was being properly enforced. This state law, passed in 1933, required that the construction of every school building in California be closely monitored by the Division of State Architects (DSA). But in 2011, California Watch, a branch of the Center for Investigative Reporting based in San Francisco at the time, revealed both that this agency had failed to fulfill its mission and that as a result of a series of regulatory failures a large number of children were at risk of being buried in the next earthquake. A series titled "On Shaky Ground" established that

- state regulators had routinely failed to enforce California's landmark earthquake safety law for public schools, by allowing children and teachers to occupy buildings with potential safety hazards reported during construction;
- most of the inspectors accused of falsification and absence had nevertheless been approved by state regulators;

- the state had made it virtually impossible for school districts to access a fund set aside for urgent seismic-safety repairs; and
- the regulation of schools' seismic safety had been largely hijacked by lobbyists and private interests.

Californians paid great attention to this revelation, which reached seven million people in three days.[1] In the weeks following the revelation, many readers were quick to question school officials, while the California State Legislature launched a public inquiry and then passed a bill to improve seismic safety in public schools. The next year, the excellence of this investigation was also recognized by the profession: the reporters were nominated as finalists for the Pulitzer Prize and received a gold medal from the Investigative Reporters and Editors association. At a time when the news business was going through an unprecedented crisis, the association's committee chair explained, this investigation proved that "investigative reporting is alive and well, and really making a difference in our society."[2]

This investigation exemplifies the first shift advocated by data journalists, as analyzed in chapter 5. By harnessing the "power of data and technology,"[3] journalists seek to hold authorities to a greater standard of transparency—in this case, the authorities responsible for earthquake-risk prevention. Thus, the investigation "On Shaky Ground" was based on the building of a database, extensive statistical and algorithmic processing, and the publication of an interactive map on the web. In the spring of 2011, anyone could check online the seismic certification level of any school building in California as well as the building's distance from the most hazardous seismic zones.

From the very beginning of the investigation, however, journalists realized the limits of what they portrayed as the "power of data." The quality of the data in question, which they had obtained from public authorities, was indeed dubious. Because the DSA was going through a major organizational crisis at the time, the data it made available to the journalists were incomplete, dirty, and full of errors, so much so that the reporters considered ending the investigation several times. They felt that there was a great

THE MAKING OF A REVELATION

risk that rather than making the authorities more transparent, any use of these data would on the contrary increase their opacity. How did the Center for Investigative Reporting ultimately overcome the tension between striving to make governments more transparent and using data produced by government authorities and thus largely questionable? Understanding how it solved this conundrum will help us sketch out what a more adequate journalistic ethics might look like.

In this chapter, I defend the counterintuitive idea that these journalists were able to make a revelation and ultimately to harness the "power of data" precisely because they refrained from approaching the data from an objectivist perspective. Rather, by remaining constructivist—in other words, by questioning the conditions of data production—they were able to produce revelations through computation. They managed to steer clear of an objectivist perspective not owing to outstanding skills or greater experience with this type of investigation but because the way they organized themselves allowed them to remain constructivist throughout the investigation. Their organization followed three key rules: (1) avoid too much division of data work within the newsroom; (2) combine data analysis with more traditional ways of knowing, such as interviews and document research; (3) and ensure that the calculations performed do not conflict with professional ethics.

I pieced together the elements of this investigation by interviewing six of the journalists involved and examining different versions of the database. I studied how over a nineteen-month period the journalists produced a revelation based on a set of material practices. My approach echoes the ethnographies of news organizations published in the 1970s[4] as well as ethnographic accounts of online journalistic work.[5] I also drew inspiration from ethnographies of scientific work, which retrace the tortuous process whereby scientists produced justified beliefs with the help of technology.[6] But unlike in most existing work in both journalism and science, I paid close attention to the ethical tensions that arose within the team surrounding computational practices and the creative solutions the journalists found to resolve these tensions.

DATA JOURNALISM IN THE MAKING

EXPOSING STATE NEGLIGENCE WITH THE "POWER OF DATA"

In September 2009, Corey Johnson had just been hired as a money and politics reporter. His first assignment was to write an article for the anniversary of the Loma Prieta earthquake. Twenty years earlier, on October 17, 1989, an earthquake had killed sixty-three people in the San Francisco Bay Area. He had previously worked as an education reporter in North Carolina, so he started off with the following question: "Are schools in California safe?" After interviewing a few experts, he sent a request to the DSA for information about the number of schools at risk. The agency returned an Excel file, which indicated that more than nine thousand schools in California did not meet seismic standards. This is when Corey realized that he had a "big story": "Once I got that, that's when I knew that there was a big story here because the law was so strict that it said not one single school can violate this law—that nine thousand in a list that appear to violate the law. So how does that happen?"[7] Corey asked his editors for more time and resources to investigate. Like a "tip" in traditional investigations,[8] the Excel spreadsheet suggested the existence of a massive problem—not just a few poorly protected schools but a more systemic failure. It also indicated that the investigation would be feasible because the spreadsheet made it possible to identify the schools affected and ultimately to retrace the chain of responsibility.

For California Watch's editors, this investigation seemed promising not only because of its topic but also because it was an opportunity to publicize the young organization. At that point, this California branch of the Center for Investigative Reporting had been in existence for only one and a half years, and as a nonprofit media organization it had to raise money from rich donors in California.[9] Since these donors had often made their fortunes in technology, what better signal to send them than an ambitious investigation demonstrating the power of data and technology to monitor government? With this in mind, the editors decided that the investigative team would produce a database of all public schools in California, combining government and geological data. As Corey explained to me, the purpose was to identify trends and interesting patterns in the data: "I then said that wouldn't it be great to now just have an analysis that looks at how many schools will perform well in an earthquake or how many schools don't comply with the safety law? But let's look at how close these schools are to earthquake faults. Let's put it all on a map, and let's see what we come up with . . . mapping it and coming up with other spreadsheets, which would then tell me interesting patterns and trends of schools to focus on."

Agustin Armendariz, an investigative reporter with experience in data analysis, was assigned to build this database. He collected three sets of data: one with data provided by the DSA relating to the seismic-risk situation of each school building; a second from the California Geological Survey on the location of hazardous seismic zones throughout the state; and a third from the California Department of Education indicating the location of each school building.

As studies of the epistemology of U.S. investigative journalism have shown, reporters highly value the comparison of accounts from different sources based on the premise that reality is necessarily coherent and not contradictory.[10] They expect this comparison to enable them to produce a new account that is more removed from the sources' interests. This is precisely what Corey and his team set out to do with the combined database they intended to create: to bring several accounts from different institutions together into a single artifact to produce a more objective account. The role that Corey and his colleagues imagined for the database in the early days of the investigation can be captured schematically (figure 6.1). The first step would be to disentangle school-inspection data from the organization that produced them, the DSA. These data would then be collated with data from other sources to ensure that the DSA data reflected the actual situation of every school, not just the agency's internal functioning. Next, the journalists would perform a set of algorithmic treatments to identify trends and patterns and through an interactive map would provide readers with personalized information about whether their children were at risk.

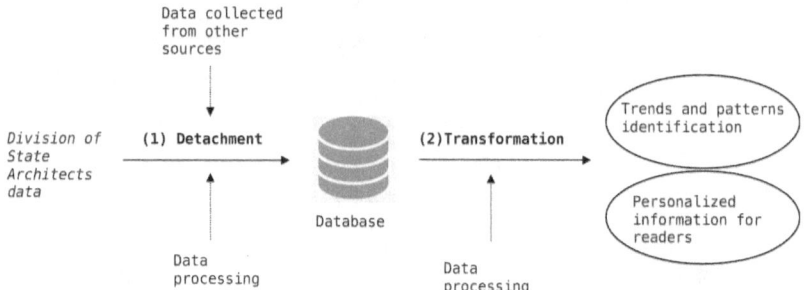

FIGURE 6.1 The data journalism process for investigating California schools' seismic safety initially imagined by the California Watch team.

Source: Based on the author's interviews with California Watch team members.

WHAT TO DO WITH SUCH DUBIOUS DATA?

Corey and Agustin soon realized, however, that they would not be able to cross-reference the DSA's data with data from other official sources or just apply a few algorithms to be able to use the data for investigation, mainly due to the poor quality of the data. The fact that the data from the agency were of poor quality came as little surprise to the reporters. Clearly, the DSA was experiencing major dysfunctions, resulting in uncertain and poorly updated data. What was more surprising was the poor quality of the data provided by the Department of Education: a single school could be designated by different names and registered at different addresses; some schools were listed even though they had closed several years earlier, and conversely, recent schools did not appear in the database. There were tens of thousands of public schools in California, so merging such messy data sets seemed almost impossible. As Agustin recalled, "It was a hard task. I mean there was the messiness of the information. There was me trying to figure out how to convey to people what I think we can and can't do in a way that they would trust. . . . The big challenge of that process is that it was very much us getting to know each other and dealing with a massive, massive, and complicated topic."[11]

THE MAKING OF A REVELATION

The inaccuracy of the data was a major source of concern for Agustin and his colleagues. The state regulators had apparently been experiencing major organizational issues for a while, so assuming that their records were accurate and factual seemed highly risky. Corey recounted that he had no idea that government authorities could work with such dirty data: "Going into this, I thought that if I could just get the data, that was cause for celebration. . . . But then once you get the data, you now have to work with that data to make sure that that data is usable, and sometimes people assume that because government is working with this data, that this data is good data. And what I learned from the data people is that, no, oftentimes that data is horrible, and it takes some work, and it takes some massaging."

The journalists were thus faced with a phenomenon that Harold Garfinkel had already highlighted in the late 1960s. While examining the files filled out by doctors at a clinic, he had noticed that they were systematically full of errors and omissions. According to Garfinkel, this poor quality of records was a normal phenomenon. Any record, he explained, could be interpreted in two different ways: either as an "actuarial record," in the sense that it showed the activity of the clinic's employees, or as a "contractual record," in the sense that each record bore the trace of an implicit contract between physician and patient, with the content of each record informed by the obligation that may have been placed on the physician to describe her interaction with the patient as having conformed to a set of expectations. The conclusion Garfinkel drew was radical: no record would tell us about activities within the organization; rather, we needed to know about the interactions between physicians and their patients to be able to read these records.[12]

Agustin's perspective was fairly close to Garfinkel's when he expressed his doubts as to whether the data could tell the reporters anything about the risk faced by California schools: "Databases are just observations, right? Sometimes it tells you more about the observer than it does about the actual thing being observed, you know. It's up to us to really try and figure that out. How accurate is my data? What can I convey to the reader? What can I tell the reader I'm seeing based on my interviews with sources and my interrogation of any available information available to me, whether that's digitized information or paper records? And I think that's our job."

During the first few months of the investigation, the journalists did feel that they could at least trust the data provided by the California Geological Survey. After all, they thought, these data had been produced by scientists. But in February 2010 Corey learned from a geologist that the seismic zones had changed a great deal in recent decades; moreover, the agency's map was not only produced by scientific expertise but also influenced by private interests and groups who had mobilized over the past few decades to change the zoning. After consulting the archives, he discovered all this to be true:

> When I met this source, that pushed me to want to know a little bit more about the history about how those maps came into being. . . . So I checked the state archives, and they didn't have everything I needed there, but they had some older maps. I was able to just look at an older map and compare it to the current map, and I could see as clear as day that the schools had been cut out of the newer map. . . . I thought that that was an interesting approach to it, which then ultimately led me to finding minutes from the board at the possibility in creating the maps. That's when I heard this debate where people were just losing their minds over the cost. They were very angry. They were pushing back on the state agency very hard to change those maps.

From the outset of the investigation, the journalists were therefore faced with a major problem of "disentanglement." The data they had collected and collated in a database, they felt, could not be disentangled from a set of considerations internal to the organizations that had produced them. It was therefore difficult to imagine that they would one day be able to complete the first step of the investigation and ultimately consider the data to accurately reflect the actual situation of California schools.

Although both Corey and Agustin were aware of the data-quality issue, they did not reach the same conclusion. When Corey asked Agustin to calculate each California school's distance from the seismic zones, this sparked a dispute between the two men. For Agustin, the data were too dirty to produce reliable measurements: "We had disputes over measurements. It was like, you know, I want to say that this building is fifty feet from a fault line. . . . Fuck no, man. This is not survey data. I don't know how these things were projected, and I reprojected them when I stitched them together. I don't know how accurate that school point is. It's not the footprint of the school, and I don't even know where that building falls on campus. I can't make a fifty-foot measurement like that."

By contrast, Corey defended a more objectivist use of the data. In his eyes, calculating the distance between the geographical locations collated in the database would provide the team with a measure of the distance between schools and seismic zones. Agustin in turn pointed out the conditions in which the data had been produced meant that the data could not be used as a basis for reliable measurements. When Corey criticized him for being overly cautious, Agustin emphasized the duties they had as journalists: "No information is ever clean. No data is ever perfect. I'm willing to accept that. But given that limitation, it's really important and really necessary and really hard to figure out what we can responsibly say with this information."

For Agustin, the team had a duty to produce responsible information: certainly, data were never perfect, but how could they make sure not to harm some families by making them think that their children were safe when they were not or vice versa? Although Corey felt that Agustin had too many scruples, he did not wish to shirk his responsibility: "The fear was you're telling mom and pop that this school could possibly kill their kid and still—this school may not even be on the list. This school may not even exist anymore. You're saying that this school may be near a fault, but if your calculations are incorrect, now you've created a fear that isn't really based on any sound facts and science."

This dispute may seem paradoxical: the journalist most skilled in statistics and computer science, Agustin, was the one showing a greater commitment to constructivism. By contrast, the journalist not skilled in these areas, Corey, was more likely to make objectivist use of the data. Agustin's approach was due largely to his professional background—he had been trained within the computer-assisted reporting community and was therefore used to dealing with data-quality issues, as we saw in chapter 1. But his view also illustrates a more general phenomenon: experience working with data protects against objectivism.[13]

Working practices at the newly formed California Watch were thus not sufficiently established for its journalists to share a common understanding of what constituted data misuse. They had to perform what Lucy Suchman calls "articulation work": they had to implement a set of tasks to bring together technologies, forms of organization, and professional practices in a coherent way.[14] This articulation was especially difficult to achieve at California Watch because the two journalists were physically distant from each other. Based in Sacramento, Corey collected documents and testimonials from all over California without being directly involved in the development and use of the artifacts developed (maps, lists, tables, etc.). Agustin worked in the San Francisco offices of California Watch, focusing on technology. He produced a set of artifacts to guide the investigation but was not part of the field investigation. The distance between the two men fueled incomprehension and created tension. As Agustin described their relationship, "It was a fight. And I think it would have been an easier fight if [Corey] hadn't been in Sacramento. If we would have sat and had interactions on a daily basis, it would have been a lot easier I think to develop that rapport earlier in the process and make it a lot smoother."

Over the first six months of the investigation, the team faced major challenges. It could neither disentangle the data from the organizations that produced them nor agree on the acceptable uses of those data within their own news organization. In the fall of 2009, the California Watch reporters found themselves in a very tense situation. The journalists were aiming to expose state negligence but were worried about increasing government opacity instead, so much so that they considered giving up on the investigation. What allowed the investigation ultimately not only to be completed but also to be recognized by the whole profession as excellent journalism?

I argue that the journalists managed to avoid an objectivist perspective by establishing an organization that made it possible for them to remain

THE MAKING OF A REVELATION

constructivist throughout the investigation and question the conditions of data production and thus enabled them to produce the revelation.

RULE NUMBER 1: AVOID TOO MUCH DIVISION OF DATA WORK

When the investigation began, California Watch was only a few months old, and it looked much more like a start-up than a conventional news organization. As mentioned earlier, the editors had high expectations for this investigation, which they hoped would earn the young organization broad professional recognition. These expectations led to two specific organizational features: the creation of a "data team," whose members were in charge of maintaining databases, designing web applications, making statistical calculations, and so on; and the significant growth of the team in charge of the investigation "On Shaky Ground." Starting with Corey and Agustin in September 2009, the investigative team eventually involved eleven people by the spring of 2011.

For some reporters, however, this movement toward specialization was becoming problematic. They were concerned about the widening gap between the reporters investigating in the field and the journalists investigating with the database. During the first few months of the investigation, Corey had collected a large number of interviews and documents from many different sources but had stayed separate from the data team, in which Agustin played a central role. Not only were the two groups involved in different activities and in some cases physically distanced, but they also did not share the same concerns, as Corey explained:

> The challenges that the data team dealt with were separate from mine. I was intimately aware of what people were dealing with, and I know that they dealt with the issue of how to do this smart, how to do this fair, and how to do this accurate in the context of all other duties and responsibilities and resources.... For me, that was less of an issue. I had my

own pulling-hair-out issues, but that was more dealing with sources—trying to pry information out of officials who didn't want me to have it and that sort of thing. So the data stuff—not so much for me. I was shielded from a lot of that.

Again, it was Agustin who raised the alarm about the excessive division of labor. It was dangerous, he argued, to think of data labor as a series of isolated operations carried out by specialized workers and cut off from the rest of the organization. Too much division of labor raised the risk of each journalist taking the work of their colleagues for granted. For Agustin, an organization modeled on the "world of engineers" was to be avoided at all cost: "We have to really kind of do this in a back-and-forth kind of way. It can't be done in this engineering style in which you say, 'Step 1 is this,' 'Step 2 is this,' 'Step 3 is this,' 'Step 4 we're done.' Right. There's revisions, there's changes, there's reporting. You might even change your entire thing at the end because you have some new pieces of information."

Taking advantage of California Watch's flexibility as a young organization, the journalists and editors tried to bridge the gap between the two groups, first by setting up regular meetings so that each group could keep the other informed about its progress and the problems it faced. As Corey recounted, "We had constant meetings. We had a project meeting that we literally had every Thursday, where we had updates on the project, but then outside of those meetings, we had conference calls and Google chats and private phone calls and emails."

More importantly, a new position was created within the data team to bridge the gap between the two sides of the investigation. In August 2010, Kendall Taggart was hired as a data reporter, first as an intern and then as a permanent staff member. Formerly a research assistant in film production, she was assigned to check the database and to collect evidence from the field, constantly moving back and forth between the data and the field: "I like the balance, though, between diving into the spreadsheet and then putting it aside and going and walking out the door and figuring out what's actually happening and then coming back to it. And the more people I talk to who sort of live in both the reporting land and the data land, [the more

I understand that] it's really important not to get stuck on the numbers and then realize two months later they don't correspond to reality, that whatever the state thinks they're measuring isn't there."[15]

Through her position as an intermediary within the organization, the data reporter helped to bring together the two sides of the investigation. Her work consisted in both knowing the data intimately and systematically opposing them with an outside view informed by interviews and documents. By establishing a constant back-and-forth between the two sides of the organization, she ensured that the work on the database was also informed by the other forms of knowledge provided by the reporters.

It was therefore primarily by adjusting the organization of their work that the journalists were able to avoid the unfortunate consequences of an excessive division of labor. By establishing the organizational conditions to allow for a back-and-forth between the data team and the more traditional reporters, they ensured that neither side took the other's work on the data for granted. The fact that California Watch was a young organization was both a constraint and a resource in this respect: it brought together people who were not used to working together but also offered flexibility.

RULE NUMBER 2: COMBINE WAYS OF KNOWING

The combination of two ways of knowing proved crucial to the investigation's success. The first way was based on the qualitative analysis of documents collected from actors (school principals, construction companies, regulators, architects, etc.). The second way was based on data analysis. For nearly one and a half years, the team members combined these two ways of knowing, first setting up a process of systematically verifying the data by means of the qualitative material collected and then relying on the data to organize field investigations.

From the fall of 2009 to the fall of 2010, the systematic verification of data required significant human resources. The journalists saw the use of human resources as a way to disentangle the data from the institutions that produced them. Instead of seeing the database itself as encapsulating a truth, the journalists considered it instead as a fragile construction that needed ongoing adjustments to make it correspond to the "real-life evidence" collected on the ground. Kendall described to me how challenging it had been for the team to match the database with the qualitative information collected on the ground:

> Two weeks before [the investigate report] went up, one of the schools that we'd written about that was in Corey's story was, in the state database it was called, like, "High School Number 2." And then in real life it was called "Southeast Middle." So when you went to that website for Southeast Middle, it showed no problems, and we just spent months writing a print story about some of the problems at that school, and Corey saw that. He was looking at stories at his own school and saw, but you can see why from a data perspective someone who's not embedded and doesn't know that High School Number 2 is Southeast Middle is going to miss it. It does happen a lot, I think, if you don't figure out ways to make sure that everything, including building an app, is a reporting process.

Like Kendall, the team concluded that to have journalistic value, a database had to be designed as a reporting process. This meant that all information in the database had to come from or be confirmed by elements that the reporters had found through personal and direct contact with sources—what Corey and Kendall called "real-life evidence." Between October 2009 and September 2010, the database was thus continuously transformed by integrating a large amount of information collected in the field (figure 6.2). This solution adopted by the California Watch journalists was rather traditional. It was consistent with the epistemology of journalism and particularly with the way U.S. investigative journalism views truth as a confrontation between accounts of reality.[16]

Through this process, a qualitative form of knowledge was mobilized to make a quantitative way of knowing possible. After one year, the team

THE MAKING OF A REVELATION

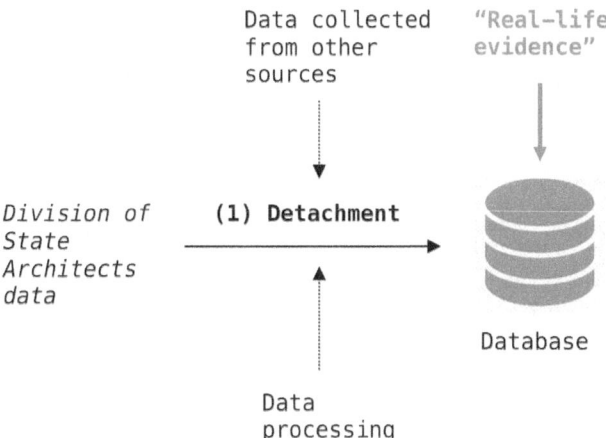

FIGURE 6.2 Adapting the data to "real-life evidence" in the data journalism investigation of California schools' seismic safety.

Source: Based on the author's interviews with California Watch team members.

members considered the disentanglement problem had been solved. Almost surprisingly, they found that there was no longer a gap between what they could see on their computers and what they observed in the field. In September 2010, Agustin produced a list of about one hundred schools that did not meet seismic-safety standards. For the first time, Corey felt that the list was a good reflection of what he saw in the field. According to Agustin, "As Corey went out [and] down this target list I gave him, he wasn't able to disprove in real life any of the things that I was finding in the technology. So as he came back, and as I understood that he was seeing the same things I was seeing, you know, the same things I was seeing in the data, he was seeing in the documents, he was seeing at the campuses, he was seeing in interviews."

By the fall of 2010, relations within the team had improved significantly, to the point where the artifacts no longer sparked controversy. The investigation thus progressed quite rapidly. A few months later, the revelations produced by the investigation would be made public without the team's journalists feeling that they had failed in their professional duties. This confidence enabled the reporters to rely on the database to gather information from actors on the ground. In October 2010, Agustin produced a "red list" of the four hundred most dangerous schools in California, extracted from the full database that the team had taken nearly a year to build. As Kendall explained, the team used the list to drive California Watch reporters to the most interesting schools, allowing them to gather new evidence in the field: "[We were] using the data to identify what schools we thought were the worst, what schools clearly had safety problems, and really drilling down on what was happening there by talking to the structural engineers and the inspectors, all the people involved in that project."

The database was used as a means of distributing the team's resources more efficiently. It allowed the reporters to collect more facts on the ground and made it easier for them to cross-compare single cases of unsafe schools. The reporters also relied on the database to gain more information from sources. Corey recalled showing the map of schools' seismic safety to geological experts in order to elicit additional information from them:

> Once we had a chance to talk to another earthquake engineer.... She knew which areas were somewhat hot zones for geological fault activity. So by seeing our map, she was able to help us to better understand threats—threats to some of the schools in a way that we just didn't have the technical understanding and knowledge of. So in that way the mapping has helped because other people were able to put other information on top of those maps and really bring the issue to life for us, so we could help the public understand why this is a big deal.

For the journalists, the artifacts produced using the data and calculation techniques allowed for better allocation of California Watch's resources, either by reducing the dispersion of human resources involved in the investigation or by increasing the quality of the information obtained from sources. This process is not specific to the world of journalism. It has its roots in the world of statistics, particularly in the tradition of data analysis that emerged in the United States in the early 1960s.[17] This tradition holds that statistics should not be used just to explain a phenomenon through a set of variables but also to allocate research efforts more efficiently by enabling a series of exploratory steps.

By combining the two ways of knowing, quantitative and qualitative, the journalists of California Watch were able to produce their revelations:

1. State regulators had routinely failed to enforce California's landmark earthquake-safety law for public schools, allowing children and teachers to occupy buildings with potential safety hazards reported during construction.
2. Most of the inspectors accused of falsification and absence had nevertheless been approved by state regulators.
3. The state had made it virtually impossible for school districts to access a fund set aside for urgent seismic repairs.
4. The regulation of school seismic safety had been largely hijacked by lobbyists and private interests.

The combination of quantitative and qualitative ways of knowing took different forms. Claims (3) and (4) were based solely on the qualitative approach (interviews and documents). This approach allowed the journalists to broaden the explanation they provided by pointing out the responsibility of actors who, because they were more distant from the DSA's day-to-day regulatory activity, did not appear in the data. Sticking to the data would have been a mistake in the journalists' eyes because they considered that their role was to identify the responsibility of all actors beyond the DSA's employees. Showing the systemic nature of the problem increased the political impact of the investigation.

To produce claims (1) and (2), which were central to the revelation, the journalists closely articulated the two ways of knowing. Data artifacts were mobilized to show the validity of claims that had been formulated through the field investigation. The team here adopted a hypothesis-driven approach, with the reporters statistically verifying a hypothesis arrived at through interactions with individuals or through documents. The deferral to the artifacts was partial here because the initial proposition was formulated through the qualitative component of the investigation.

The first claim was that there was a massive regulatory crisis surrounding the protection of schools from seismic activity. Evidence of this crisis had accumulated from the start of the investigation: as we saw earlier, it had all begun with the Excel file that the DSA sent to Corey, which disclosed that nearly nine thousand schools were not certified as earthquake safe. The field investigation subsequently confirmed the magnitude of the crisis. The journalists then sought to use the data to prove this hypothesis by precisely quantifying the number of California schools that were not protected. Given their lack of confidence in the data, they chose to randomly select a sample of 370 schools to verify the situation of each school and concluded that 60 percent of the state's schools had at least one building that had not been certified as safe from seismic risk.

The team followed the same process to prove the second claim: that the DSA had wittingly recruited substandard or even criminal inspectors. The reporters first learned from school principals that inspectors sent by the agency had not come to inspect buildings or that they had certified buildings with obvious defects. The team thus deduced that the agency had failed to vet its inspectors and even encouraged them to break the rules. To prove this hypothesis, the reporters created a new database using the seventeen thousand evaluation forms filled out by the eighteen hundred inspectors who had served over a thirty-year period. They extracted a sample of the three hundred worst-rated inspectors and based on a cross-tabulation found that 66 percent of them had continued to be recruited despite the poor evaluations they had carried out. Here again, the data reinforced a claim based on field sources.

This combination of the two ways of knowing had several benefits for the journalists. First, it was largely consistent with the epistemology of investigative reporters. As James Ettema and Theodore Glasser explain, reporters never collect facts before assessing the overall situation.[18] They always rely on stories to collect relevant facts, and the facts allow them to confirm the stories or develop new ones. To arrive at claims (1) and (2), the journalists started with a story ("the agency hired incompetent inspectors") before gathering data (the inspectors' evaluation sheets) and coming up with a new story. Second, this combination considerably facilitated the articulation of the revelations with the moral order at the heart of investigative reporters' work. From the outset, the hypotheses to be confirmed were articulated with a shared moral order—exposing the inability of public authorities to fulfill their mission. The process of moral articulation preceded the elaboration of the artifacts: the database of inspectors was produced after the agency's responsibility for the inspectors' misconduct was signaled.

During their investigation, the California Watch journalists thus closely combined two different ways of knowing. They maintained a high degree of reflexivity regarding the data and calculations they used and were able to reconcile the data processing with their professional standards. At no time did one way of knowing fully overshadow the other. Although there was far greater collective trust in the data artifacts by the end of the investigation, that trust was never absolute.

RULE NUMBER 3: SUBJECT ALGORITHMS TO ETHICAL STANDARDS

Several times over the course of the investigation, the team's reporters considered which calculations they could perform and which ones were ethically problematic. They felt that some calculations conflicted with the news organization's legal and ethical responsibility. They addressed these concerns by setting limits on the operations delegated to algorithms. As a result, they decided not to disseminate some of the data collected and to integrate professional standards in the algorithms.

The team ruled out certain ways of using the data it had collected. This was the case for information on the evaluations filled out by the inspectors in charge of checking school buildings under construction. As mentioned earlier, the journalists developed a database of seventeen thousand evaluation forms filled out by eighteen hundred inspectors. In their view, sharing these data was of real editorial interest; the very fact that public money was spent on recruiting inspectors justified the dissemination of their evaluations to the public. The team, however, refused to disseminate the data on the web, preferring to use this database for internal purposes only.

The journalists made this choice for both moral and legal reasons. From a moral perspective, the poor quality of the data meant that disseminating the evaluation forms comprehensively would have involved a considerable workload. The reporters would have had to ensure that individuals were not defamed because the agency had confused them with other people. Checking each file that was to be posted online would have added to an already very large budget. From a legal standpoint, the dissemination of this information on the web raised another legal challenge. Because the DSA did not allow the inspectors it recruited to access their evaluation files, the news organization could easily have been sued in court by a disgruntled inspector.

On other occasions, the California Watch reporters went further, modifying algorithms to meet professional standards. This led them to build public-accountability requirements into the calculation process. Let us remember that at the start of the investigation Agustin had alerted his colleagues to the problem of measuring each school's distance from the seismic zones. Although he recognized the value of making an interactive map of the schools in the danger zones available to the public, in his view this publication conflicted with the professional standards to which he was committed. The whole team agreed with him regarding their duty not to stir unfounded fears among readers. Through the dispute with his colleagues, Agustin came to propose an alternative conception of measurement. He defended the idea that precision should be defined not in absolute terms but in relation to the public: "Sometimes people don't think about the level of precision that they convey to readers. My favorite example is you tell your friend, 'I'm going to be there at 15.53 seconds. They'd laugh their fucking ass at you. Right? I mean, this level of precision you cannot achieve. So you don't want to convey that level of precision to a reader. You say, 'I'll be there in about fifteen minutes.'"

Because an accurate measurement was impossible to achieve and was not expected by readers, Agustin proposed defining a level of accuracy that would satisfy two conditions. First, the accuracy would be high enough that a school would not be too likely to appear in a danger zone on the map when it was actually a distance away from that zone. This would avoid stirring unfounded fears among readers. Second, the accuracy would be low enough that a school would not be too likely to appear on the map outside a danger zone when it was actually within that zone. Accordingly, Agustin decided to modify the algorithm informing the interactive school map. He built a "buffer" into the algorithm—that is, an interval that increased the size of the area around each school: "What I did is that once you stitch together a map of the seismic hazards in California, and you put the schools in proximity to those, can I lay a buffer, a half-mile buffer around that point at which they say the school is at and see if there are features, you know, hazards that fall within it?"

An ethical consideration was thus written into the algorithm. On the map, yellow dots indicated schools located near a danger zone (figure 6.3).

This process fits what Madeleine Akrich calls the "script" of a technical object.[19] Part of innovators' work consists in embedding a vision of the world or a set of predictions about the actors involved in the objects they develop. Here, Agustin embedded a set of expectations about how the public would use the online application in the algorithm, which allowed California Watch to uphold the professional ethical standards requiring it to convey information to the public in a responsible way.

The third rule established during the investigation required the news organization to subject algorithms to journalistic standards. In the case of the investigation "On Shaky Ground," this process translated into occasional discussions between team members. Although not frequent, these discussions paved the way for setting up arenas within the organization that would allow reporters, data analysts, application developers, and possibly also lawyers and legal advisers to exercise that rule in a more collective way.

Most news organizations, whether in France or in the United States, are obviously unable to conduct such complicated and expensive investigations. California Watch devoted nineteen months to this investigation and spent more than $500,000, mostly on staff costs.[20] Undoubtedly, such resources

DATA JOURNALISM IN THE MAKING

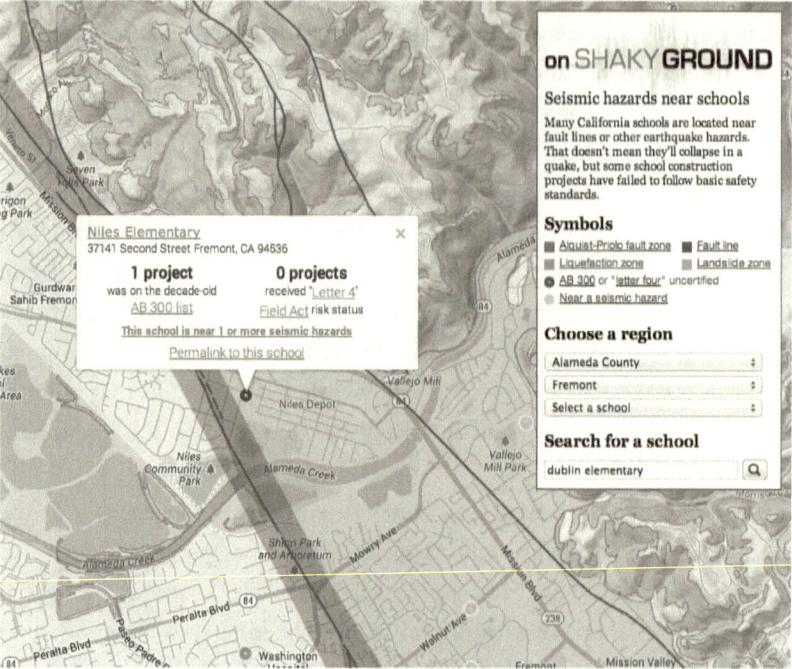

FIGURE 6.3 Writing an ethical consideration into the mapping algorithm for the investigation of California schools' seismic safety.

Source: Based on the author's interviews with California Watch team members.

are out of most news organizations' reach. Nevertheless, the rules identified by Corey and his colleagues have a broader significance.

* * *

This chapter has demonstrated that steering clear of objectivism can allow journalists to produce revelations consistent with the standards of the profession. Although the California Watch reporters wanted to leverage the "power of data" to uncover aspects of government that were both unknown and outrageous, they realized that the data themselves provided them with very limited power. Most of the time, especially when the data did not come from official statistical institutions, their quality was dubious because they were difficult to disentangle from the organizations that produced them. But the main lesson from this chapter is that for journalists to steer clear of an objectivist approach to data and algorithms, they need more than just extraordinary personal skills. On a more fundamental level, they need to establish a form of organization that avoids too much division of data work within the newsroom, allows for a combination of different ways of knowing, and makes it possible to decide collectively on the limits to be imposed on the algorithms.

This brings into relief the sociological value of analyzing how journalists and their organizations resolve the tensions they face when confronted with computational artifacts. Social scientists' conventional criticism of the "positivism of data" is not enough because the actors acknowledge the constructed nature of the data and algorithms. It is far more productive for sociology to adopt a pragmatic stance—that is, to reconstruct the processes that actors and organizations implement to mitigate the problems that arise while respecting the principles to which they are committed.

Crossing the Atlantic, the next chapter analyzes another aspect of the evolution of journalistic ethics: the relationship between journalists and researchers.

7
HOW NOT TO GET ACADEMIC

> *After [my story] went out on the wire, I overheard a bit of conversation between two of my colleagues. It was in the men's room, and I was out of sight in a stall. "Did you see Meyer's story on Carter and religion?" one of them asked. "Yeah," said the other. "Meyer is getting pretty academic."*
>
> —PHILIP MEYER, *PAPER ROUTE*

In 1976, Philip Meyer, one of the American pioneers of data journalism, had just published a story based on a national preelection poll that he had carried out to determine whether Jimmy Carter's religiosity would motivate a greater number of churchgoers to vote for him in the upcoming presidential election. Of interest here is the reaction of Meyer's colleagues, who felt that he was "getting pretty academic" and therefore was not quite journalistic enough. Because his article focused on the relationships between variables related to voters' religion and age, they may have been reproaching him with losing sight of his readers and seeking primarily to contribute to political science scholarship. In fact, Meyer did "get pretty academic" on several occasions, publishing academic articles,[1] attending political science conferences, and ultimately becoming a full-time academic in the early 1980s.

As an academic, I do not have any particular reason to be concerned about journalists "getting pretty academic." Like many of my fellow sociologists, I am inclined to think of the social sciences as a resource for journalism.[2] Moreover, the boundaries between journalism and social science long remained blurred in the United States and in France until the late

1930s.[3] For this reason, the rise of data journalism and computational journalism more broadly could be seen as a good opportunity to bridge the gap, as Chris Anderson puts it, between "journalists [who] interpret" and "sociologists [who] scientize."[4] In this chapter, however, I take the criticism voiced by Meyer's colleagues as my starting point. Because my objective here is to sketch the contours of a renewed ethics for journalism, it is critical to understand how journalists should relate to science and scientists. Turning newsrooms into "calculation centers" involves relying on computational resources, including scientific knowledge and science practitioners. Accordingly, the main questions here are: What relationships should journalists foster with scientists? What mistakes are they likely to make in their interactions with scientists within the framework of a data journalism project? Although I use the word *mistakes*, my intention is not to judge the actions of journalists from a scientific point of view or to point out their lack of rigor or of compliance with scientific standards. Following Cyril Lemieux,[5] my aim is rather to identify attitudes that journalists might have toward scientists that can cause them to lose sight of their own professional obligations. A fairly obvious type of mistake would involve journalists using science merely as a facade of objectivity. By remaining totally detached from scientific reasoning, journalists would stray from the professional ethics that encourage them to investigate facts objectively. Conversely, journalists might behave too much like scientists—for instance, by not paying enough attention to the time constraints they face as news professionals or by focusing on topics of interests only to the scientific community. Because data journalism is disrupting the established relationships between journalists and scientists, it is crucial to investigate how journalistic ethics should adapt to this upheaval.

To determine the direction that the ethics of journalism should take regarding journalists' relations with scientists, I investigated a news project led by two journalists with the French magazine *Paris Match* between 2016 and 2019. This project, "The Weight of Words" ("Le poids des mots"), originally aimed to cover the French presidential campaign of 2016–2017 in a more objective way by collating all the speeches made by the main candidates in a database. By means of quantitative text analysis, the main purpose of the collation was to reveal ideological differences between candidates and to hold them accountable for their statements. After the election of Emmanuel Macron in May 2017, the journalists renamed the project "The Weight of the President's Words" ("Le poids des mots du président") and continued collecting all of the speeches Macron made until early 2019. Because Macron was relatively new to politics at the time and had not belonged to any established political party, the quantitative analysis of his speeches was supposed to help readers better understand his ideological standpoint and to hold him accountable for the promises he had made during his campaign.

With respect to journalistic ethics, this project is interesting in two ways. First, the two journalists worked with a dozen social scientists and developed strong relationships with a research laboratory that specialized in the quantitative analysis of political discourse. Having trained in the social sciences before becoming journalists, the reporters attached great importance to their relationship with knowledge and researchers in the social sciences. Far from merely seeking scientific endorsement, they engaged with the academic world by reading research papers, taking part in seminars, and building strong relationships with researchers over time. In so doing, they experienced the tensions raised by close interactions with researchers. Second, the value of this project has been recognized by the profession, as attested to by the amount of media coverage that the *Paris Match* journalists have received and the number of collaborations they have engaged in with other French news organizations to quantitatively investigate political discourse.

Through interviews with the *Paris Match* team and the researcher with whom they engaged most extensively, I was able to see how the journalists successfully avoided the two pitfalls mentioned earlier—losing sight of their professional obligations and behaving too much like scientists. By establishing a symmetrical relationship with the scientists, finding trade-offs between scientific standards and journalistic constraints, and adjusting the data infrastructure to the imperative of newsworthiness, the *Paris Match* journalists explored rules particularly well suited to the challenges that data journalism raises in the relationship between journalists and scientists.

AN UNEXPECTED HOME FOR DATA JOURNALISM

In the French media landscape, *Paris Match* was certainly not thought of as the news organization most likely to engage in data journalism. Primarily known as a photonews magazine since its creation in 1949, with a wide and popular audience and a strong focus on celebrities and human-interest stories,[6] it has often been criticized for being sensationalist.[7] And yet in 2013 editor in chief Olivier Royant decided to create a team called "Data Match" as part of a new format for the magazine. Royant had been a correspondent in the United States for a long time, and so his task was to modernize the image of the magazine by exploring a new format alongside photography, text, and illustration. The *Guardian* and major U.S. newspapers served as examples for the editor in chief, who believed that it was important to keep up with the data journalism trend that was starting to reach France. At *Paris Match*, even more clearly than in the case of the other media organizations mentioned in chapters 6 and 8, data journalism was introduced as a way to change the news organization's image. As Adrien Gaboulaud, one of the reporters involved in the project, explains, "We're often considered a people magazine. Of course, there's Miss France inviting us over to her place. But if you turn the page, you will find a story on Syria. Our frequent readers know that, but those who read us less often do not. I'm speculating a bit here—we didn't have a brief to change the image of the newspaper, but it was an opportunity to show that we know how to innovate."[8]

The Data Match team, established in 2013, was assigned to Anne-Sophie Lechevallier, a reporter who had been covering the economy for the magazine for twelve years. Her weekly mission thus became to produce "one page answering positively or negatively to a question" by representing data graphically.[9] In the following years, the team grew to three people, bringing Adrien onboard as a second reporter and Dévrig Plichon as a graphic designer. Together, they developed a format enabling them to cover a great variety of topics through histograms, tables, and pie charts. Moreover, the team gradually managed to produce this page by relying on its own resources rather than on technical assistance from external agencies. With good audience figures and positive feedback from the profession, data journalism soon made its way into a magazine that seemed largely foreign to it. As Anne-Sophie put it recently, "The few studies of which I have seen, the results show that the page has always been popular with the readership. . . . This whole data journalism endeavor has therefore been recognized externally as journalistically valid and legitimate. Also, we were finalists for the award for the best financial article. . . . Management can only have been attentive to that."

As data journalism found its way into *Paris Match*, the Data Match team started working on a more ambitious project in the summer of 2016. This initiative was driven primarily by management, which wanted to experiment with more autonomous ways of producing news within the magazine: "When we threw ourselves into 'The Weight of Words,'" explained Anne-Sophie, "it was also an opportunity for management to test a 'start-up approach.' The aim was to see what it would look like if we were given a great deal of autonomy. It was management's idea back then. This explains why we were able to do it. And I'm not sure it would be possible in every newspaper."

The context was therefore conducive to envisaging a more ambitious project as the team had guaranteed access to the necessary resources. With the presidential elections scheduled for the following year, Anne-Sophie and Adrien contemplated engaging in a political project. During a training session on computer coding funded by the magazine, they learned about a project called "At the National Conventions, the Words They Used," published by the *New York Times* in 2012.[10] Based on transcripts of speeches given at U.S. Democratic and Republican Party conventions, Mike Bostock, Shan Carter, and Matthew Ericson had visually represented the words most used by both parties. Anne-Sophie and Adrien then decided to launch a similar project surrounding the candidates for the French presidential election. There were several reasons for this choice. First, this project aligned well with the magazine's editorial strategy, for which the presidential campaign was once again going to be a major topic of interest. Moreover, both reporters already had experience in quantitative text analysis. In the early

DATA JOURNALISM IN THE MAKING

2000s, Anne-Sophie had trained in lexicometric analysis as part of her master's degree in history. She and Adrien had also devoted a few pages of Data Match to the statistical analysis of texts sourced from social media platforms. Thus, as Anne-Sophie put it, "when we thought about the presidential election, we figured that discourse would be our primary material." Finally, the technological context also informed this choice because the reporters believed that it had become easier to collect, handle, and process large volumes of text.

In the early summer of 2016, Anne-Sophie and Adrien put down on paper their initial ideas about "The Weight of Words"—a title referring to the magazine's historical motto magazine: "The weight of words, the shock of photographs." First, they would incorporate a wide variety of transcribed speeches given by candidates: not just speeches made at political rallies but also those delivered in TV or radio broadcasts, interviews published in newspapers and news magazines, and even statements made in videos posted on social media platforms. Second, they figured that counting the number of words in candidates' speeches should allow them to cover politics in a more objective way in a context where electoral polls had shown their limits. This would enable them to clarify each candidate's ideological positions and above all to reveal contradictions in their discourse. As Anne-Sophie explained, "Capturing contradictions in discourse . . . allows us to confront the politician with the commitments they make verbally and to look at their actions, which is the basis of democracy. You get elected on the basis of words, and that also serves as a democratic memory. It's a big word, but from a journalistic point of view it's very interesting."

In more concrete terms, from the outset they considered how they, their colleagues, and readers could use this project. Within the newsroom, the database of every candidate's discourse would make it possible to generate new story ideas during the campaign, whether to verify political statements, to compare statements to candidates' past actions, or to reveal ideological contrasts between candidates. As Adrien recalled in mid-2020, "There was the ambition that a tool like this could be used by the editorial staff to support its own coverage of the campaign." Furthermore, from the beginning the two journalists wanted to give their readers the opportunity to check on the magazine's website how often a word was used by the different candidates. They created visual representations inspired by the *New York Times* series, showing the word count in bubbles.

The emergence of such a project was therefore owed largely to the organization of the magazine and the editorial strategy adopted by management but also to the profiles and interests of the two journalists involved. I now consider how in the summer of 2016 the two journalists envisaged the role of science and scientists in the project.

LOOKING FOR MORE THAN SCIENTIFIC SHELLAC

From the outset, the two journalists planned to make science central to this project, which would distinguish it from many data journalism projects conducted in France and the United States. As both journalists told me, they felt the need to "integrate a scientific approach as closely as possible." Of course, they needed some form of scientific endorsement, both to reassure the magazine's management and to give some authority to their analyses. They were claiming to analyze political discourses using statistical means, so they needed to "arm themselves" against the suspicion of incompetence that they would inevitably encounter. Anne-Sophie thus emphasized the need for the method to be irreproachable: "I was absolutely convinced that there was interest among the readership. Beyond that, as always, we had not to give up on the methodology. Addressing as many people as possible doesn't mean oversimplifying and doing something that isn't carefully thought out. . . . On the contrary, I thought it was necessary for the method to be totally irreproachable for the result to be valid and exploitable."

The two reporters have very explicitly stated that they did not just want to display a scientific guarantee of the reliability of their data. Beyond what they called "scientific shellac," their intention was to rely on scientists to build their method simply because they were venturing in an area with which they were not familiar as news professionals: "We submitted our main methodological choices to researchers working on discourse analysis," Anne-Sophie clarified. "This desire came early on because we felt that it would increase the value of all the editorial outcomes of this work. It would give us a bit of an armor. And beyond the communication aspect or this varnish that we wanted to display, we in any case didn't know how to do it. So we needed this contribution from researchers to really build our tool."

The two reporters' desire to build a strong and meaningful collaboration with researchers was closely linked to Anne-Sophie's prior engagement with social science research. This link was pivotal to the project by providing the team with the resources to establish relationships and dialogue with social scientists. After studying literature and history, Anne-Sophie had undertaken a master's degree at Sciences Po when she started working at *Paris Match* in 2001. Alongside her work as a journalist, she had also trained in research by doing a master's degree in U.S. history at the École des hautes études en sciences sociales (EHESS) in Paris. She had then taken part in a collective research project on oral history and begun training to use textual-analysis software. While still working at *Paris Match*, she started a PhD in American history. Although she did not complete her PhD thesis, her interest in the social sciences remained strong: "Anyway, I never said I wouldn't do my thesis. I continued to be on standby, albeit less assiduously. In history, what interested me was oral history. It was the only way to do my thesis because there were very few written sources. I was interested in it both because it was a new field and because it was the EHESS, which is an extraordinary place that allows you to cross boundaries between disciplines—with sociology, for example. For sure, it was very intellectually enlightening."

The other members of the team were also trained in social science: both Adrien and Steven Lebolloch, the web developer hired for the project, had a master's degree in political science.[11] More importantly, however, Anne-Sophie's familiarity with research made it fairly easy to build a network of people gathered in a "scientific committee." Turning to her former research supervisors, she was rapidly able to identify the individuals who could help them design a methodological framework and produce analyses throughout the presidential race. The committee comprised three historians (Romain Huret, Agnès Callu, Patrick Eveno), a political scientist (Marc Lazar), a literature scholar (Cécile Alduy), and the dean of Sciences Po (Bénédicte Durand). But it was by reading academic literature that Anne-Sophie and her colleagues identified the last member of the committee, with whom they had the most fruitful interactions, Damon Mayaffre. "I've revived a lot of my academic connections," Anne-Sophie stated, "the people I've come across. . . . And Damon, it's because we read all the literature on lexicometry and textual analysis. And quite quickly Damon Mayaffre's lab appeared to be a very dynamic lab on these topics. We subscribed to *Mots*, to other journals, and I did a bit of a survey of social science research on political discourse before getting into it."

It thus appears that the importance that the journalists attributed to science in "The Weight of Words" was closely linked to their personal trajectories. As a result of their prior acquaintance with social science, they viewed science as offering a set of cognitive resources more than a guarantee or shield against criticism. As Anne-Sophie put it, "This project synthesizes all my lives, my different inspirations."

The desire to give science an important role in a journalistic project, however, tells us little about the concrete ways in which the journalists interacted with scientists. How did the Data Match team manage to steer clear of the two pitfalls identified at the start of this chapter: instrumentalizing scientists simply as a source of superficial endorsement and adopting an attitude so respectful of the scientific approach that they would lose sight of their obligations as journalists? As we shall see, the *Paris Match* journalists explored a range of practices that played a decisive role in their ability to avoid these two dangers. I propose to consider these practices as rules for a renewed ethics of journalism.

RULE NUMBER 1: BUILD A SYMMETRICAL RELATIONSHIP WITH SCIENTISTS

A first rule that can be derived from the project carried out by Anne-Sophie Lechevallier and her colleagues is that a symmetrical and natural relationship needs to be established between the journalists and the researchers. To be more precise, the interactional framework must challenge the expected distribution of roles between the expert scientist, who would normally have the monopoly on the use of scientific reasoning, and the lay journalist, who would passively expect the former to open his or her eyes to what needs to be done to implement "science." Introducing symmetry between the two parties is not easy and can result only from deep and repeated interactions. Beyond symmetry, a natural relationship also needs to form; in other words, both parties need to feel confident enough to give reciprocally without fear of being instrumentalized. Such a relationship occasionally develops between a journalist and a source[12] and must also be built between the journalist and the scientist.

For Damon Mayaffre and his colleagues at the University of Nice, it was initially highly unlikely that a symmetrical and natural relationship could develop with the *Paris Match* journalists. As a researcher in linguistics who specialized in the quantitative study of political discourse and highly recognized in his field, Damon was used to interacting with local and national media, especially during electoral campaigns. Based on all his contact with journalists, he had already concluded that most of them did not know what they were talking about:

> I don't want to give the impression of a scientist who is a bit contemptuous; that's not it at all. I remember a journalist who was interviewing me about a book I had just published on Jacques Chirac. And I could see that he didn't know much about it. Finally, he asked me, "Couldn't you write the report for me?" And how many times have my words been completely distorted when I've been quoted? And then I felt powerless about the situation. I've done a few TV interviews; it's tragic. It's a fake live

show, and then it's edited afterward. I say this without bitterness; these are the rules of the game, and I feel sorry for them.[13]

Unsurprisingly, Damon received Anne-Sophie and Adrien's email in July 2016 with some apprehension. For him, *Paris Match* was a people magazine, and he did not see how it could relate to his research. He was also concerned that Anne-Sophie and Adrien might be trying simply to obtain their database from his laboratory when he was in the process of developing a research project on the upcoming presidential elections: it was one of those times when journalists and social scientists compete to describe society.[14] But most of all Damon was afraid of being manipulated: "And repeatedly I wondered: Do they want to take a stance in the campaign? Aren't they just looking for scientific backing? As it was *Paris Match*, I feared that they would then call on readers to vote for a specific candidate. What do I do then if I am the scientific sponsor?"

Despite these initial reservations, the relationship between the researcher and the journalists stabilized fairly quickly. When I interviewed Damon four years after their collaboration, he concluded that the journalists' approach was "serious, both ethically and scientifically." The relationship smoothed out over time, and the researcher came to view Anne-Sophie and her colleagues as exceptions among their peers. However, this was not the result of extraordinary skills on the journalists' part. On a more fundamental level, they behaved in a way that challenged the expected division of roles between expert researchers and lay journalists. First, before their initial meeting with the researchers, they made a few cognitive choices directly informed by their journalistic practice. For example, they chose not to collect copies of the candidates' speeches from their campaign teams but to transcribe these speeches as they were actually delivered. This cognitive choice was informed by a situation Adrien had witnessed a few years earlier: "I had experienced this during the 2012 campaign. I think it was Nicolas Sarkozy's meeting in Villepinte [a city in the suburbs of Paris]. The press service had distributed a speech at the beginning of the meeting. In fact, he didn't stick to it at all. So I knew that you can't rely on these [staff-provided copies of] speeches. . . . Researchers would use these documents for their analyses. So it was very important for us to have the speech that was actually delivered."

Drawing on his own journalistic practice, from the very beginning of the project Adrien formulated a methodological requirement that was justifiable from a social science perspective. Moreover, this choice signified a rejection of researchers' tendency to rely on the printed texts provided by campaign staff. From the outset, therefore, the journalists took a cognitive stance, in a way refusing to expect the researcher to choose the method of doing research based on abstract considerations. This choice had tough consequences on the team because they had to find a way to transcribe hundreds of hours of audio files. Given the limitations of most speech-to-text services, they had to identify and pay for the service they found most efficient.[15] Even then, they spent many hours manually checking the transcripts. Nevertheless, as we will see later, this choice was decisive in bringing balance to the relationship between the journalists and the researchers.

The two journalists then engaged in a series of interactions with Damon and his team, adopting a similar attitude to that held in academia. In July 2016, they spent a day at the laboratory in Nice to meet Damon and discuss the project's methodology with him and his colleagues. The meeting was pleasant, but the discussion was not superficial. As Anne-Sophie recalled, she and Adrien had their questions prepared: "We quickly agreed to come and see him. This is also what we do as journalists. We went there with Adrien, and we were welcomed by Damon, his PhD students, and Etienne Brunet, the creator of Hyperbase [a quantitative text-analysis software program]. . . . We had prepared our methodological questions. . . . They helped us. For them, it was obvious; they had had these questions for a long time. That morning was really exciting. We came with our questions, they had their answers, and at the same time we could talk."

Damon was surprised by the nature of the discussion that took place that day, which he described as "almost scientific." He found that the journalists asked specific and informed questions about the method, starting with the list of terms that should be excluded from the count because they were too general (e.g., adverbs, pronouns, etc.). To him, they demonstrated an understanding of the methodological choices made by the members of his laboratory. Even more surprising to Damon, the two journalists took the time to attend a research seminar, where they asked questions. Anne-Sophie's familiarity with social science research was striking to him: "When you talk to her, you see that she knows the rules of the game. And better yet, she has the feeling, the attitude. . . . She doesn't just do anything with language."

The journalists did not just adopt or mimic the codes of academia. By drawing on knowledge derived from their journalistic practice and embracing the codes of scientific discussion, they were able to challenge the distribution of roles between journalists and researchers that Damon had anticipated. Even more significantly, however, they managed to symmetrize their relationship with the researcher by providing him with data. Whereas Damon had expected the reporters to be chasing data from his laboratory, the opposite occurred:

> They understood that our resources were scarce. They themselves had a fair amount of money. So it was a win-win situation: on their side, they needed my name to put together a credible scientific committee and because they wanted to do something serious. And on our side, they could do small things—since they had contracts with private companies to do speech-to-text, they had a corpus that was bigger than mine. I had a hard time, alone or with colleagues. And always in a very nice way, when I told them I was missing a speech, they would send it to me within the day.

Over time, the relationship thus became "natural" in the sense that each party came to make a series of gifts and countergifts. For the journalists, the contribution from the researcher was obvious—Damon both helped them to build a reliable methodology and enabled them to display scientific support. But the *Paris Match* journalists also made sure that Damon and his colleagues benefited from the collaboration, both by extending to them the media notoriety associated with the magazine, which has become a key dimension of the evaluation of academic research in France,[16] and, more surprisingly, by providing data to the researchers.

The two-way working exchange marked a significant departure from the way in which relations between journalists and researchers have historically unfolded.[17]

This exchange of gifts undoubtedly helped to balance the relationship and maintain this equilibrium over the course of the three-year project. Certainly, through this project the reporters were able to demonstrate a strong familiarity with academia. But it is important to remember that such familiarity in and of itself cannot have any journalistic value. It could even have led the two journalists to fail to follow their journalistic ethics if they had forgotten their obligations as journalists. It was precisely by finding trade-offs between scientific standards and journalistic constraints that the two journalists were able to preserve their autonomy.

RULE NUMBER 2: FIND TRADE-OFFS BETWEEN SCIENTIFIC STANDARDS AND JOURNALISTIC CONSTRAINTS

Despite their familiarity with the researchers, the *Paris Match* journalists did not embrace all of the methodological standards that Damon and his colleagues viewed as fundamental. On the contrary, they made an informed choice not to observe or only partly to observe some of these standards so they could abide by the constraints they faced as journalists. These constraints, which have been widely studied by the sociology of journalism,[18] involve product considerations (Is the news product tailored to an audience?), substantive considerations (Is the news product likely to be newsworthy enough?), and the resources available for producing news content (Are there enough budget, time, and human resources to produce the news?). How journalists negotiate between these constraints and the scientific standards they face in the practice of data journalism, however, has yet to be explored. I argue that to remain journalists, Anne-Sophie and Adrien had to make trade-offs between scientific standards and the requirements of the news organization.

A first trade-off revolved around the way to count words. Linguistics researchers traditionally measure the frequency of a word's appearance—for example, the word *France* appears 5.34 times per 1,000 words. But for the *Paris Match* journalists, this measure was not easy enough for the public to read, and they felt that it was "better to keep the indicator as simple as possible." They preferred to measure a raw number of words because "it was easier to understand at first glance." Thus, out of concern for the magazine's audience, they deviated from the scientific measurement standard because they considered the audience unfamiliar with that statistical indicator. From the summer of 2016, they drew bubbles with the graphic designer showing the raw word counts and the distribution of those counts across the five candidates. This representation was included in the web application at the launch of the project (figure 7.1). For example, during the entire campaign the word *travail*, which denotes "work," "job," and "labor" at the same time, was mentioned 483 times by the socialist candidate Benoît Hamon but only 93 times by the far-right candidate Marine Le Pen.

Although this choice was seen as more convenient for the audience, it raised difficulties for the team. By measuring raw numbers, the journalists ran the risk of concluding that one word was used more by one candidate simply because that candidate had spoken more than the others. For this reason, Anne-Sophie and Adrien had to ensure that they analyzed exactly the same amount of speech for all candidates.[19] They thus found a trade-off that was fully satisfactory to Anne-Sophie, probably because it was informed by a governing principle of journalistic work—providing readers with a product that is appealing to them: "Of course, we don't have the same standards as some researchers. I'm very comfortable with the fact that we take more liberties—for example, counting occurrences instead of counting frequencies like researchers do. In this case, we discussed our respective positions. And they [the researchers] didn't have any major methodological problems with that."

Another trade-off related to the choice of texts to be included in the database. For Damon and his colleagues, it was particularly important to ensure that the texts were not too different from one another. For a presidential candidate, speaking on YouTube is not the same as giving a TV

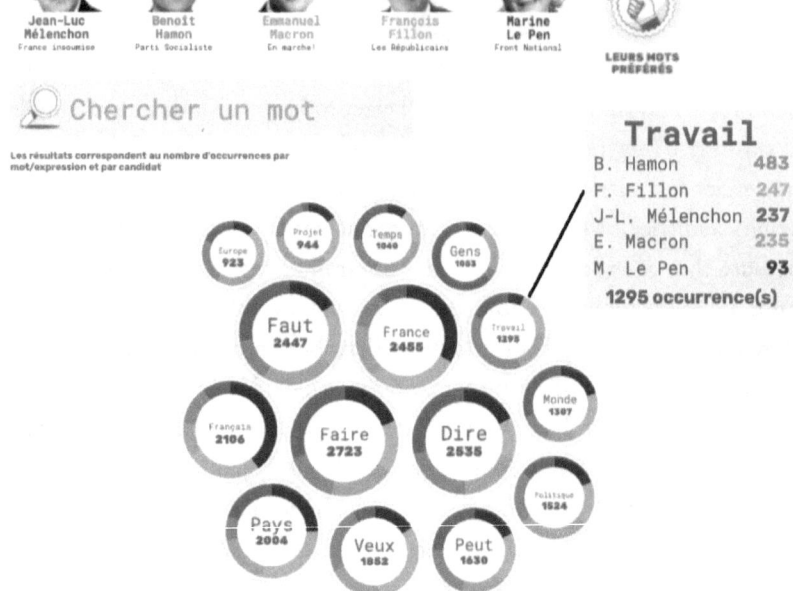

FIGURE 7.1 Word counts for French presidential candidates' speeches shown as raw occurrences, not frequencies, 2017.

Source: Screenshot from "Le poids des mots" [The weight of words] website, *Paris Match*, June 15, 2020, https://www.parismatch.com/Le-Poids-des-Mots.

interview, which is in turn different from delivering a speech at a rally. According to Damon, because the contexts of enunciation differed greatly from one text to another, it was crucial to pay close attention to the design of the corpus. Failing to do so would raise the risk of measuring differences that were merely the result of different contexts of enunciation:

> For us, the problem is the consistency of the corpus. For example, if I take the speeches by Jean-Luc Mélenchon and Emmanuel Macron, I can't have one with only YouTube speeches and the other without any because these are different genres. . . . I also have to do a chronological breakdown. I can't have one candidate speaking before the COVID crisis

and another speaking only after the COVID crisis. . . . Adrien and Anne-Sophie were aware of this, we spoke about it, but they didn't have time to go into it. At one point, they had this Google-like claim—to take it all.

This position is in no way dominant in current research; many researchers today leverage digital technology to pursue a comprehensive approach.[20] But for Anne-Sophie and Adrien, comprehensiveness was a goal informed by several considerations. First, having a large volume of texts was a good way to promote the project's scientificity: at the launch of the project, they were able to write that the project "relies on a database of more than 628 speeches, that is, over 2.9 million words."[21] On a more fundamental level, it was also a way for the two journalists to ensure the feasibility of the project given the constraints of the news organization. When the project was launched in January 2017, there were five months of campaigning left before the election, and many texts had to be integrated into the database every week. In practice, it was therefore very difficult for Anne-Sophie and Adrien to determine which speeches had to be selected or discarded. In order not to dismiss Damon's criticism, they defined a set of metadata allowing them to identify the context of enunciation for each text. As Adrien explained, "We defined a series of metadata we were interested in: date, candidate, location, categories of discourse (a short statement on the front steps of a building, a major speech, a meeting, a press conference), type of media (national or local). We had about ten categories. The purpose was to identify changes in discourse based on geographic location, media, etc." The journalists followed this approach to be able to take into consideration the context of enunciation as they queried the database, which would allow them to put into perspective any differences in the number of appearances of a given word in the candidates' speeches.

Similarly, the journalists chose not to use the algorithms that most researchers commonly use when working with textual corpuses. They ruled out lemmatization techniques, used to group together the inflected forms of a word (e.g., *walk*, *walking*, and *walked*), as well as disambiguation techniques, designed to distinguish between the different meanings of a word (e.g., a "fair" trial as opposed to an art "fair"). That is not to say that the team members considered these operations unnecessary. Rather, they felt that the operations were too complicated to complete within three months and likely to draw criticism from the public. As Steven Lebolloch, the web developer hired for the project, recalled,

> Intuitively, I thought that it was important to know in what context and how a word is used. To say that someone says the word *travail* [work] more often than another candidate doesn't necessarily mean much. But I could already see that doing this in three months would be a real pain in the ass.... I told myself that I couldn't reinvent everything in three months. And also because *Paris Match* could be accused of favoring this or that candidate, we couldn't take any risks. For the two journalists, we had to be beyond reproach, especially since *Paris Match* belongs to [Arnaud] Lagardère, and [Denis] Ollivennes is friends with what's-his-name. The best thing was to be simple and transparent.[22]

Here again the team pointed to organizational considerations to explain the decision to break with scientific standards. Not only were the resources required to meet these standards too great, but trying to achieve these standards would also have jeopardized the whole project by raising doubts about the alterations made to the corpus—even though from the researchers' point of view these "alterations" would on the contrary have reduced errors of interpretation due to the variability of linguistic forms. After discussing this issue with the scientific committee, the journalists decided to stick to counting strings. However, they also decided to systematically check the context in which the words appeared and thus to disambiguate manually. As Adrien explained, "We tried to correct for the lack of lemmatization through systematic consultation of the database. In other words, when we were interested in a specific word, we went to see precisely in what context it had been uttered. So we disambiguated manually."

Clearly, this series of trade-offs arrived at by Anne-Sophie and her colleagues did not amount to a dismissal of scientific standards. Rather, it was concerned with finding practical ways to reconcile these standards with the constraints of the news organization, particularly surrounding the production and distribution of news. From a journalistic point of view, it would have been wrong for Anne-Sophie and Adrien to lose sight of the interest that the information product must have for the audience or to engage in a project that would have required time or means unavailable to the magazine. Damon and the researchers at the University of Nice reacted positively to all of these trade-offs. While maintaining that as researchers they could never make such choices, they recognized that these trade-offs were the best option given the constraints that Anne-Sophie and Adrien faced as journalists.

RULE NUMBER 3: BUILD INFRASTRUCTURE THAT ENABLES NEWSWORTHINESS

Timeliness is one of the major points of difference between journalists and researchers. Whereas most social scientists are not expected to produce content relating to current events, journalists have to speak about the present moment, be it recent events or topics that have become the focus of public discussion. The rise of online journalism has made the structuring role of time in journalistic work all the more decisive, with some news organizations increasingly compelled to cover events as they unfold.[23] Nevertheless, timeliness is not the only value informing journalists' work,[24] and the previous chapter shows how it can sometimes be considerably relegated. In the case of *Paris Match*, this value was important because the organization had to cover a presidential campaign marked by a series of key events: party primaries, electoral rounds, televised debates, scandals affecting some candidates, and so on. But how can journalists be expected to say something about these unfolding events while also processing data and performing calculations? How can they avoid the trap of producing analyses that are not timely? What the *Paris Match* case teaches us is precisely that the design of the data infrastructure is critical to ensuring the timeliness of editorial outputs.[25] I understand infrastructure here not only as the technical choices made by the news organization but also as the way in which technology articulates with the news organization as a community of practice.

The editorial outcomes of "The Weight of Words" database demonstrate that the *Paris Match* journalists were able to produce timely content. They managed not only to provide users with a regularly updated application so as to enable users to grasp the differences in the words used by candidates but also to publish a significant body of stories covering the campaign. The project was initially not intended to produce "hard" or "breaking" news but rather to offer an analytical overview of the campaign. Thus, in the month preceding the first round of the election on April 23, 2017, about twenty articles published in the magazine covered the campaign based on word counts. These articles analyzed each candidate's ideological stance, revealing, for example, that the left-wing candidate Jean-Luc Mélenchon had ceased using communist lexicon and had replaced it with populist terminology[26] and that the right-wing candidate François Fillon was the one who most strongly asserted that the state should stop imposing constraints on entrepreneurs.[27] Over the course of the campaign and especially between the two rounds of the election, the number of articles related to the events of the campaign noticeably increased. For example, a few hours after the televised debate between the two finalists on May 4, Anne-Sophie and Adrien published an article titled "Breaking News: The Words of the Toughest Debate of the Fifth Republic."[28] On the day of Emmanuel Macron's victory, the magazine published an analysis within a few hours of the newly elected president's very first speech.[29]

To understand how the *Paris Match* journalists managed to produce content in tune with the campaign's new developments, we must pay particular attention to the data infrastructure they built (figure 7.2). As mentioned earlier, the team was guaranteed some technical autonomy from the outset, with Steven Lebolloch hired as a freelance developer. This autonomy allowed the team to make several decisive choices in the design of the infrastructure. First, data verification was given an important role through the

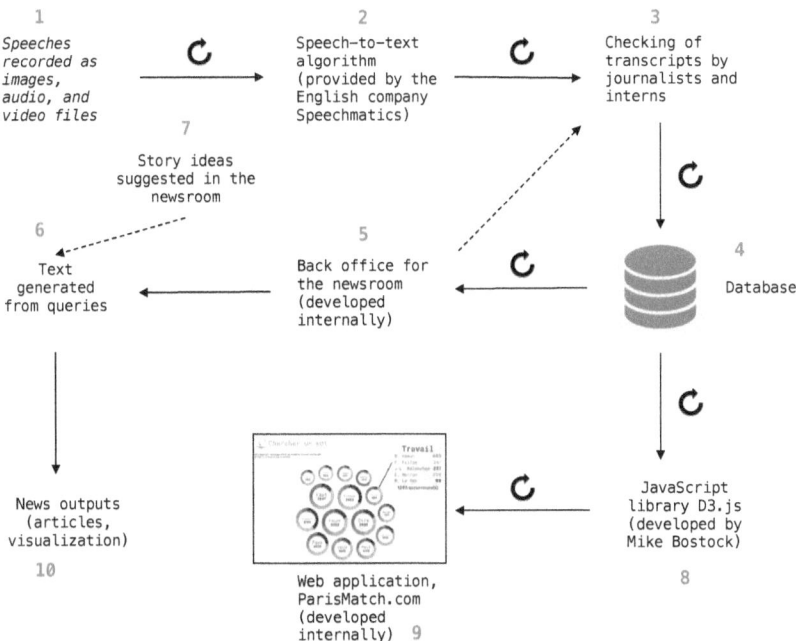

FIGURE 7.2 The infrastructure underpinning "The Weight of Words" project.

Source: Based on the author's interviews of project team members and examination of "The Weight of Words" website.

allocation of human resources (step 3 in figure 7.2) and the design of a back office allowing users to generate lists of words according to their frequency and thus to identify misspelled words and correct them (step 5).

Second, the back office allowed users to build subcorpuses from word queries or metadata (step 6). The journalists thus had access not only to word counts but also to the texts themselves, which meant they were able not only to produce their own analyses by accessing the texts directly but also to communicate these subcorpuses to their colleagues, who could do their own analyses. As Steven explained, "[The journalists] also needed another display to do editorial work around the word counts. . . . They had their own back office. This allowed them to dig through the mass of data to write their content around it. And so in their story, they would take a topic, and they would go snooping around to see more closely who was saying what. They had to be able to explore the data themselves. Because otherwise the raw counts don't say anything."[30]

These technical choices were instrumental to the success of the project, allowing the organization to articulate word counting with developments in the campaign. From a researcher's perspective, such an interface would surely have seemed highly unsatisfactory both because it offered very limited calculation possibilities and because it was closely linked to an organization whose members were unfamiliar with lexicometry. But for the journalists, this interface made it possible to mobilize the entire editorial staff and to react quickly to new events. Adrien explained, "There had been an alleged terrorist attack at Orly airport. A possible angle would have been to see if [the word] *terrorism* appeared in the speeches after this attack. It's for these kinds of circumstances that the whole project was conceived—to see if elements of current events that happen during the campaign are reflected in the speeches. . . . There was this back-and-forth between the current events of the campaign and the speeches that we were trying to identify."

Similarly, ideas raised at editorial conferences or by other media organizations could quickly lead to querying the database and publishing stories. For example, when a television channel noticed that Emmanuel Macron often used the expression "at the same time," the *Paris Match* journalists performed a query and soon published an analysis of a phenomenon that was beginning to fuel campaign discussions. The *Paris Match* journalists' experience thus teaches us one final lesson: journalists' ability to produce newsworthy content hinges on the design of the data infrastructure. To be more precise, it depends on the possibility for journalists to generate intermediary objects (such as subcorpuses) with great flexibility, so that, for example, word counts can become newsworthy.

Finally, these technological practices echo one of the standards originally established by American computer-assisted reporters in the early 1990s: journalists must start from a hypothesis before exploring the data. Enabled by this data infrastructure, compliance with this standard played an important role in exploring fruitful relationships with researchers, at least from the journalists' perspective.

* * *

This chapter opened with Philip Meyer, who was undoubtedly a pioneer in the use of quantitative social science in journalism. In fact, it is only natural that the Investigative Reporters and Editors association gives the annual Philip Meyer Journalism Award to recognize the best work using data journalism techniques and social science research. But in a way Meyer is not a model for data journalists, especially not in the context of the current major economic crisis in journalism. Today's data journalists cannot be those extraordinary individuals whose inclination to follow a scientific approach ultimately leads them to embrace an academic career. Hence, we must think about how journalists can integrate a social science approach into their work when handling data but remain full-fledged journalists. This is one of the major dimensions of the renewal of journalistic ethics imposed by data and computation. In this chapter, I argued that journalists have to avoid two opposite pitfalls: using social science only as a facade of objectivity and not being sufficiently attentive to their constraints as journalists working in news organizations. The case of *Paris Match* shows that journalists need to implement new rules that will govern how they interact with researchers, the trade-offs they must accept between scientific standards and journalistic constraints, and the design of the data infrastructure.

This second case study sheds new light on long-standing debates on the relationship between journalism and the social sciences. For decades, many social scientists have urged journalists to adopt a more scientific approach, with some hoping for the boundaries between journalism and social science to become less clear-cut. In this respect, the rise of computational forms of journalism has raised great expectations among researchers. But as this chapter has shown, for journalists to truly benefit from social science, they must not sacrifice their autonomy. On the contrary, they need to develop close contacts with researchers but at the same time keep them at a distance; they need to become familiar with scientific standards, while also knowing when to break with them. Paradoxically, the success of the social sciences in journalism requires social scientists to accept that their practices must be adjusted to the constraints of journalistic work.

I now turn to the final dimension of a renewed journalistic ethics: the type of public that news organizations are likely to form using computational means.

8
THE ART OF BRINGING ABOUT PUBLICS

The same tragedy keeps repeating itself in most metropolitan areas of the United States. Day after day, people are murdered, most of them from minority groups living in disadvantaged neighborhoods. This problem, which has reached a magnitude unknown to other Western countries,[1] has raised questions about how the media cover lethal violence and crime more generally. For decades now, journalists have been accused of treating this problem in a biased and sensationalist manner, focusing on a small proportion of homicides affecting white and/or rich individuals.[2] Over the past few years, even within the profession this problem has been highlighted as a sign that objectivity as a professional ideal only serves to justify white reporters' and editors' gaze on American society.[3] Some journalists have therefore turned to data and algorithms to raise citizens' awareness of this problem and mobilize them to address it. Using interactive maps and searchable databases, they have sought to generate "publics"—that is, citizens who discuss a problem and try to solve it together. But how can journalists bring about such publics by treating homicides as data and by providing citizens with data products?

In this chapter, I explore this question by focusing on a homicide map launched by the *Los Angeles Times* in 2010. This project, the Homicide Report, exemplifies data journalists' quest for objectivity. Initiated by Jill Leovy, a reporter who wanted to break with the common journalistic practice of covering only a small number of what were considered newsworthy homicides, it has evolved into a database designed not only to offer "a story for every victim" (the Homicide Report's motto) but also to give readers "a more realistic view of the people who are dying" by means of comprehensive and standardized coverage of every homicide committed in Los Angeles County. The Homicide Report is becoming a reference in the United States regarding the use of data and algorithms in journalism[4] and has attracted a large and popular audience, making it one of the most visited and commented sections on LATimes.com.[5]

How journalism can help citizens engage with public issues is a major concern within American journalism. This concern developed particularly as a result of advocacy for "engaged journalism" and its precursor "public journalism."[6] Bringing about publics though interactive maps and searchable databases, however, is in no way straightforward. Many essayists and researchers have become pessimistic about the publics of news products supported by data. This stance stems from a concern about the personalization possibilities offered by these products, which they argue allow users to pay attention only to distinct and localized occurrences—a single crime in a neighborhood, the pollution level on a particular street, and so on. In exploring a map or searching a database, users allegedly pay attention only to news occurrences that affect them personally as residents, parents, or consumers. Cass Sunstein, who was one of the first to voice this criticism, suggests that such editorial products will not encourage people to behave like citizens—that is, to pay attention to occurrences that happen far away or that they did not experience personally.[7] This criticism is often driven by considerations surrounding the crisis of mass media and its ability to foster social integration. In the age of mass media, people had access only to a small number of occurrences selected by news professionals, which led them to share topics of conversation and interest.[8] But with the rise of data journalism, people are increasingly able to select from a large number of occurrences. As a result, it has been argued that they are no longer able to form a "public" in the strong sense of the word but merely an assemblage of individuals focused on their own private concerns.

This criticism echoes another much older concern, which arose in the United States and France with the industrialization of the press at the turn of the twentieth century. In the 1920s, John Dewey, for example, worried that the vast majority of news stories published by newspapers constituted "breaches of continuity"; in other words, they presented news items such as crimes or accidents in isolation, disconnected from one another. And yet, he wrote, the "meaning [of a news story] depends upon relation to what it imports, to what its social consequences are. This import cannot be determined unless the new is placed in relation to the old, to what has happened and been integrated into the course of events."[9] Dewey's main concern was that a public opinion could not form if newspapers provided people with isolated and uncoordinated news occurrences. On the other side of the Atlantic, in the late nineteenth century French writers and journalists were similarly worried that "the newspaper was no more than an amorphous, indigestible heap of small facts that accumulated, without any ferment of ideas to make the dough rise."[10] Today, the same concern has resurfaced all the more acutely as the progress of industrialization has allowed journalists to disseminate a very large number of occurrences in the form of data.

Studying how the journalists behind the Homicide Report were able to bring about publics through data products highlights another challenge surrounding the types of metrics that journalists and scholars use to represent news audiences. These metrics typically depict the public as a sum of individuals who engage in actions—viewing, commenting, sharing, or liking a news item. Although such metrics represent the public in a comprehensive way, they fail to capture how users actually interpret content. To understand how journalists can generate collectives of citizens who will interpret a problem they face together—in other words, as a public—we therefore need to move beyond the behavioral metrics commonly used in the news industry and research. Focusing on the case of the Homicide Report, I studied the traces that some internet users leave on the platform in the form of comments. Together with Jean-Philippe Cointet, a computational social scientist, I developed a new way of representing publics based on the analysis of 28,828 comments posted on the Homicide Report between 2010 and 2017. We found that this platform had successfully gathered two publics around the problem of homicides in Los Angeles: one comprising individuals close to the victims who paid tribute to them and demanded justice, the other consisting of activists who debated the cause of the prevalent lethal violence in Los Angeles.

This chapter argues that journalists' ability to bring about publics with data news products is contingent on a twofold shift. First, they must show a certain humility by relinquishing part of their gatekeeping prerogative, a shift already advocated by proponents of "public journalism" and, more recently, by the promoters of "engaged journalism." They must neither select individual occurrences worthy of coverage nor impose their own interpretations. But relinquishing this prerogative cannot in and of itself bring about publics—that is, collectives of people trying to interpret and solve a problem. Journalists must also adopt a set of practices aimed at fostering and channeling the development of publics. These practices include, in particular, creating spaces for discussion, defining rules to allow for a wide range of people to engage with and debate issues, and producing editorial content based on the data at stake. The case of the Homicide Report highlights that journalistic ethics must integrate these practices for journalism to fulfill one of its fundamental missions: to foster the emergence of publics.

"GIVING READERS A MUCH MORE REAL VIEW OF WHO IS DYING"

Originally, the journalists behind the Homicide Report wanted to break with the way most news organizations cover crime. They criticized the journalistic tendency to cover only a small number of homicides to the detriment of the vast majority of homicides, which were considered to be of no editorial value. Judging by these journalists' public statements and the interviews they gave to the journalism scholars Mary Lynn Young and Alfred

Hermida,[11] this criticism appears to have been at the root of the project. As Megan Garvey, the editor of the Homicide Report, put it, "The white teenage girl who was killed—which is the outlier, the exception to the rule—gets a lot of attention. . . . Or a mass shooting. But the people who are getting killed day-in, day-out, the 17- to 22-year-old black male living in a poor neighborhood, those homicides had gotten to the point, with constraints in print and everything else, where they were not newsworthy."[12]

Social scientists have made this observation for decades.[13] In the case of the *Los Angeles Times* between 2010 and 2012, only 10 percent of all homicides committed in the city were covered in the printed edition.[14] The reporter Jill Leovy, seeing this lack of coverage as a major problem, launched a blog in 2007 in an attempt both to cover every homicide in the county and to treat them all equally. But with six hundred to nine hundred homicides in Los Angeles each year, the task quickly became overwhelming, and the blog was eventually shut down the following year. In January 2010, the project was completely redesigned by two data journalists from the *Los Angeles Times*, Ben Welsh and Ken Schwencke. To better implement Leovy's principles—comprehensiveness and the equal treatment of all homicides—they built a database that captured each homicide through a set of structured information, including the date, location, time, and jurisdiction of the homicide as well as the ethnicity, age, and gender of the victim. To users, the Homicide Report then appeared as an interactive map and a searchable database (figure 8.1), allowing them to look for a person by name, to visually check the number of people killed in a given area in the past twelve months, and to browse homicides based on criteria relating to the person murdered (ethnicity, age, gender) or to the circumstances of the crime (cause of death, involvement of a police officer).

Users are able to view different scales, ranging from the entire county to the street level. When it comes to a specific homicide, they can access not only a set of structured information about the homicide but also a photograph of the victim and a story outlining the circumstances of the crime. For example, by clicking on a dot on the map, we learn that a twenty-nine-year-old Black man, identified by name, was killed by

DATA JOURNALISM IN THE MAKING

FIGURE 8.1 The Homicide Report: an interactive map and a searchable database.

Source: Screenshot from the home page of the Homicide Report, *Los Angeles Times*, October 1, 2021, http://homicide.latimes.com/.

gunshot on 1301 E. Culver Avenue in Compton on February 28, 2011, and that the case was handled by the Los Angeles County Sheriff's Department. According to witnesses, the victim was shot on his way to open the door to his home (figure 8.2).

Like the work of the reporters studied in chapter 6, the algorithms and the database designed by the data journalists behind the Homicide Report were informed by journalistic standards.[15] With extensive experience in computer-assisted reporting, Ben Welsh was particularly well equipped to adjust computational tools to these standards. The descriptive criteria that organize the database were selected for their editorial significance, and the Los Angeles County Coroner's Office was chosen as the main source of data for the database and the algorithm that generates stories because the journalists assumed that this institution would provide more complete and reliable information about homicides than the Los Angeles Police Department (LAPD). Because LAPD officers are involved in a significant

THE ART OF BRINGING ABOUT PUBLICS

FIGURE 8.2 One homicide covered in the Homicide Report in 2011.

Source: Screenshot from Homicide Report, *Los Angeles Times*, June 15, 2019, http://homicide.latimes.com/.

proportion of homicides (7.2 percent between 2010 and 2017, according to the Homicide Report's database), using the LAPD as their sole source of data was obviously problematic for the journalists.

The journalists in charge of this platform envisioned two different publics. First, they wanted to address the people who lived in the neighborhoods where the murders took place. Ben Welsh thus stated that "[the platform] is something that could be of interest to people who care about what happens near [where] they live."[16] They wanted to reach out to the victims' families and relatives, in particular the "weeping mothers who say their sons' deaths were never covered by the press," according to Jill Leovy.[17] But they also targeted another public that, albeit less precisely defined, brought together people interested in better understanding the causes of urban violence. With this second audience in mind, the platform was designed to allow for identifying general trends and sorting homicides according to various criteria, with a view to giving users "a more realistic view of the people who are dying," as Jill Leovy put it.[18]

From the start, the journalists opened up each homicide on the map to comments so that users could "share a memory or thought about" the victim. The response has been quite significant, with tens of thousands of comments posted on the platform since 2010. The way in which the invitation to contribute is expressed reflects the journalists' recognition of the two publics to whom they wished to give a voice. As Ken Schwencke explained, "People who lived there said 'hey, this is what it's like.' 'This tells my story and here are some more thoughts on it.' And people who didn't live there gave their feelings too, and we really want to have that conversation with the community."[19]

It is worth noting that these two audiences are very different and possibly conflicting: on the one hand, grieving people who above all want to pay tribute to the person they loved; on the other hand, people who consider the fate of an individual human through the prism of a much-debated issue in the United States. The journalists here faced a tension that runs through the moral fabric of our societies: the tension between love and justice.[20] How could they accommodate both a public driven by love and a public driven by justice?

Before delving into the study of these publics, however, I first explain how I investigated their emergence through their textual traces.

HOW TO CAPTURE THE EMERGENCE OF PUBLICS

The study of news publics has always been challenging for social scientists. A wide variety of methods have been developed over nearly a century, which can roughly be organized into two categories. On the one hand, behavioral approaches view a public as a sum of individuals who engage in a similar action—viewing, commenting, sharing, or liking a news item. The strength of these metrics, commonly used in the news industry and research, lies in their ability to provide a comprehensive representation of the public. Their main weakness, however, is that they fail to capture how people actually interpret content. If we consider the public as a collective of individuals who share concerns and interpretations and eventually mobilize around an issue, these metrics singularly lack depth. Reception approaches, on the other hand, have addressed this shortcoming by closely examining how people make sense of news content.[21] Although the scope of reception studies is limited because they typically involve a few dozen individuals at most, the analysis goes much further into the processes that lead different individuals to share interpretations about the news. Such an approach allows us to access publics, as defined earlier, but significantly lacks scope.

In recent years, social scientists have explored digital methods to bridge the gap between quantitative and qualitative research on social phenomena.[22] In particular, the quantitative study of the textual traces left by social media users has emerged as a promising avenue to capture how people interpret news items. Not only does the volume of textual material involved provide access to interpretations relating to specific news content, but this material also has the benefit of not having been elicited by researchers. Combined with new text-analysis techniques,[23] this material makes it possible to reconcile the wider scope of behavioral approaches to publics with the depth of reception approaches. This is the path Jean-Philippe Cointet and I adopted to capture the way publics emerged from the *Los Angeles Times* Homicide Report.

More specifically, we built a new database compiling the 4,506 homicides listed on the Homicide Report between February 2010 and December 2016. For each homicide, we collected the information provided by the platform about the victim (name, age, gender, ethnicity) and the homicide (date, location, crime scene, causes, circumstances).[24] We then scraped the 28,828 comments posted on the 4,506 homicides committed during this seven-year period. For each comment, we collected the textual content of the comment, the name of its author, and the publication date.

Capturing the emergence of publics based on a corpus of comments posted on the Homicide Report was not an easy task.[25] We faced two main challenges. The first was the lack of information available on the individuals who posted comments. We knew only the name that identified each user on the platform; we did not know the person's gender, age, profession, socioeconomic status, family situation, or political preferences. We learned a bit more about the users by looking at how they contributed to the platform. As at many online platforms, participation was highly unequal.[26] The authors' activity was unevenly distributed (figure 8.3): in a total of 16,147 authors, 83 percent posted only one comment, and 1.3 percent posted more than ten comments.

In light of these statistics, we distinguished between two groups of authors: a group of "superposters" who commented on at least ten different homicides and a group of "occasional posters" who commented on a smaller number of occurrences. The first group totaled seventy-six authors, who together accounted for 16 percent of all comments. A quick look at their publications suggested that these superposters pursued a specific political agenda, some of them systematically defending police action, others denouncing police violence. Syscom3 was by far the most active contributor, with 1,142 comments published on 449 homicides. This contributor

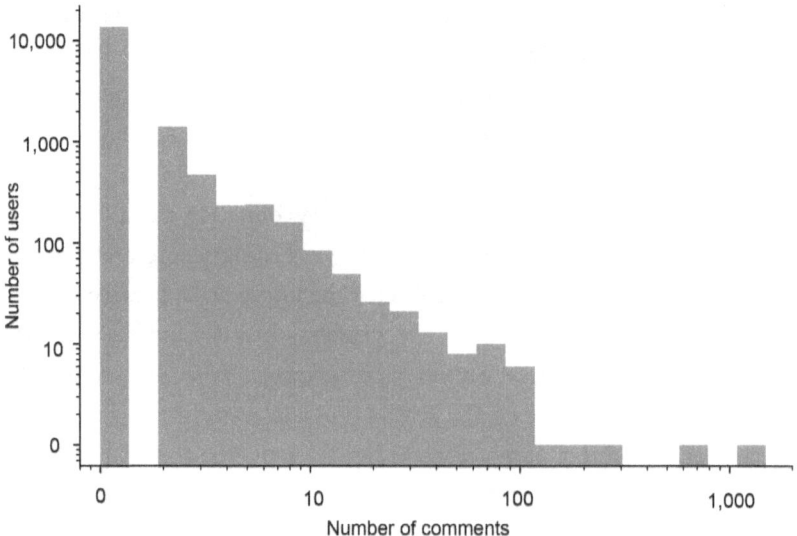

FIGURE 8.3 Distribution of authors who posted comments on the Homicide Report according to the number of their comments, 2010–2016.

Source: Based on data compiled by Sylvain Parasie and Jean-Philippe Cointet from the Homicide Report, *Los Angeles Times*, http://homicide.latimes.com/.

systematically spoke out to denounce the role of gangs in urban violence. By contrast, Jag regularly spoke out against racial discrimination by the police. During this period, he posted 350 comments concerning 186 homicides. The second group comprised the overwhelming majority of contributors, most of whom commented only once or twice. As we will see, the majority of "occasional posters" commented to pay tribute to a victim.

The second challenge was to find a text-analysis method that could capture the emergence of publics. We needed to be able to grasp the dynamics whereby speakers came to make sense of an occurrence in connection with other contributors. We therefore designed a text-processing method that built on the theoretical framework developed by Luc Boltanski in his pioneering work on the analysis of public speaking.[27] Drawing on semiotics, he conceptualized speaking as the construction of relationships between several "actants." In the Homicide Report case, the actants were the author of the comment, the deceased, the individual(s) or collective(s) who may have been blamed for the killing, and the larger platform readership whose compassion was sought or who was called to witness an injustice (figure 8.4). We thus conceptualized any comment posted on the Homicide Report as a way of linking some or all of these actants together.

After reading a significant part of the corpus, we established four main variables capturing the diversity of possible configurations of the relationships between the actants:

1. Author–victim relationship: This variable coded for the explicit mention of an existing relationship between the poster and the victim. In the comment, the author mentioned a personal link with the deceased. This link could be conveyed in various forms depending on whether the speaker addressed the victim directly ("you were special"), demonstrated a family or friendship tie ("he was a dear friend"), mentioned memories shared with the victim ("we had so many good laughs"), or showed acquaintance in another way ("I lost someone very special").

2. Affection for the victim and the victim's relatives: This variable captured situations where the speaker showed love or affection for the deceased ("rest in peace," "you will not be forgotten," "You're Forever in our Hearts")

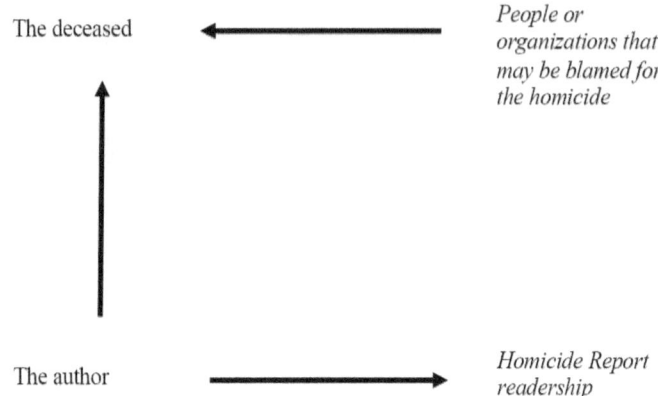

FIGURE 8.4 Measuring agency in Homicide Report comments, 2010–2016.

Source: Visualization based on the theoretical model of public speaking built by Luc Boltanski.

or for the relatives of the deceased by conveying their condolences ("my prayers go to the family").

3. Moral evaluation of individuals: This variable identified the presence of a judgment about the moral values of the victim or the suspects. It could be a positive judgment ("he was a loving and devoted husband and father," "my nephew was so loving," "He stood out as an employee, always smiling, dressed nicely and eager to help people in need") or a negative judgment ("this guy was evil"; "He was a known notorious gangster"; "a 15 year old punk"). In the latter case, the author sought to assign exclusively individual responsibility—whether blaming the victim for his or her lifestyle or other individuals (a parent, a police officer, etc.), whom they accused of misconduct or negligence. Here, the homicide was considered the consequence of individual behaviors and was not associated with more general concerns.

4. Search for collective responsibility: The last variable corresponded to situations where the author identified collective responsibility to make an argument implicating more than just the individuals involved in a

particular homicide. We organized this last variable into three different subvariables capturing three forms of generalization:

4.1. Issues: This subvariable identified comments in which the author mentioned more general issues beyond the details of a particular homicide—urban violence, gang culture, police brutality, the crisis of the education system, and so on. The author did not necessarily assign explicit blame or pitch solutions but did consider the particular occurrence as indicative of a more general problem ("with all the violence in our society," "these killing fields neighborhoods," "plenty of murders like this," "We as society have to come to accept that certain young teens are damaged goods").

4.2. Institutions: This subvariable aimed to detect comments in which the responsibility of an institution was invoked—the federal, national, or local government; the judiciary; the police; schools; churches; or the media. These institutions could either be denounced as the cause of the problem ("the failure of the religious leaders") or identified as a possible solution ("start DEMANDING action by your elected representatives").

4.3. Socioethnic groups: The third subvariable identified comments in which social or ethnic groups were mentioned ("black on black, latino on latino crime," "low income residents," "You white people are funny as hell").

Because each of these variables could involve various lexical and syntactic forms, we had to rule out a strict lexicometric approach, wherein each variable is identified based on a comprehensive list of expressions. We instead opted for supervised machine-learning algorithms to code all comments according to these different variables (see appendix 1 at the end of this chapter).

A COUNTERPUBLIC SEEKING TO DIVERT THE SPOTLIGHT

Our analysis first showed that the *Los Angeles Times* journalists successfully brought about a public that is interested primarily in homicides usually ignored by the media. This public is a counterpublic in the sense that it seeks to divert the spotlight and shine it on the main victims of urban violence—young Black and Hispanic males killed in poor neighborhoods, often with real or alleged connections to gangs—who are largely ignored by the media. This finding confirmed the journalists' intuition that many people are frustrated by the way traditional media cover homicides. Yet this public does not pay the same attention to all homicides. Although comment contributors can access any occurrence, they focus their attention on a small number of occurrences. Figure 8.5 shows the unequal attention homicides receive from the various users of the website. The comments follow the curve, which indicates a high concentration of comments on a small number of occurrences—80 percent of all comments pertain to 23.5 percent of homicides. Admittedly, the selection made by users is not as restricted as that of gate-keeping news editors, who allow only 10 percent of all

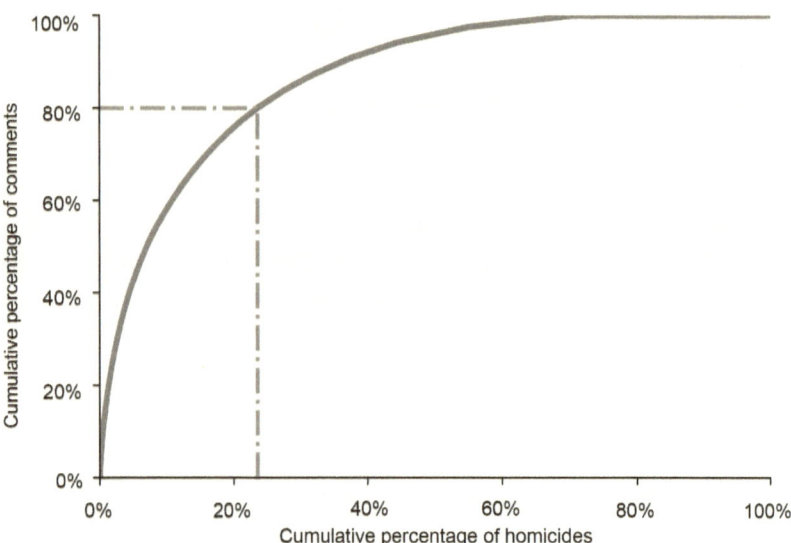

FIGURE 8.5 Distribution of the number of comments received with respect to homicides on the Homicide Report, 2010–2016.

Source: Based on data compiled by Sylvain Parasie and Jean-Philippe Cointet from the Homicide Report, *Los Angeles Times*, http://homicide.latimes.com/.

homicides to be included in the *Los Angeles Times*' printed edition. Nevertheless, a similar selection process emerges, albeit slightly less pronounced. Just as journalists and editors select the occurrences they find newsworthy, so, too, users select the homicides they find interesting.

Let us first examine the criteria mobilized by *Los Angeles Times* journalists when they cover a homicide in the printed newspaper. Statistical regression shows that these reporters predominantly cover murders that occur in safer neighborhoods and affect older people.[28] They systematically exclude homicides that occur on the street and give greater coverage to those that occur following a burglary or involved police officers. These results confirm what research has found for decades: journalists favor exceptional occurrences, which are not related to the street violence that affects mostly young Black and Hispanic men in poor neighborhoods; over the period we studied, homicides involving young Black and Hispanic males killed by firearms accounted for 65 percent of all homicides.[29]

By contrast, the users of the Homicide Report comment primarily on homicides that affect young Black males and show less interest in the murders of older people. Their focus is primarily on homicides that are systematically neglected by traditional media and that make up the mass of homicides committed in Los Angeles—those of young Black males, often in connection with gangs. However, there is some overlap between journalists' and users' selections. First, they do share two common criteria—the involvement of the police in the homicide and the fact that a homicide is allegedly gang related—although users give these criteria far greater importance. Second, a homicide being covered by a newspaper increases its chances of being commented on by users.

The Homicide Report journalists were thus faced with a public that seized the opportunity to shift the spotlight on the victims of urban violence in major U.S. metropolitan areas, in particular the victims of police violence. However, if we look more closely, it appears that they fostered the emergence of two distinct publics, with specific populations developing their own interpretation of homicides: here I refer to these two publics as the "collective of inquiry" and the "loving relatives."

A COLLECTIVE OF INQUIRY

The Homicide Report brought about a public that comprises highly involved users who engage in discussions about the problem of urban violence.[30] By treating a great number of homicides in the same way, this public articulated a cognitive and political repertoire to collectively identify more general explanatory frameworks for the problem of violence. Jean-Philippe and I decided to name this public a "collective of inquiry" in reference to John Dewey's conceptualization of the public. In *The Public and Its Problems*, originally published in 1927, Dewey argued that a collection of people could form a "public" only by carrying out an inquiry to interpret the problem they collectively faced.[31] Yet such an inquiry is difficult to conduct, for people have to rely on fragmented information, particularly from newspapers. Thus, according to Dewey, the main challenge for a public to emerge is that it needs to investigate these fragmented occurrences in order to interpret them and put them into a series. The interpretative work here is considerable and requires significant cognitive resources.[32]

The members of the "collective of inquiry" take an interest in a great number of homicides. As "superposters," they differ from other users by commenting on ten or more different homicides, often far more—Syscom3, for example, posted 1,142 comments on 449 homicides. They are likely to leverage the possibilities of equivalence offered by the platform to quickly identify "interesting" murders. They are more specifically interested in the homicides that affect young people, are allegedly gang related, and involve police officers (see the statistical table in appendix 2 at the end of this chapter). Compared to regular posters, they also focus far more on homicides covered in the *Los Angeles Times* printed edition as well. Thus, superposters are arguably interested primarily in homicides linked to the problem of urban violence and specifically to the role of the police.

Further analysis reveals that superposters significantly differ from nonsuperposters in the way they make sense of homicides. Beyond the considerable number of homicides they comment on, superposters also strongly differ from nonsuperposters in the construction of their arguments (figure 8.6). The radar chart in figure 8.6 shows that they very often express no personal connection to the victim (in our study, 13.1 percent of superposters expressed a personal connection, compared to 67 percent of nonsuperposters) and speak far more about institutions (31 percent versus 8.3 percent), societal issues (13.3 percent versus 4.2 percent), and socioethnic groups (7.3 percent versus 4.5 percent). Thus, most superposters can be

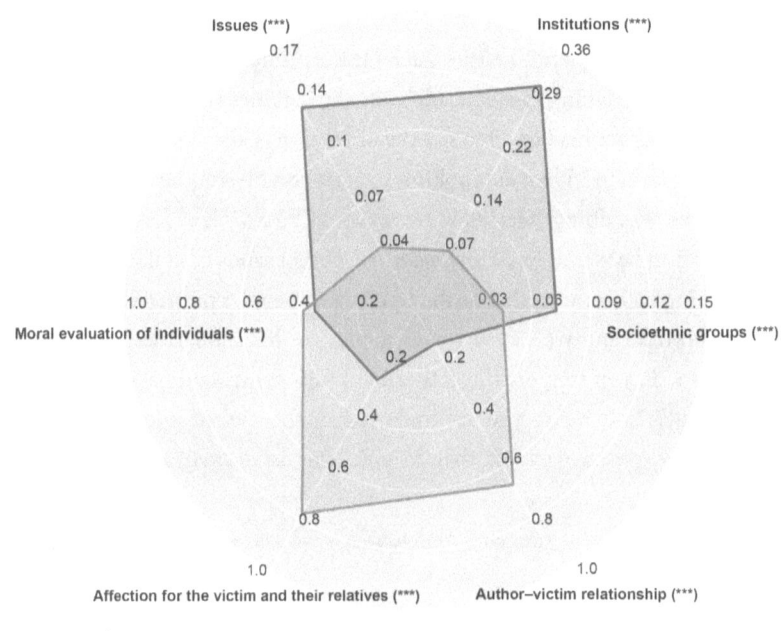

FIGURE 8.6 Radar chart comparing how superposters and nonsuperposters on the Homicide Report make sense of homicides, 2010–2016. The top polygon shows the argumentative profile of superposters. It links six points corresponding to the proportions of their comments coded in each variable. Thus, 30 percent of comments from superposters mention institutions, whereas only 8 percent of comments from nonsuperposters include such references. (Fisher exact test: *$p < 0.05$; **$p < 0.01$; ***$p < .0001$.)

Source: Based on data compiled by Sylvain Parasie and Jean-Philippe Cointet from the Homicide Report, *Los Angeles Times*, http://homicide.latimes.com/.

considered activists or at least individuals highly involved in the issue of urban violence.

Their involvement is informed by a specific political agenda and cognitive repertoire. For instance, Syscom3, who posted the greatest number of comments between 2010 and 2017, adopted the "cop supporter" stance, systematically blaming the behavior of "sociopathic" gang members for the murders commented on and highlighting the huge burden they represent for society:

> Why should anyone like this guy? He's a primary reason these neighborhoods are falling to pieces. He's like the harbinger of doom and crime. I would expect his family to say the usual things about him. But for the rest of you why? He went looking to start trouble and he knew exactly what he was doing. He knew there would be a violent reaction to the vandalism he was doing. How many 10's of thousands of dollars was spent cleaning up his mess, that he did upon other peoples property? This state is bankrupt and we get to spend money on his thoughtless activities! heavan, do you support the activities of miscreants and barbarians like this guy? Why? Are you so immersed in the violent and sociopathic world he was a part of, that to you, this is normal and acceptable behavior?
>
> (Syscom3, April 15, 2010, 10:46 p.m.; homicide of Jose Castillo)

On the other end of the spectrum, Jag posted 350 comments about 186 distinct homicides. He regularly denounced racial discrimination and criticized unfair law enforcement by the LAPD:

> The under privilege people, which are for the most part minorities, are the ones who get the short end of the stick. Many have to take deals in order to avoid serving more time for a crime they did not commit. I avoid playing the race card, but when a white homeless man gets killed by cops in fullerton, some cops are actually held accountable. I'm all for justice, but when a cop kills a hispanic or black justice is not served. Syscom3, you like stats and I was wondering if you happen to have the demographic

THE ART OF BRINGING ABOUT PUBLICS

breakdown of people who are charged with a crime and are actually found guilty. I'm almost certain the White people get more of a break than minorities. It's sad but true.

(Jag, November 17, 2012, 10:00 a.m.; homicide of Armondo Casillas)

As these comments show, some superposters address each other directly. Because they have been using the platform for a long time, a new homicide is an opportunity for them to continue a discussion that has been ongoing for months, if not years. Moving from one homicide to another, they defend the same two strong positions, which oppose police defenders ("cop supporters") and police critics ("police bashers"). Clearly, these positions are closely associated with forms of activism and political repertoires that originate outside the platform. Thus, the journalists behind the Homicide Report did not create this public out of thin air but gave it both the resources to browse, sort, and compare homicides quickly and efficiently as well as a discussion space to test its conflicting interpretations with the latest homicides.

THE LOVING RELATIVES

Another public emerged that did not exist before the Homicide Report. Its members are "occasional posters"—that is, most of them have commented on only one homicide. They have lost a loved one and leave a comment to honor and remember that person. It is usually not the issue of violence but love that drives them to post a comment.[33] As shown in figure 8.6, in our study 67 percent of occasional users expressed a personal relationship to the victim, with 77 percent of those users showing the victim love and affection. Conversely, they rarely mentioned civic-oriented interpretations of the homicide. These contributors therefore constitute a very different kind of public that aims to highlight the value of each deceased person and seeks the compassion of anyone visiting the platform. The *Los Angeles Times* journalists undoubtedly played a more decisive role in the emergence of this particular public, giving people from various backgrounds the opportunity to speak out publicly and defend the memory of their loved ones:

> Olga, I can't believe you are gone so quick, . . . I will always cheris our wonderful memories in school . . . i love you and will miss you always . . . you'll forever be missed . . . may god bless ur kids and ur family in this hard times. . . . May u rest in heavenly peace.
> Always
> Letty
>
> (Letty M., May 14, 2010, 9:55 p.m.; homicide of Olga Martinez)

In addition to these love-centered tributes, a large number of comments stress the moral qualities of the deceased: the murdered person was a "wonderful son," a "loving father," a "strong woman," and so on. These tributes take on particular significance in a context where most victims of gun violence in U.S. metropolitan areas are suspected of belonging to a gang or being involved in illegal activities. The platform thus becomes a space in which the value of the deceased can be fully recognized and even celebrated in spite of any involvement in gang-related activities—as in the case of David Cota, who was stabbed to death at twenty-three: "Cota was and will remain in the memories of those who knew him as a warm, loving, fun, down-to-earth person. The Most High God welcomes all of us with open arms and love, and I pray for the family to keep their faith and conviction that another angel joined heaven. Our world pushes good people into dangerous places sometimes, and only God can judge what happens here. One love!" (Natalie; July 6, 2010, 11:01 p.m.; homicide of David Cota).

The expression of love thus takes an oppositional form, contrasting with the discourses that blame the victims for their life choices. Far from a sign of withdrawal into the private sphere, these tributes can be viewed as acts of resistance: they are public affirmations that the victim was loved, no matter how one may judge that person's life. The contrast between these tributes and the judgments passed by the members of the "collective of inquiry," who in each homicide seek a confirmation or refutation of a more general explanatory scheme, is particularly stark.

THE ART OF BRINGING ABOUT PUBLICS

Under certain circumstances, however, this public does depart from a love-centered discourse to discuss public issues and institutions. When the homicide involved the police—in other words, when a police officer caused the victim's death—occasional posters' comments are more informed by civic-oriented considerations (figure 8.7). In our study, when a police officer was involved, 14.1 percent of occasional posters interpreted the

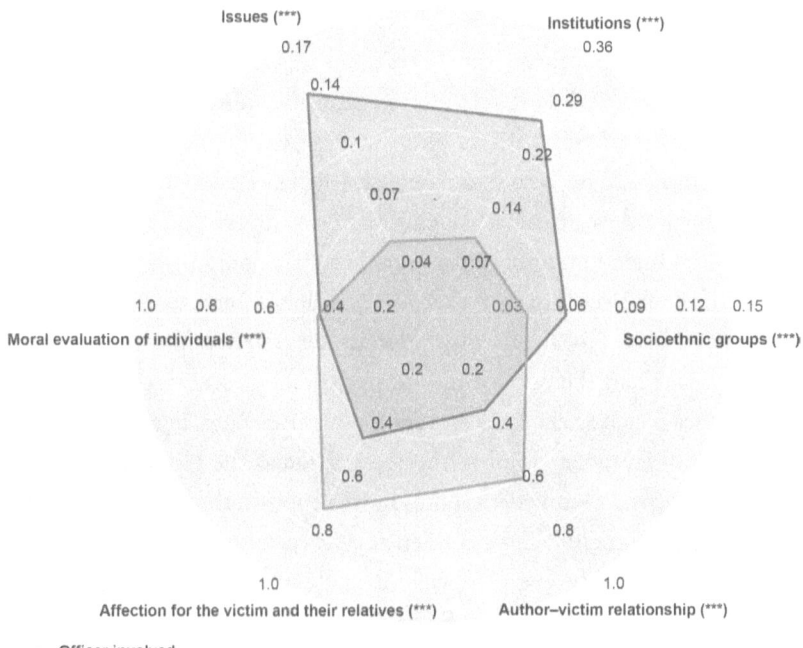

FIGURE 8.7 Radar chart showing how occasional posters on the Homicide Report make sense of homicides involving police officers in Los Angeles County, 2010–2016. The top polygon shows the argumentative profile of nonsuperposters commenting on homicides that involved the police. It links six points corresponding to the proportions of their comments coded in each variable. Thus, 5 percent of comments from nonsuperposters mention issues when a police officer was not involved in the homicide, compared to 14 percent when a police officer was involved. (Fisher exact test: *p < 0.05; **p < 0.01; ***p < 0.001.)

Source: Based on data compiled by Sylvain Parasie and Jean-Philippe Cointet from the Homicide Report, *Los Angeles Times*, http://homicide.latimes.com/.

occurrence within the context of particular issues, compared to 4.7 percent when a police officer was not involved. For these specific homicides, this public also made far more mentions of institutions (26.1 percent versus 10.4 percent) and socioethnic groups (6.7 percent versus 4.8 percent). Clearly, homicides involving police officers are a major source of outrage for residents, which is informed not only by a long history of this phenomenon within African American communities in Los Angeles[34] but also by a broader movement to combat police violence against Black people across the United States, embodied by the Black Lives Matter movement.

Through this platform, the *Los Angeles Times* journalists have thus allowed a public of "loving relatives" to grow and consolidate. Unlike the "collective of inquiry," which is likely to more easily find other arenas in which to form and become aware of itself (such as Reddit and other social media platforms), the public of "loving relatives" appears to be more dependent on the intervention of journalists. First, the journalists have offered the victims' relatives a space for recognition that is particularly significant because it is linked to a major institution in Los Angeles. These people presumably have had the opportunity to pay tribute to the victims in semipublic spaces, such as churches and community meetings, but none of those spaces offer such wide visibility and recognition as the Homicide Report. Furthermore, the Homicide Report allows people to share their memories anonymously, without being identified as gang mates or suspects.[35] The anonymity guaranteed by the platform has made it possible to bring about a public that is inherently fragile. By designing the Homicide Report in this way, the journalists have been able to generate a public whose members are often denied a public voice.

HOW TO BRING ABOUT PUBLICS

The case of the Homicide Report shows that allowing for publics to emerge through a data application is a paradoxical process. On the one hand, the journalists successfully brought about publics by showing great modesty,

THE ART OF BRINGING ABOUT PUBLICS

giving users full control over the selection of what they consider the most interesting or significant homicides, and, as discussed earlier, users seized this opportunity to give greater visibility to homicides involving young Black males. The journalists relinquished their prerogative to select newsworthy homicides, which previously constituted a major tenet of their professional identity. On the other hand, they have been able to shape the publics that have emerged from the platform, in particular the one I have referred to as the "loving relatives." Beyond simply encouraging the emergence of these publics by providing the conditions for their development, they initiated a policy that encourages Los Angeles residents to widely discuss the causes of violence. Rather than just inviting users to pay tribute to the deceased, this policy subtly prompts them to discuss the broader causes behind each tragic occurrence.

This policy was closely linked to the moderation system introduced at the *Los Angeles Times* in 2010, which required staff members to check all posted comments prior to publication. Rather than contracting a third-party firm, the journalists themselves moderated the comments, suggesting that in their view this task fell within the remit of their editorial activity. As the data journalist Ken Schwencke explained, their main purpose was of course to block insulting or threatening comments but also nevertheless to be "a little more lenient . . . since homicide is a tough subject to talk about."[36] More specifically, the journalists behind the Homicide Report did not want to secure a space for comments intended only for those who wished to pay tribute to victims. This is what Ken Schwencke explained in response to a user who asked why a certain comment was not blocked: "It was never our intention for this blog only to be a memorial. We want people to feel free to share memories of their loved ones and to grieve openly, but we don't want to discourage people from asking questions about the circumstances surrounding someone's death."[37]

On several occasions, the journalists intervened in the discussions to explain why a particular comment was not deleted. In response to one user, for example, Megan Garvey, the editor of Homicide Report, argued that an aggressive comment could shed new light or contain interesting information on a homicide: "While we do our best to moderate posts, as a matter of practice we retain the ability to remove material determined to be inappropriate. Since the subject matter of this site is so raw, there are times when that line is hard to determine. We often have to weigh the potential of a comment to reveal information about an incident against the possibility it will offend."[38]

This deliberate editorial choice thus put occasional posters in an unsecured space, where attacks could always occur—a superposter blaming a victim or another user passing harsh judgment on a victim. Part of the journalists' goal was indeed to compel users to discuss the more general factors that made a particular tragedy possible. In fact, our analyses show that these editorial choices have been effective. In our study, when superposters began to comment on a homicide, this had a significant effect on how occasional posters related to homicides (figure 8.8). They came to mention their relationship with the victim less often (60.5 percent after interaction with superposter comments versus 74.8 percent before interaction), expressed their love for the victim less often (72.2 percent after versus 84.6 percent before), and spoke more about issues (6.3 percent after versus 1.6 percent before), institutions (10.5 percent after versus 5.6 percent before), and socioethnic groups (5.3 percent after versus 3.5 percent before). In other words, the voluble presence of superposters forced them to consider the homicide they were focusing on from a more general perspective. That is precisely what the journalists sought to achieve: to encourage residents to discuss the broader causes of violence.

In addition to their moderation work, the journalists behind the Homicide Report regularly produce editorial content to fuel conversation among residents. In 2014, for example, they published the article "South Vermont Avenue: L.A. County's 'Death Alley'" (figure 8.9), showing that in a two-mile portion of Westmont Avenue sixty people had been killed in the past seven years, most of them by gunshot. Based on an analysis of the Homicide Report database as well as field research among residents, this article both identified homicide trends and provided photos of residents, personal testimonials, and graphs (figure 8.10). Although this article was published only on the newspaper's online platform, it attracted more than one hundred thousand views in the first week.[39] Producing news content using the

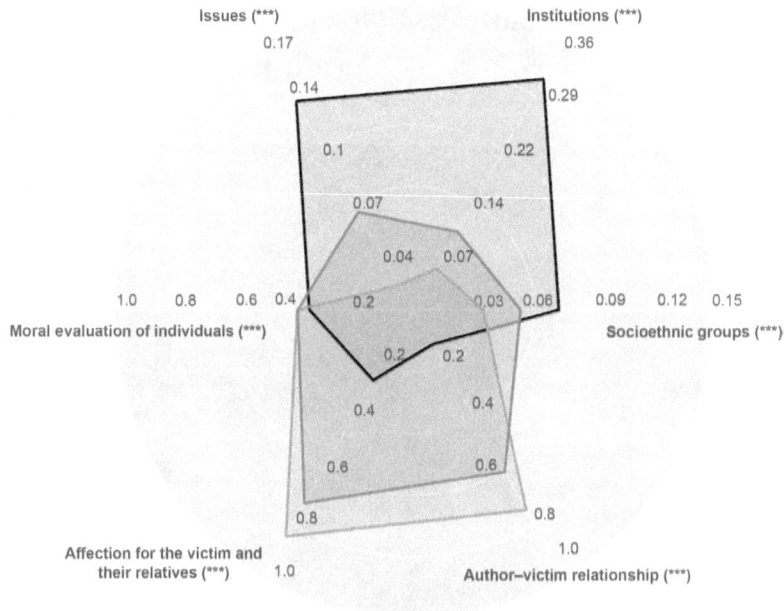

FIGURE 8.8 Radar chart showing how occasional posters on the Homicide Report make sense of homicides before and after their interaction with superposters, 2010–2016. The middle polygon draws the argumentative profile of nonsuperposters before interaction with superposters. It links six points corresponding to the proportions of their comments that were coded in each variable. Thus, 2 percent of comments from nonsuperposters mention issues before interaction, compared to 6 percent after interaction. (Fisher exact test: *p < 0.05; **p < 0.01; ***p < 0.001.)

Source: Based on data compiled by Sylvain Parasie and Jean-Philippe Cointet from the Homicide Report, *Los Angeles Times*, http://homicide.latimes.com/.

database therefore appears to be another practice that has been mobilized to foster the emergence of publics.

It thus becomes apparent that these journalists are not passive in relation to the public, even if they have relinquished their prerogative to select newsworthy occurrences. On the contrary, not only have they created the conditions for the emergence of publics, but they have also shaped the way

DATA JOURNALISM IN THE MAKING

South Vermont Avenue: L.A. County's 'death alley'

Tiny Westmont has highest homicide rate in the county.

BY NICOLE SANTA CRUZ AND KEN SCHWENCKE | PHOTOGRAPHY BY GENARO MOLINA | JANUARY 19, 2014

FIGURE 8.9 Title and title-page photograph of the online article "South Vermont Avenue: L.A. County's 'Death Alley,'" 2014.

Source: From Nicole Santa Cruz and Ken Schwencke, "South Vermont Avenue: L.A. County's 'Death Alley,'" *Los Angeles Times*, January 19, 2014, https://homicide.latimes.com/post/westmont-homicides/.

users make sense of occurrences. By creating spaces for discussion, moderating them, and producing editorial content, these journalists have explored how to bring publics into existence through data products.

★ ★ ★

In contrast with the alarmist rhetoric about audience fragmentation in the digital age, this chapter has shown that through data applications journalists have the ability to bring publics into existence—that is, collectives of individuals who together make sense of a problem. This outcome requires

THE ART OF BRINGING ABOUT PUBLICS

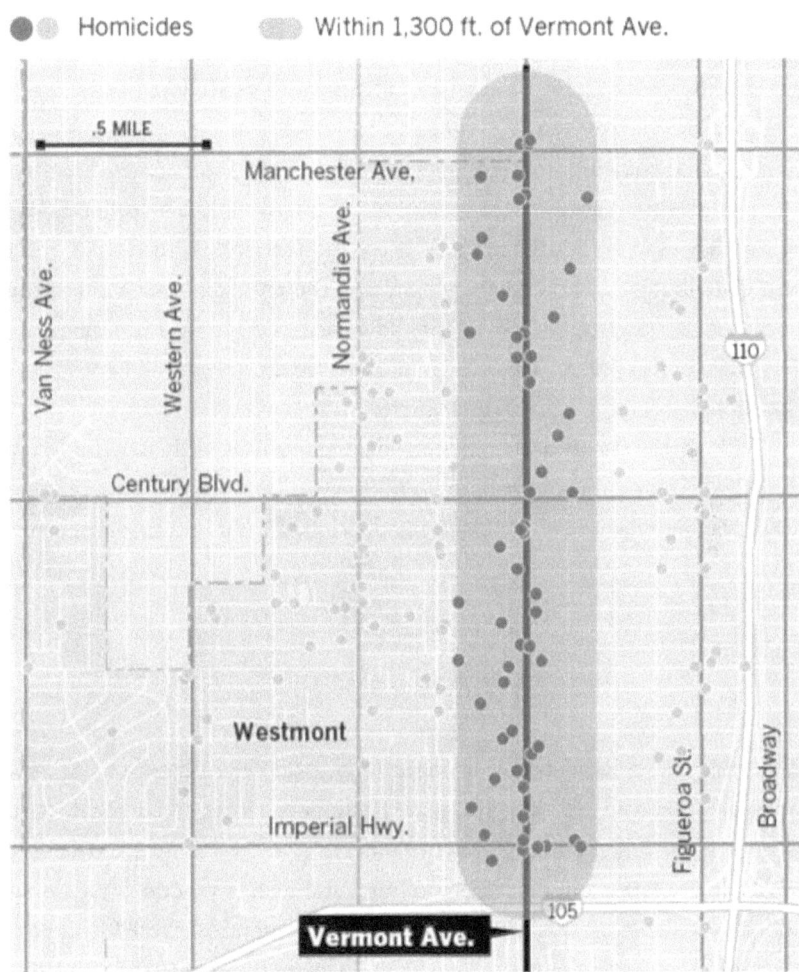

FIGURE 8.10 Graph locating the homicides committed on Vermont Avenue since 2007.

Source: From Santa Cruz and Schwencke, "South Vermont Avenue."

journalists to develop a trend that has been emerging within journalism over the past two decades, which endeavors to give people greater autonomy to form their own interpretations of the facts they consider most important. But it also requires journalists to subtly intervene to ensure that individuals engage with one another and consider the patterns that explain why the world is the way it is. Although these interventions are distinctly complicated by the rise of social media platforms as the place where most people get and discuss the news, major news organizations still have the ability to weigh in on the way people gather and make sense of their problems.

This final chapter also highlights the need for new ways of representing the public—in other words, to provide an alternative to the behavioral metrics widely used within the news industry and research. Although journalism contributes to democracy by fostering the emergence of publics, the audience metrics used today do not allow journalists to measure their performance in this regard. This is an important research avenue to which computational social science can contribute.

With this series of case studies on "data journalism in the making" now complete, I conclude the book by outlining an "ethics of reflexivity" that would be better suited to the emerging division of labor within journalism.

APPENDIX 1

To classify the comments posted on the Homicide Report based on the variables described in this chapter, Jean-Philippe Cointet and I relied on a machine-learning method. We used Prodigy, an active-learning system that works in combination with Spacy, a linguistic-analysis module (including morphosyntactic processing, semantic vectors, semantic parser). On a technical level, we used the text classifier implemented in Spacy (v2), which is a neural-network architecture. A list of terms was provided to the system to prime the examples presented in the interface and ensure balanced learning. As the training progressed, the examples were chosen by the machine to make the learning process as fast and efficient as possible. Several hundreds of comments were manually labeled for each variable, until the efficiency of the classifier (measured by an F-score) was deemed satisfactory. The models corresponding to each variable were then used to code the entire corpus. Finally, we evaluated a random sample of three hundred automatically coded comments.

Comments posted on the Homicide Report, *Los Angeles Times*: evaluation of the classifier's efficiency for each variable

VARIABLES	TESTING SET	EX POST RANDOM SET
1. Author–victim relationship	Precision: 0.87 Recall: 0.92 F-score: 0.90 Baseline: 0.64 Accuracy: 0.86	Precision: 0.78 Recall: 0.92 F-score: 0.85 Baseline: 0.54 Accuracy: 0.82
2. Affection for the victim and the victim's relatives	Precision: 0.94 Recall: 0.94 F-score: 0.94 Baseline: 0.63 Accuracy: 0.92	Precision: 0.90 Recall: 0.85 F-score: 0.87 Baseline: 0.62 Accuracy: 0.85
3. Moral evaluation of individuals	Precision: 0.69 Recall: 0.87 F-score: 0.77 Baseline: 0.58 Accuracy: 0.78	Precision: 0.77 Recall: 0.68 F-score: 0.72 Baseline: 0.60 Accuracy: 0.69
4.1 Search for collective responsibility—issues	Precision: 0.90 Recall: 0.65 F-score: 0.76 Baseline: 0.78 Accuracy: 0.91	Precision: 0.74 Recall: 0.57 F-score: 0.64 Baseline: 0.90 Accuracy: 0.94
4.2 Search for collective responsibility—institutions	Precision: 0.89 Recall: 0.70 F-score: 0.78 Baseline: 0.70 Accuracy: 0.88	Precision: 0.84 Recall: 0.67 F-score: 0.74 Baseline: 0.82 Accuracy: 0.92
4.3 Search for collective responsibility—socioethnic groups	Precision: 0.94 Recall: 0.63 F-score: 0.76 Baseline: 0.84 Accuracy: 0.93	Precision: 0.70 Recall: 0.64 F-score: 0.66 Baseline: 0.96 Accuracy: 0.98

APPENDIX 2

Focusing on a three-year period from 2010 to 2012 and on the 1,699 homicides in those years (out of a total of 4,506 homicides committed in Los Angeles between 2010 and 2016), Jean-Philippe Cointet and I performed a statistical regression based on the ordinary least-squares method. For this subcorpus, we manually checked which of the homicides mentioned on the platform were covered in the *Los Angeles Times* printed edition. We also manually checked whether each entry in the Homicide Report mentioned the victim's real or alleged gang ties.

OLS regression predicting the number of comments posted in the Homicide Report and the coverage of homicides in the *Los Angeles Times* printed edition, 2010–2012

	A. COVERAGE IN THE LOS ANGELES TIMES PRINTED EDITION	B. NUMBER OF COMMENTS PER MONTH (ALL USERS)	C. NUMBER OF COMMENTS PER MONTH (SUPERPOSTERS ONLY)	D. NUMBER OF COMMENTS PER MONTH (OCCASIONAL POSTERS ONLY)
Victim's age				
0–19	-0.0037	0.4081***	0.1176***	-0.4416*
	(0.0207)	(0.1088)	(0.0308)	(0.2284)
20–24	0.0030	0.0702	0.0403	0.1376
	(0.0206)	(0.1081)	(0.0306)	(0.2268)
25–31	-0.0243	0.0972	0.0294	0.2565
	(0.0202)	(0.1063)	(0.0300)	(0.2229)
32–43	-0.0275	-0.0811	-0.0336	0.5024**
	(0.0203)	(0.1069)	(0.0302)	(0.2244)
44–97	0.0001	-0.3054***	-0.0679**	0.3831*
	(0.0205)	(0.1076)	(0.0304)	(0.2258)
Victim's gender				
Female	0.1129	-0.1109	0.0263	-1.4866
	(0.1056)	(0.5557)	(0.1571)	(1.1657)
Male	0.0176	-0.1789	0.0053	-0.9258
	(0.1063)	(0.5592)	(0.1581)	(1.1732)

Victim's ethnicity			
Black	0.0417	0.3713**	0.0609	-0.2240
	(0.0306)	(0.1613)	(0.0456)	(0.3384)
Hispanic	0.0259	0.2220	0.0796*	-0.0864
	(0.0295)	(0.1550)	(0.0438)	(0.3251)
Asian	0.0582	-0.2214	-0.0362	0.2762
	(0.0456)	(0.2399)	(0.0678)	(0.5034)
White	0.0528	0.1262	0.0335	0.1791
	(0.0326)	(0.1719)	(0.0486)	(0.3606)
Other	-0.0650	-0.3539	-0.0841	0.2216
	(0.1242)	(0.6534)	(0.1847)	(1.3708)
Circumstances of the homicide			
Domestic violence	-0.0781***	-0.3502**	-0.0794*	0.1260
	(0.0302)	(0.1589)	(0.0449)	(0.3334)
Drive-by	-0.0734***	0.1245	-0.0065	0.3493
	(0.0259)	(0.1368)	(0.0387)	(0.2869)
Fight	-0.0624***	-0.1293	-0.0292	-0.3473
	(0.0224)	(0.1181)	(0.0334)	(0.2477)
Police officer involved	0.0918***	0.7587***	0.3902***	-0.3681
	(0.0274)	(0.1446)	(0.0409)	(0.3033)

(continued)

OLS regression predicting the number of comments posted in the Homicide Report and the coverage of homicides in the *Los Angeles Times* printed edition, 2010–2012 (continued)

	A. COVERAGE IN THE LOS ANGELES TIMES PRINTED EDITION	B. NUMBER OF COMMENTS PER MONTH (ALL USERS)	C. NUMBER OF COMMENTS PER MONTH (SUPERPOSTERS ONLY)	D. NUMBER OF COMMENTS PER MONTH (OCCASIONAL POSTERS ONLY)
Party	0.0702	−0.0640	−0.1376	−0.5746
	(0.0619)	(0.3255)	(0.0920)	(0.6828)
Robbery	0.1576***	−0.0687	0.0455	0.3996
	(0.0394)	(0.2082)	(0.0589)	(0.4368)
Walk-up shooting	−0.0535**	0.0078	−0.0814***	0.1509
	(0.0209)	(0.1102)	(0.0312)	(0.2313)
Cause of homicide				
Blunt force	−0.0010	−0.0053	0.0253	−0.6884**
	(0.0316)	(0.1660)	(0.0469)	(0.3482)
Gunshot	0.0157	0.0020	0.0135	−0.3001
	(0.0191)	(0.1004)	(0.0284)	(0.2106)
Other	0.0949**	−0.0563	0.0025	−0.2447
	(0.0380)	(0.2001)	(0.0566)	(0.4197)
Stabbing	−0.0098	−0.0571	−0.0419	0.2191
	(0.0245)	(0.1290)	(0.0365)	(0.2706)
Strangling	−0.0452	0.2328	−0.0220	−0.3680
	(0.0445)	(0.2341)	(0.0662)	(0.4911)

	(1)	(2)	(3)	(4)
Mention of the word *gang* in the article	0.0170** (0.0086)	0.1265*** (0.0454)	0.0370*** (0.0128)	-0.2104** (0.0953)
No coverage in the *Los Angeles Times* printed edition	—	-0.2152*** (0.0644)	-0.0753*** (0.0182)	0.2471* (0.1351)
Main ethnicity of the neighborhood's residents				
Asian	-0.0611 (0.0422)	0.1699 (0.2223)	0.0788 (0.0629)	-0.9299** (0.4664)
Black	0.0032 (0.0241)	0.1030 (0.1270)	-0.0567 (0.0359)	0.3914 (0.2664)
Hispanic	-0.0230 (0.0177)	0.0058 (0.0933)	-0.0115 (0.0264)	0.1751 (0.1956)
Neighborhood's average income (log)	-0.0160 (0.0261)	0.0488 (0.1372)	-0.0142 (0.0388)	0.2563 (0.2877)
Neighborhood's homicide rate (log)	-0.0778*** (0.0242)	0.0521 (0.1278)	0.0268 (0.0361)	-0.2769 (0.2680)
Intercept	0.6506* (0.3368)	0.4707 (1.7716)	0.2837 (0.5009)	2.2773 (3.7166)
R-squared	0.07	0.09	0.12	0.04

No. observations: 1,699

Note: *p < 0.05; **p < 0.01; ***p < 0.001. Standard errors in parentheses.

CONCLUSION

An Ethics of Reflexivity

With the COVID-19 outbreak, a growing number of journalists around the world have begun to think of their work in computational terms. Health statistics and epidemiological modeling have become topics of heated public discussion, and the experts who produce them have been systematically and vigorously challenged, so journalists can no longer rely merely on calculations made outside their news organizations. To report on the epidemic in a journalistic way, some have felt the need to compute the data. For example, they have found new ways to calculate the virus's fatality rate without relying on official death counts, have developed epidemiological-modeling expertise to reveal the inequalities affecting underprivileged populations and racial minorities, and have designed visualization formats that enable citizens to grasp the human reality of the epidemic behind the abstraction of numbers. As a result, many journalists around the world have come to see their own organization as a "calculation center": rather than viewing news organizations as repositories for calculations performed externally by health officials, researchers, or citizens, they have come to realize that producing news about the virus requires them, journalists, to perform the computations.

CONCLUSION: AN ETHICS OF REFLEXIVITY

Yet the case of COVID-19 illustrates that computing the news in and of itself is not a protection against misinformation. Many media outlets have compared infection and fatality rates across countries and over time based on data generated using nonstandardized procedures and so provide the public with a misleading picture of the pandemic and government responses.[1] Even some data-visualization specialists have argued that the data are so dubious and the modeling so complex that it is probably best to let the experts do the calculations to avoid the risk of creating unwarranted fears among the public or a false sense of security. As one data-visualization specialist has explained, "With the stakes as high as they are, and with the state of the current data on the outbreak, this kind of reporting should be left to the experts, not used as a fun weekend coding project."[2]

Since the late 2000s, news-production practices involving computational techniques have become more widespread, with a coalition of data journalists from around the world rallying around the banner of journalistic objectivity. Faced with the major economic crisis afflicting the news industry and an unprecedented level of public mistrust of that industry, they argue that integrating data practices and computational skills within newsrooms as well as properly recognizing these practices as fully-fledged journalism will allow the profession as a whole to better fulfill its missions. Specifically, they claim that through interactive maps, search engines, and other web applications, news organizations can help citizens make better-informed decisions, make governments more transparent, shed light on systemic processes within society, and open up media coverage to events and people usually excluded from that coverage. As discussed in this book, the rise of data journalism practices stems from two distinct movements. The first is internal to the profession and has arisen from a questioning of traditional conceptions of journalistic objectivity. In the United States, as in France, large sections of the profession consider it crucial for them to be able to express their views on the substance of a situation rather than just to report stakeholders' contradictory statements. Easier access to data and computational techniques is thus seen as a step toward greater objectivity for the profession. The second movement originated outside journalism and is rooted in the transformation of the social and political meanings of the

CONCLUSION: AN ETHICS OF REFLEXIVITY

computational possibilities afforded by the web. The unprecedented development of computing infrastructure as well as the emergence of an international movement promoting the civic potential of data technologies have brought the profession face to face with actors who claim to be fixing journalism with databases and algorithms. As a result, data journalists have come to embody considerable hope placed in technology, challenging the way in which the profession was built, both in the United States and in France, with technology kept at a distance.

Over the past decade, these journalistic practices have thus developed in various cultural contexts far beyond the United States. In the United States, deep mistrust of government and bureaucracy created an environment conducive to the advent of quantification practices in American public life, where the need to base public judgments on numbers and calculations has been historically far more pronounced than in any other country. Against this backdrop, a movement emerged within U.S. journalism from the late 1960s that took advantage of the computational possibilities afforded by social science and computer science to promote these news-production practices within the profession. In France, although a number of particularities long made journalism rather inhospitable to practices involving the collection and processing of digital data, data journalism has nevertheless been able to establish itself sustainably. As we saw in this book, this development is closely linked to that of the web: the web has contributed to destabilizing the news industry, but it has concomitantly given rise to its own antidote as a variety of actors, primarily young journalists struggling in a business in crisis, have come to see data-oriented technology as an opportunity to reboot journalism.

As the case of COVID-19 has shown, however, the claim that computational techniques allow journalists to more efficiently fulfill the missions they set for themselves as professionals is in no way straightforward.[3] First, the very notion of objectivity has come to be deeply questioned in journalism as a consequence of the criticism that what is considered objective truth is decided almost exclusively by a journalistic establishment historically dominated by white male reporters and editors. Second, more broadly, the adoption of these data journalistic practices raises major questions regarding

CONCLUSION: AN ETHICS OF REFLEXIVITY

journalistic ethics. Many journalists have realized that it is not easy to make governments more transparent by processing public data, either because the data are incomplete or of poor quality or because they are based on choices that are inconsistent with journalistic imperatives. It also quickly became apparent that data-management infrastructures, statistical software, and computer languages for data processing not only require significant skills absent from most news organizations but are also designed in environments far removed from the news industry. How, then, can journalists ensure that they are the initiators of computing and not just marginal contributors? Most importantly, it has become clear that disseminating data to the people is not enough to effectively make them better informed or to enhance democratic life. It can sometimes have the opposite effect—for instance, when journalistic calculations contribute to weakening the most fragile institutions or when they prevent citizens from becoming aware of broader issues affecting them beyond their personal situations.

As discussed in the book, these ethical tensions are not recent. From the 1980s on, the pioneers of investigations based on statistics in the United States and the creators of journalistic rankings of institutions on both sides of the Atlantic faced issues surrounding either the quality of the data or the unanticipated effects of calculations on the public. However, recent developments in computing and the web have given greater prominence to deterministic views of technology, suggesting that the mere adoption of computational techniques could save journalism. As we reach the end of this book, I focus on three points that appear crucial for understanding how computing the news can benefit the democratic mission of journalism.

DATA JOURNALISM AND THE SEARCH FOR OBJECTIVITY

Throughout this book, I have developed a critique of this quest for objectivity, taking it seriously without assuming that it is always successful or that it is systematically deceptive. To this end, I focused on the practical

CONCLUSION: AN ETHICS OF REFLEXIVITY

problems that journalists encounter when they start to produce news based on data and calculations. I examined these emerging news-production practices from the perspective of journalists' own professional ethics. By becoming dependent on a broader array of human and nonhuman actors, data journalism has disrupted the ethical rules that journalists set for themselves as professionals. First, data collection affects the relationship established with sources, especially official ones, as journalists are confronted with materials in such quantity and of a quality that make their conventional standards for assessing the value of a document impractical. As a result, even when they do manage to obtain data from government sources, they are faced with a range of difficult questions regarding the way the data were produced. In the words of Agustin Armendariz, the journalist involved in the investigation of seismic safety in California schools discussed in chapter 6, "Sometimes [a database] tells you more about the observer than it does about the actual thing being observed." The ways in which journalists organize their relations with sources are thus challenged when they become data providers.

Second, the practice of data journalism requires new relationships to be established with computational professionals, including algorithm designers, application designers, and scientists. Journalists have traditionally viewed these professionals as experts or technicians—in other words, as people whose work is generally taken for granted. However, as soon as journalists themselves venture into performing calculations, they paradoxically become more dependent on these practitioners, who do not or may not share their values regarding what constitutes worthy, useful, or responsible information. Consequently, performing calculations requires journalists to stop taking the activity of these professionals for granted and to build new relationships with them.

Finally, these practices are disrupting the relationship between journalists and their audiences. On the one hand, they have enabled journalists to offer citizens a greater role in the selection and interpretation of information and thus to address a criticism long leveled at the profession, which has been accused of conveying a biased image of reality by overlooking large groups of people and a large proportion of the events affecting people. On the other hand, it soon became clear that citizens have neither the time nor the resources to interpret such large volumes of information, which raises the great risk that they will pay attention only to what affects them personally. Hence, the need for journalists who embrace computational techniques to rethink their relationship with news audiences.

This book has thus contributed to the critique of journalists' technological practices by revealing the ethical difficulties that journalists face when they engage in these practices. It both demonstrates the inadequacy of their professional ethics and outlines the direction that this ethics should take. My critique is therefore reformist in the sense that it aims to bring to attention computational practices that constitute a tool of weakness or that merely serve as a facade of objectivity. Let us now turn to this new ethics that is better suited to the current division of labor, which I call an "ethics of reflexivity."

AN ETHICS OF REFLEXIVITY

By investigating several news projects carried out on either side of the Atlantic, all of which have been widely acclaimed within the profession, this book has outlined the contours of a renewed ethics of journalism. This "ethics of reflexivity" is guided by the general principle that journalists' work must take into account the actions of the other actors they encounter in their data journalism practices. However, such reflexivity is particularly challenging for journalists because the data are often depicted as a medium for accessing accounts of reality that transcend the views of the specific actors or organizations that produce them. The crisis facing the news industry and the cultural status of digital technologies today sustain the belief that data and algorithms hold a power that journalists need only harness to reveal reality as it is. Contradicting this stance, an ethics of reflexivity would ensure that journalists take into account all the actors who contribute to the production, processing, and interpretation of data. It involves considering both the data and the computational apparatus (software, scripts,

CONCLUSION: AN ETHICS OF REFLEXIVITY

algorithms) used to process them, two elements that are in fact often difficult to disentangle.[4] Far from being reducible to a set of skills or knowledge, such an ethics is embodied by specific ways of organizing news production. Four dimensions of this ethics emerged from the cases studied in part III of the book.

First, this ethics urges journalists to resist an objectivist approach to data and to question the conditions of data production. This principle in itself is not new; in fact, it resonates with the way journalists deal with more traditional sources of information, such as paper archives and personal accounts. However, it is far more difficult to observe when handling large volumes of digital data from a variety of sources and when specialized workers are involved in different parts of the data work. As evidenced in chapter 6, the remedy is organizational. Avoiding too much division of data work within the newsroom, creating roles in charge of checking the quality of data, and combining data analysis with more traditional ways of knowing, such as interviews and document research, are all valuable organizational solutions. This reorganization, of course, requires significant resources—in particular personnel—that may not be available to all organizations. Thus, the extent to which computational techniques reduce the cost of news production ought to be strongly reconsidered.

A second dimension of this renewed ethics has to do with the way news organizations relate to ever-changing technologies. The core of the promise of data journalism is to ensure that journalists control the choice and implementation of computational technologies—in other words, to outsource as little as possible of the relationship with technology to nonjournalists, particularly to consultants who are foreign to the concerns of the profession. As described in part III, embracing technology is indeed likely to enable journalists to better accomplish the missions they set for themselves as professionals by revealing public problems on a global and local scale (chapter 6), by confronting election candidates with the speeches they have made (chapter 7), or by allowing a public to emerge around an issue (chapter 8). But technology evolves at such a fast pace and comes from social worlds so far removed from journalism that in practice all journalists must accept some level of delegation. The key is therefore to create the conditions

CONCLUSION: AN ETHICS OF REFLEXIVITY

for the profession as a whole to gain an understanding of technologies so that the technologies can be integrated into and put at the service of journalism. In concrete terms, opening the profession to technological profiles as well as establishing trading zones between journalists, data scientists, and researchers are crucial.[5] Several conferences are facilitating this connection today in both the United States (e.g., the Computation + Journalism Symposium) and Europe (e.g., the European Data and Computational Journalism Conference and SciCAR), bringing together journalists, academics, practitioners, social scientists, and industry technologists. They are relatively diverse, with some created at the initiative of computer scientists and others by journalists or academics. The history of computer-assisted reporting suggests that journalists must play an active role if not in creating then in maintaining these spaces. Only then will the constraints of journalists and news organizations be central to their interactions with computer scientists, academics, and technologists. A renewed ethics would thus require journalists to engage in these trading zones and to ensure that certain journalists play the role of translators.

Establishing new relationships with academia is another component of this ethics of reflexivity. As we saw in chapter 7, by collecting and processing data, journalists build more symmetrical and egalitarian relationships with researchers so long as they do not seek to use science as a facade of objectivity: they must indeed engage in scientific reasoning but also remain aware of their constraints as journalists. Such a relationship is not easy to build, particularly because of the skills and resources required to make compromises between the two worlds. From this perspective, data journalism should not be seen as the work of specialized workers applying these techniques to a great variety of topics but rather as a set of techniques that can be mobilized by journalists specializing in health, crime, the environment, or any other social issue.

Finally, a major dimension of this ethics concerns the relationship between the journalist and the public. Disseminating news in the form of data or designing research tools for the public in no way guarantees that citizens will become more involved in public affairs. On the contrary, users may focus on their individual situations and lose sight of the systemic nature

CONCLUSION: AN ETHICS OF REFLEXIVITY

of the difficulties they face collectively as citizens. Journalists' responsibility here is twofold. First, they must consider the effects of these news-production practices on the public by developing ways of representing the public that are more meaningful than conventional audience metrics. Second, they need to develop a set of practices to enable users not only to become aware of the systemic dimension of issues but also to discuss them with each other. Disseminating information in the form of data requires journalists to consider how they bring about publics in a democracy.

These are some of the dimensions needed in a renewed ethics that would be better suited to journalism's growing dependence on a variety of actors as the newsroom is transformed into a calculation center. The outlines of such an ethics are still in the making, and many gray areas remain, waiting to be explored by journalists. In this process, the social sciences have a major responsibility to help journalists equip themselves with rules that take better account of the expectations being placed on technology.

FRENCH AND U.S. PERSPECTIVES

Computing the News has focused on two countries where journalists have endeavored, to varying degrees, to harness the rise of computational technologies for the fundamental missions they set for themselves in a democracy. Although similarities have emerged in the constitution of a professional segment around data journalism in the United States and France, significant differences remain that affect the possibility of implementing this ethics of reflexivity in both countries. First, in the United States these news practices enjoy high visibility within the profession, which encourages journalists to discuss them. In France, by contrast, these practices remain poorly visible. As a result, the challenge they represent for professional ethics is not as obvious there. Thus, even though some French journalists are exploring new dimensions of journalistic ethics, as evidenced in chapter 7, a greater temptation remains for them to assume that only the traditional rules of journalism still apply. Second, the division of

CONCLUSION: AN ETHICS OF REFLEXIVITY

computational work is, overall, more extensive in the United States than in France, with major news organizations hiring a set of people with specialized skills. Their French counterparts, by contrast, usually recruit a single "data journalist" who is expected to perform a range of tasks. This limitation also contributes to the lack of awareness of the need for a renewed ethics among French journalists. Finally, the way the profession is structured in both countries also influences the evolution of journalistic ethics. For example, the greater rigidity of professional boundaries in France clearly does not facilitate the creation of trading zones with the technological worlds.

The fact nevertheless remains that better alignment of journalists' practices with this ethics of reflexivity will increase journalists' ability to fulfill their fundamental role in democracy. In a context where more and more actors are pointing to the strength of data to support their arguments, it is crucial for the quality of public debate that journalists take on the role of arbiter.

NOTES

INTRODUCTION: TRYING TO BE NONJUDGMENTAL

1. Many news publishers such as the BBC, the *New York Times*, and *Le Monde* have calculated excess mortality rates using official mortality data from previous years. They are thus able to estimate the number of deaths caused by the outbreak without relying on the official death count.
2. See, for example, the investigation published by the *Washington Post* in May 2020: Aaron Williams and Adrian Blanco, "How the Coronavirus Exposed Health Disparities in Communities of Color," *Washington Post*, May 26, 2020, https://www.washingtonpost.com/graphics/2020/investigations/coronavirus-race-data-map/.
3. For an overview of data visualizations designed in the United States, see Ben Shneiderman, "Data Visualization's Breakthrough Moment in the COVID-19 Crisis," April 30, 2020, https://medium.com/nightingale/data-visualizations-breakthrough-moment-in-the-covid-19-crisis-ce46627c7db5.
4. A growing body of research has documented the development of data journalism around the world. For North America, see Katherine Fink and Christopher W. Anderson, "Data Journalism in the United States: Beyond the 'Usual Suspects,'" *Journalism Studies* 16, no. 4 (2015): 467–81; Alfred Hermida and Mary Lynn Young, "Finding the Data Unicorn: A Hierarchy of Hybridity in Data and Computational Journalism," *Digital Journalism* 5, no. 2 (2017): 159–76; and Constance Tabary, Anne-Marie Provost, and Alexandre Trottier, "Data Journalism's Actors, Practices, and Skills: A Case Study from Quebec," *Journalism* 17, no. 1 (2016): 66–84. For Europe, see Megan Knight, "Data

INTRODUCTION: TRYING TO BE NONJUDGMENTAL

Journalism in the UK: A Preliminary Analysis of Form and Content," *Journal of Media Practice* 16, no. 1 (2015): 55–72; Eddy Borges-Rey, "Unravelling Data Journalism: A Study of Data Journalism Practice in British Newsrooms," *Journalism Practice* 10, no. 7 (2016): 833–43; Juliette De Maeyer et al., "Waiting for Data Journalism: A Qualitative Assessment of the Anecdotal Take-Up of Data Journalism in French-Speaking Belgium," *Digital Journalism* 3, no. 3 (2015): 432–66; and Markus Beiler, Felix Irmer, and Adrian Breda, "Data Journalism at German Newspapers and Public Broadcasters: A Quantitative Survey of Structures, Contents, and Perceptions," *Journalism Studies* 21, no. 11 (2020):1571–89. But also see for Africa, David Cheruiyot, Stefan Baack, and Raul Ferrer-Conill, "Data Journalism Beyond Legacy Media: The Case of African and European Civic Technology Organizations," *Digital Journalism* 7, no. 9 (2019): 1215–29; Last Moyo, "Data Journalism and the Panama Papers: New Horizons for Investigative Journalism in Africa," in *Data Journalism in the Global South*, ed. Bruce Mutsvairo, Saba Bebawi, and Eddy Borges-Rey (Cham, Switzerland: Palgrave Macmillan, 2019), 23–38; for the Middle-East, Norman P. Lewis and Eisa Al Nashmi, "Data Journalism in the Arab Region: Role Conflict Exposed," *Digital Journalism* 7, no. 9 (2019): 1200–214; for South America, Eddy Borges-Rey, "Data Journalism in Latin America: Community, Development, and Contestation," in *Data Journalism in the Global South*, ed. Mutsvairo, Bebawi, and Borges-Rey, 257–83; and for Asia, Shuling Zhang and Jieyun Feng, "A Step Forward? Exploring the Diffusion of Data Journalism as Journalistic Innovations in China," *Journalism Studies* 20, no. 9 (2019): 1281–300.

5. Karthik Madhavapeddi, "Hate Crime Watch," *FactChecker.in*, October 2018, https://factchecker.in/our-new-hate-crime-database-76-of-victimsover-10-years-minorities-90-attacks-reportedsince-2014/. See Global Editors Network, "Data Journalism Website of the Year," 2019, https://datajournalismawards.org/2019-winners/.

6. The Offshore Leaks (2013), Panama Papers (2016), and Paradise Papers (2017) were based on massive volumes of leaked data and involved hundreds of journalists and media organizations from all over the world.

7. This definition of computational journalism was coined in 2011 by Nicholas Diakopoulos in "A Functional Roadmap for Innovation in Computational Journalism," *Nick Diakopoulous* (blog), April 22, 2011, http://www.nickdiakopoulos.com/2011/04/22/a-functional-roadmap-for-innovation-in-computational-journalism. For a discussion of the consistency of the label, see Tania Bucher, "'Machines Don't Have Instincts': Articulating the Computational in Journalism," *New Media & Society* 19, no. 6 (2017): 918–33; and Mark Coddington, "Clarifying Journalism's Quantitative Turn: A Typology for Evaluating Data Journalism, Computational Journalism, and Computer-Assisted Reporting," *Digital Journalism* 3, no. 3 (2015): 331–48.

8. On how objectivity emerged as a professional ideal within U.S. and British journalism in the early twentieth century, see Michael Schudson, "The Objectivity Norm in American Journalism," *Journalism* 2, no. 2 (2001): 149–70.

9. See Edson C. Tandoc Jr. and Soo-Kwang Oh, "Small Departures, Big Continuities?," *Journalism Studies* 18, no. 8 (2017): 997–1015.

INTRODUCTION: TRYING TO BE NONJUDGMENTAL

10. Simon Rogers, *Facts Are Sacred* (London: Faber and Faber, 2013), 4.
11. Nate Silver, Twitter, October 6, 2017, https://twitter.com/natesilver538/status/916075565349826560.
12. Lorraine Daston and Peter Galison, *Objectivity* (New York: Zone, 2007). For a discussion of how this concept is applied in journalism, see Matt Carlson, "News Algorithms, Photojournalism, and the Assumption of Mechanical Objectivity in Journalism," *Digital Journalism* 7, no. 8 (2019): 1117–33.
13. I draw here on the vast literature on journalism's contribution to democracy. See, for example, Michael Schudson, *Why Democracies Need an Unlovable Press* (Cambridge: Polity, 2008); Herbert Gans, "What Can Journalists Actually Do for American Democracy?," *Harvard International Journal of Press/Politics* 3, no. 4 (1998): 6–12; and Clifford Christians, *Normative Theories of the Media: Journalism in Democratic Societies* (Urbana: University of Illinois Press, 2009). For a more recent study, see Natali Helberger, "On the Democratic Role of News Recommenders," *Digital Journalism* 7, no. 8 (2019): 993–1012.
14. An investigation on drinking water in Brazil was conducted jointly by two Brazilian news organizations, Repórter Brasil and Agência Pública, and by the Swiss nongovernment organization Public Eye. See Ana Aranha and Luana Rocha, "'Coquetel' com agrotóxicos foi achado na água de 1 em cada 4 municípios," Repórter Brasil, April 15, 2019, https://reporterbrasil.org.br/2019/04/coquetel-com-27-agrotoxicos-foi-achado-na-agua-de-1-em-cada-4-municipios/.
15. See Mike Tigas et al., "Dollars for Docs: How Industry Dollars Reached Your Doctors," ProPublica, 2019, https://projects.propublica.org/docdollars/.
16. See Daniel Lathrop and Laurel Ruma, *Open Government: Collaboration, Transparency, and Participation in Practice* (Sebastopol, CA: O'Reilly, 2010).
17. Sylvain Parasie and Éric Dagiral, "Data-Driven Journalism and the Public Good: 'Computer-Assisted-Reporters' and 'Programmer-Journalists' in Chicago," *New Media & Society* 15, no. 6 (2013): 853–71; Stefan Baack, "Practically Engaged: The Entanglements Between Data Journalism and Civic Tech," *Digital Journalism* 6, no. 6 (2018): 673–92.
18. See James T. Hamilton, *Democracy's Detectives: The Economics of Investigative Journalism* (Cambridge, MA: Harvard University Press, 2017).
19. The *Guardian* was the first in 2009 to carry out a large-scale investigation into the expenses of British MPs based on 5,500 PDF files compiling the receipts they submitted for reimbursement of their expenses. The newspaper solicited the help of its readers to transform these files into a unique database. See "MPs' Expenses: The *Guardian* Launches Major Crowdsourcing Experiment," *Guardian*, press release, June 23, 2009, https://www.theguardian.com/gnm-press-office/crowdsourcing-mps-expenses.
20. On tax evasion, in addition to the investigations conducted by the International Consortium of Investigative Journalists, the Organized Crime and Corruption Reporting Project conducted similar investigations, which in 2019, among other things, exposed the complex financial system allowing Russian oligarchs to hide their money abroad,

INTRODUCTION: TRYING TO BE NONJUDGMENTAL

launder it, and secretly invest in Russia and abroad. See Paul Radu, "Vast Offshore Network Moved Billions with Help from Major Russian Bank," Organized Crime and Corruption Reporting Project, March 4, 2019, https://www.occrp.org/en/troika laundromat/vast-offshore-network-moved-billions-with-help-from-major-russian-bank.

21. Schudson, *Why Democracies Need an Unlovable Press*, 16–17.
22. These pioneering projects are discussed in chapter 1.
23. See European Data Journalism Network, "Glocal Climate Change," n.d., https://climatechange.europeandatajournalism.eu/en/.
24. In chapter 8, I explore how through this platform *Los Angeles Times* journalists have managed to generate publics around victims of urban violence.
25. Several data journalism projects have focused on gender violence ("Sobrevivientes," Colombia, 2014, http://especiales.datasketch.co/sobrevivientes/index.html), women dying during pregnancy (ProPublica's "Lost Mothers," 2017, https://www.propublica.org/series/lost-mothers), female infanticide in China and India (Quartz's "World Sex Map: A Story of Drinkers, Genocide, and Unborn Girls," https://qz.com/335183/heres-why-men-on-earth-outnumber-women-by-60-million/), and the underrepresentation of women in European politics (*Der Spiegel*'s "Frauen an der Macht," 2019, https://www.spiegel.de/politik/ausland/internationaler-frauentag-paritaet-in-der-eu-frauen-an-der-macht-a-1256576.html).
26. In 2014, a coalition of European journalists attempted to count the number of men, women, and children who had died as a result of European Union member states' migration policies ("The Migrant Files," http://www.themigrantsfiles.com/). See also Reuters's project from 2017 documenting the situation of Rohingya refugees in Bangladesh using satellite imagery and data ("Life in the Camps," http://fingfx.thomsonreuters.com/gfx/rngs/MYANMAR-ROHINGYA/010051VB46G/index.html).
27. For an analysis of the rise of counterhegemonic media criticism, see Dominique Cardon and Fabien Granjon, *Médiactivistes* (Paris: Presses de Sciences Po, 2010).
28. Candis Callison and Mary Lynn Young's recent book *Reckoning Journalism's Limits and Possibilities* (Oxford: Oxford University Press, 2020) offers a comprehensive and highly relevant analysis of contemporary critiques of journalistic objectivity. In *The View from Somewhere: Undoing the Myth of Journalistic Objectivity* (Chicago: University of Chicago Press, 2019), the reporter Lewis Raven Wallace offers a vivid personal critique of this "view from nowhere," the limits of which he experienced as a transgender reporter, particularly as part of the Black Lives Matter movement.
29. Wesley Lowery, "A Reckoning Over Objectivity, Led by Black Journalists," *New York Times*, June 23, 2020, https://www.nytimes.com/2020/06/23/opinion/objectivity-black-journalists-coronavirus.html.
30. This criticism was voiced by Emily Bell, professor at the Columbia Journalism School, who deplored the lack of attention paid to diversity in journalism start-ups. See Emily Bell, "Journalism Startups Aren't a Revolution If They're Filled with All These White

INTRODUCTION: TRYING TO BE NONJUDGMENTAL

Men," *Guardian*, March 12, 2014, https://www.theguardian.com/commentisfree/2014/mar/12/journalism-startups-diversity-ezra-klein-nate-silver.
31. See Safiya Umoja Noble, *Algorithms of Oppression: How Search Engines Reinforce Racism* (New York: New York University Press, 2018).
32. See John Abraham, "Climate Change in 2016: The Good, the Bad, and the Ugly," *Guardian*, January 2, 2017, https://www.theguardian.com/environment/climate-consensus-97-per-cent/2017/jan/02/climate-change-in-2016-the-good-the-bad-and-the-ugly.
33. This outcome has been highlighted by social science research on fact-checking journalism. See Lucas Graves, *Deciding What's True: The Rise of Political Fact-Checking in American Journalism* (New York: Columbia University Press, 2016).
34. Allison Schrager, "The Problem with Data Journalism," *Quartz*, March 19, 2014, https://qz.com/189703/the-problem-with-data-journalism/.
35. Geoffrey C. Bowker and Susan Leigh Star, *Sorting Things Out: Classification and Its Consequences* (Cambridge, MA: MIT Press, 2000).
36. This criticism is cogently put in Daniel Kreiss, "Beyond Administrative Journalism: Civic Skepticism and the Crisis in Journalism," in *The Crisis of Journalism Reconsidered: Democratic Culture, Professional Codes, Digital Future*, ed. Jeffrey C. Alexander, Elizabeth Butler Breese, and María Luengo (Cambridge: Cambridge University Press, 2016), 59–76.
37. In *Exit, Voice, and Loyalty: Responses to Decline in Forms, Organizations, and States* (Cambridge, MA: Harvard University Press, 1970), Albert O. Hirschman analyzes the risks that exit strategies present for organizations.
38. See Cass R. Sunstein, *#Republic: Divided Democracy in the Age of Social Media* (Princeton, NJ: Princeton University Press, 2018); and Markus Prior, *Post-broadcast Democracy: How Media Choice Increases Inequality in Political Involvement and Polarizes Elections* (Cambridge: Cambridge University Press, 2007).
39. See Theodore M. Porter, *Trust in Numbers: The Pursuit of Objectivity in Science and Public Life* (Princeton, NJ: Princeton University Press, 1995); Isabelle Bruno, Emmanuel Didier, and Tommaso Vitale, "Statactivism: Forms of Action Between Disclosure and Affirmation," *Partecipazione e conflitto: The Open Journal of Sociopolitical Studies* 7, no. 2 (2014): 198–220.
40. See Stefania Milan and Lonneke Van der Velden, "The Alternative Epistemologies of Data Activism," *Digital Culture & Society* 2, no. 2 (2016): 57–74; and Miren Gutiérrez, *Data Activism and Social Change* (London: Palgrave Macmillan, 2018).
41. Among the most important representatives of this stream, see Gaye Tuchman, "Objectivity as Strategic Ritual: An Examination of Newsmen's Notions of Objectivity," *American Journal of Sociology* 77, no. 4 (1972): 660–79; and Daniel Hallin, *We Keep America on Top of the World: Television Journalism and the Public Sphere* (London: Routledge, 2005).
42. Christopher W. Anderson, *Apostles of Certainty: Data Journalism and the Politics of Doubt* (Oxford: Oxford University Press, 2018), 15.

INTRODUCTION: TRYING TO BE NONJUDGMENTAL

43. See Wendy Nelson Espeland and Mitchell L. Stevens. "A Sociology of Quantification," *European Journal of Sociology / Archives européennes de sociologie* 49, no. 3 (2008): 401–36; Michael Power, *The Audit Society: Rituals of Verification* (Oxford: Oxford University Press, 1997); and Marilyn Strathern, *Audit Cultures: Anthropological Studies in Accountability, Ethics, and the Academy* (Hove, U.K.: Psychology Press, 2000).
44. Wendy Nelson Espeland and Michael Sauder, "Rankings and Reactivity: How Public Measures Recreate Social Worlds," *American Journal of Sociology* 113, no. 1 (2007): 1.
45. See Isabelle Bruno and Emmanuel Didier, *Benchmarking: L'état sous pression statistique* (Paris: Zones, 2015); and Alain Desrosières, *Pour une sociologie historique de la quantification: L'argument statistique I* (Paris: Presses des Mines, 2013).
46. See, for instance, Karin Knorr Cetina, *Epistemic Cultures: How the Sciences Make Knowledge* (Cambridge, MA: Harvard University Press, 1999). In the area of journalism, this perspective was introduced by Robert E. Park in "News as a Form of Knowledge: A Chapter in the Sociology of Knowledge," *American Journal of Sociology* 45, no. 5 (1940): 669–86.
47. See Pablo J. Boczkowski, *Digitizing the News: Innovation in Online Newspapers* (Cambridge, MA: MIT Press, 2005); and Angèle Christin, *Metrics at Work: Journalism and the Contested Meaning of Algorithms* (Princeton, NJ: Princeton University Press, 2020).
48. See Simon Susen and Bryan S. Turner, eds., *The Spirit of Luc Boltanski: Essays on the "Pragmatic Sociology of Critique"* (London: Anthem, 2014); and Yannick Barthe et al., "Pragmatic Sociology: A User's Guide," *Politix* 3 (2013): 175–204.
49. This perspective is based on actor-network theory. For an analysis of the rise of this theory in journalism studies, see Fred Turner, "Actor-Networking the News," *Social Epistemology* 19, no. 4 (2005): 321–24.
50. See Christopher W. Anderson, *Rebuilding the News: Metropolitan Journalism in the Digital Age* (Philadelphia, PA: Temple University Press, 2013). Technological actors play a growing role in this division of news labor, as evidenced in Mike Ananny and Kate Crawford, "A Liminal Press: Situating News App Designers Within a Field of Networked News Production," *Digital Journalism* 3, no. 2 (2015): 192–208. Moreover, studies have shown that web algorithms were designed based on an elaborate conception of democracy; see, for example, Dominique Cardon, "Inside the Mind of PageRank: A Study of Google's Algorithm," *Réseaux* 1, no. 177 (2013): 63–95.
51. Stephen J. A. Ward, *Disrupting Journalism Ethics: Radical Change on the Frontier of Digital Media* (London: Routledge, 2019).
52. See Jean-Gustave Padioleau, *Le Monde et le Washington Post: Précepteurs et mousquetaires* (Paris: Presses universitaires de France, 1985).
53. See Jean K. Chalaby, "Journalism as an Anglo-American Invention: A Comparison of the Development of French and Anglo-American Journalism, 1830s–1920s," *European Journal of Communication* 11, no. 3 (1996): 303–26.
54. See Éric Dagiral and Sylvain Parasie, "Presse en ligne: Où en est la recherche?," *Réseaux* 2 (2010): 13–42.

1. REVEALING INJUSTICE WITH COMPUTERS, 1967-1995

55. See Denis Ruellan, *Le professionnalisme du flou: Identité et savoir-faire des journalistes français* (Grenoble: Presses universitaires de Grenoble, 1993).

1. REVEALING INJUSTICE WITH COMPUTERS, 1967-1995

1. Bill Dedman, "The Color of Money," *Atlanta Journal-Constitution*, May 1-4, 1988.
2. Margaret H. DeFleur, *Computer-Assisted Investigative Reporting: Development and Methodology* (New York: Routledge, 2013); Bruce Garrison, *Computer-Assisted Reporting*, 2nd ed. (Mahwah, NJ: Lawrence Erlbaum, 1998); Melisma Cox, "The Development of Computer-Assisted Reporting," paper presented to the Newspaper Division, Association for Education in Journalism and Mass Communication, Southeast Colloquium, University of North Carolina, Chapel Hill, March 17-18, 2000.
3. Chris W. Anderson, *Apostles of Certainty: Data Journalism and the Politics of Doubt* (New York: Oxford University Press, 2018); Sylvain Parasie and Éric Dagiral, "Data-Driven Journalism and the Public Good: 'Computer-Assisted-Reporters' and 'Programmer-Journalists' in Chicago," *New Media & Society* 15, no. 6 (2013): 853-71; Michael Schudson, "Political Observatories, Databases, & News in the Emerging Ecology of Public Information," *Daedalus* 139, no. 2 (2010): 100-109.
4. Anderson, *Apostles of Certainty*, 16-49.
5. Philip Meyer, "The Non-rioters: A Hopeful Majority," *Detroit Free Press*, August 20, 1967.
6. David Burnham, "Murder Rate for Blacks in City 8 Times That for White Victims," *New York Times*, August 5, 1973.
7. Donald Barlett and James Steele, "Crime and Injustice," *Philadelphia Inquirer*, February 18, 1973.
8. See, for example, Thomas Maier and Rex Smith, "The Confession Takers," *Newsday*, December 7-19, 1985.
9. See, for example, Maria Miro Johnson and Elliot Jaspin, "R.I. System Fails to Fully Check Driving Records of Bus Applicants: Traffic Violators, Some Felons Certified to Drive School Buses," *Providence Journal*, May 11, 1986.
10. See, for example, David Burnham, *A Law Unto Itself: Power, Politics, and the IRS* (1989; reprint, New York: Open Road Media, 2015).
11. Stephen Doig, "What Went Wrong?," *Miami Herald*, December 20, 1992.
12. See James G. Bradsher, "A Brief History of the Growth of Federal Government Records, Archives, and Information 1789-1985," *Government Publications Review* 13, no. 4 (1986): 491-505.
13. James L. Aucoin, *The Evolution of American Investigative Journalism* (Columbia: University of Missouri Press, 2005), 84-116; James S. Ettema and Theodore L. Glasser, *Custodians of Conscience: Investigative Journalism and Public Virtue* (New York: Columbia University Press, 1998).
14. Aucoin, *Evolution of American Investigative Journalism*, 97.

1. REVEALING INJUSTICE WITH COMPUTERS, 1967–1995

15. Terence Ball, "American Political Science in Its Postwar Political Context," in *Discipline and History: Political Science in the United States*, ed. James Farr and Raymond Seidelman (Ann Arbor: University of Michigan Press, 1993), 207–21.
16. David H. Weaver and Maxwell E. McCombs, "Journalism and Social Science: A New Relationship?," *Public Opinion Quarterly* 44, no. 4 (1980): 477–94.
17. Philip Meyer, *Paper Route: Finding My Way to Precision Journalism* (Bloomington, IN: iUniverse, 2012), 246.
18. Philip Meyer, *Precision Journalism: A Reporter's Introduction to Social Science Methods* (Bloomington: Indiana University Press, 1973).
19. Philip Meyer, "Social Science Reporting," paper presented at the Conference on Education for Newspaper Journalists in the 1970s and Beyond, Boston, October 31–November 2, 1973, https://files.eric.ed.gov/fulltext/ED089269.pdf.
20. Meyer, *Paper Route*, 266.
21. Meyer, *Precision Journalism*, 13.
22. Meyer, *Precision Journalism*, 4.
23. Meyer, "Social Science Reporting."
24. As analyzed in Weaver and McCombs, "Journalism and Social Science."
25. Elliott Jaspin, telephone interview by the author, September 19, 2014.
26. *Long v. U.S. Internal Revenue Service*, U.S. Court of Appeals, case no. 76-3734 (1979).
27. To understand how reporters experienced these legal limitations in the early 1990s, see Elliot Jaspin and Mark Sableman, "News Media Access to Computer Records: Updating Information Laws in the Electronic Age," *Saint Louis University Law Journal* 36, no. 2 (1992): 349–408.
28. *Dismukes v. Department of Interior*, U.S. District Court for the District of Columbia, case no. 84-0757 (1984).
29. *Kele vs. U.S. Parole Commission*, U.S. District Court for the District of Columbia, case no. 85-4058 (1986), quoted in DeFleur, *Computer-Assisted Investigative Reporting*, 58.
30. Clarence Jones, quoted in Scott R. Maier, "The Digital Watchdog's First Byte: Journalism's First Computer Analysis of Public Records," *American Journalism* 17, no. 14 (2000): 79.
31. Curtis D. MacDougall, "Schools of Journalism Are Being Ruined," Southern Illinois University, School of Journalism, Carbondale, 1972, https://files.eric.ed.gov/fulltext/ED088043.pdf.
32. On such networks, see Bruno Latour and Steve Woolgar, *Laboratory Life: The Construction of Scientific Facts* (Princeton, NJ: Princeton University Press, 2013).
33. Meyer, *Paper Route*, 260–64.
34. D. O. Sears and J. B. McConahay, "Participation in the Los Angeles Riot," *Social Problems* 17, no. 1 (1969): 3–20.
35. Dedman, "The Color of Money."
36. About these two professional norms in American journalism, see Herbert J. Gans, *Deciding What's News: A Study of CBS Evening News, NBC Nightly News, Newsweek, and Time*, 25th anniversary ed., with a new preface by the author (Evanston, IL:

1. REVEALING INJUSTICE WITH COMPUTERS, 1967-1995

Northwestern University Press, 2004), 214–20. For a theorization of news formats, see Cyril Lemieux, *Mauvaise presse: Une sociologie compréhensive du travail journalistique et de ses critiques* (Paris: Métailié, 2000), 261–69.

37. For a definition of infrastructure, see Susan L. Star, "The Ethnography of Infrastructure," *American Behavioral Scientist* 43, no. 3 (1999): 377–91.
38. In current dollars, this would be between $18,000 and $24,000.
39. Jaspin, telephone interview.
40. See David Burnham, *The Rise of the Computer State* (New York: Random House, 1983).
41. David Burnham, "Tracking the Fed with TRAC—the Transactional Records Access Clearing House," paper presented at the Computers, Freedom, and Privacy Conference, Burlingame, CA, March 26–28, 1991, http://cpsr.org/prevsite/conferences/cfp91/burnham.html/.
42. Burnham, "Tracking the Fed with TRAC."
43. Brand Houston, "Changes in Attitudes, Changes in Latitude," in *When Nerds and Words Collide: Reflections on the Development of Computer-Assisted Reporting*, ed. Nora Paul (St. Petersburg, FL: Poynter Institute for Media Studies, 1999), 6–7.
44. Jaspin, telephone interview.
45. Brand Houston, "A Summary of Problems Using Nine-Track Tapes," NICAR Tipsheet No. 136 (1993), 9, archived at https://www.ire.org/resources/.
46. This "evangelizing" approach, which involved small groups of journalists organizing to persuade their colleagues of the merits of new practices, is one of the driving forces of change in the profession today—for instance, with the rise of "public journalism," "solution journalism," and "engaged journalism."
47. Bob Port, "The Contraption," in *When Nerds and Words Collide*, ed. Paul, 37–39.
48. Port, "The Contraption."
49. George Landau, "Objects in Mirror Are Closer Than They Appear," in *When Nerds and Words Collide*, ed. Paul, 28–30.
50. Fred Turner, *From Counterculture to Cyberculture: Steward Brand, the Whole Earth Network, and the Rise of Digital Utopianism* (Chicago: University of Chicago Press, 2006), 97–98.
51. Among these women was Erin McCormick, who became interested in computer programming as a teenager in the early 1980s because of her family background (her father was an electronics engineer). In the late 1980s, she turned to journalism without making the connection with computer science, then met Elliott Jaspin, who hired her as an intern. She then became passionate about computer-assisted reporting, which led to her being recruited by the *San Francisco Examiner* in 1993. Until 2000, she specialized in working with databases, auditing government financial records, and following the money trail in campaign finance reports (Erin McCormick, telephone interview by the author, September 25, 2012).
52. For example, Bruce Garrison, *Computer-Assisted Reporting* (Mahwah, NJ: Lawrence Erlbaum Associates, 1995); and Brand Houston, *Computer-Assisted Reporting: A Practical Guide* (New York: St. Martin's, 1996).

1. REVEALING INJUSTICE WITH COMPUTERS, 1967-1995

53. Penny Loeb, "Tips on Computer-Assisted Reporting," NICAR Tipsheet No. 160 (1993), 1, archived at https://www.ire.org/resources/.
54. Bruce Garrison, *Computer-Assisted Reporting*, 2nd ed. (Mahwah, NJ: Lawrence Erlbaum, 1998), 342.
55. See Ettema and Glasser, *Custodians of Conscience*, 131–53.
56. Garrison, *Computer-Assisted Reporting* (1998), 303.
57. Garrison, *Computer-Assisted Reporting* (1998), 303–4.
58. Ettema and Glasser, *Custodians of Conscience*, 131–53.
59. Philip Meyer, "Reporting in the 21st Century," presentation at the Association for Education in Journalism and Mass Communication Annual Conference, Montreal, August 1992, cited in DeFleur, *Computer-Assisted Investigative Reporting*, 204.
60. David Burnham, "Investigating the Investigators—David Burnham's All-Purpose Cook Book," TRAC, Syracuse University, 1999, archived at https://www.ire.org/resources/.
61. Doig, "What Went Wrong?"
62. Jaspin, telephone interview.
63. For example, Anderson, *Apostles of Certainty*; Parasie and Dagiral, "Data-Driven Journalism and the Public Good"; and Schudson, "Political Observatories, Databases, & News."
64. Gaye Tuchman, "Objectivity as Strategic Ritual: An Examination of Newsmen's Notions of Objectivity," *American Journal of Sociology* 77, no. 4 (1972): 660–79.
65. See Jean K. Chalaby, "Scandal and the Rise of Investigative Reporting in France," *American Behavioral Scientist* 47, no. 9 (2004): 1194–207.

2. RANKINGS; OR, THE UNINTENDED CONSEQUENCES OF COMPUTATION, 1988-2000

1. Dean quoted in Robert J. Vickers, "Some Ga. Colleges Climb US News Ranking, Some Slip," *Atlanta-Journal Constitution*, September 24, 1993.
2. Frédéric Pierru, "La fabrique des palmarès: Genèse d'un secteur d'action publique et renouvellement d'un genre journalistique. Le cas du palmarès des hôpitaux," in *La presse écrite: Objets délaissés*, ed. Jean-Baptiste Legavre (Paris: L'Harmattan, 2004), 265.
3. For a discussion of the rise of these policies in Western countries, see Christopher Hood, "The 'New Public Management' in the 1980s: Variations on a Theme," *Accounting, Organizations, and Society* 20, nos. 2–3 (1995): 93–109.
4. Sisi Wei, Olga Pierce, and Marshall Allen, "Surgeon Scorecard," ProPublica, 2015, https://projects.propublica.org/surgeons/.
5. Among many others, the French local newspaper *Le Parisien* regularly provides a ranking of the most active MPs in the Paris region. See Marie-Anne Gairaud, with Christine Henry and Julien Duffé, "Découvrez notre classement des députés de Paris," *Le*

2. RANKINGS

Parisien, June 17, 2018, https://www.leparisien.fr/paris-75/decouvrez-notre-classement-des-deputes-de-paris-17-06-2018-7777770.php.
6. See Wendy N. Espeland and Michael Sauder, "Rankings and Reactivity: How Public Measures Recreate Social Worlds," *American Journal of Sociology* 113, no. 1 (2007): 1–40.
7. In France, journalistic rankings have often been stigmatized as evidence of the harmful U.S. influence on French journalism.
8. Pierru, "La fabrique des palmarès," 256.
9. About the rise of an anti-institutional sentiment in French journalism at that time, see Cyril Lemieux, *Mauvaise presse: Une sociologie compréhensive du travail journalistique et de ses critiques* (Paris: Métailié, 2000).
10. See Jean-Gustave Padioleau, "Systèmes d'interaction et rhétoriques journalistiques," *Sociologie du travail* 3 (1976): 256–82.
11. Quoted in Julie Bouchard, "La fabrique d'un classement médiatique de l'enseignement supérieur et de la recherche: Le cas du *Monde de l'éducation* (1976–1988)," *Quaderni* 77, no. 1 (2012): 28.
12. Frank D. Roylance, "Alvin P. Sanoff, Former *Sun* Reporter, Helped Launch Annual College Rankings at *US News & World Report*," *Baltimore Sun*, May 21, 2007.
13. Mel Elfin, "Going to College Has Become an Almost Inalienable Right," in "America's Best Colleges," special issue of *U.S. News & World Report*, September 25, 1995.
14. *Science & Avenir* reporter quoted in Pierru, "La fabrique des palmarès," 259.
15. Compared to their French counterparts, American journalists more frequently made the argument that rankings contributed to the improvement of institutions. This tendency may be due to the importance of the libertarian tradition in the United States, which expects public exposure of wrongdoing to contribute to the improvement of the system as a whole. See Jean K. Chalaby, "Scandal and the Rise of Investigative Reporting in France," *American Behavioral Scientist* 47, no. 9 (2004): 1194–207.
16. On the rise of the consumer press in Europe, see Alan Aldridge, "The Construction of Rational Consumption in *Which? Magazine*: The More Blobs the Better?," *Sociology* 28, no. 4 (1994): 899–912; and Joachim Marcus-Steiff, "L'information comme mode d'action des organisations de consommateurs," *Revue française de sociologie* 18 (1977): 85–107.
17. Norman I. Silber, *Test and Protest: The Influence of Consumers Union* (New York: Holmes & Meier, 1983).
18. See William Aspray, "One Hundred Years of Car Buying," in *Everyday Information: The Evolution of Information Seeking in America*, ed. William Aspray and Barbara M. Hayes (Cambridge, MA: MIT Press, 2011), 16–17.
19. Jillian Kinzie et al., *Fifty Years of College Choice: Social, Political, and Institutional Influences on the Decision-Making Process* (Indianapolis, IN: Lumina Foundation for Education, 2004), 55.
20. Alvin P. Sanoff, "The *US News* College Rankings: A View from the Inside," in *College and University Ranking Systems*, ed. Institute for Higher Education Policy (Washington, DC: Institute for Higher Education Policy, 2007), 9–21, https://eric.ed.gov/?id=ED497028.

2. RANKINGS

21. Robert Ballion, *La bonne école: Évaluation et choix du collège et du lycée* (Paris: Hatier, 1991).
22. Sylvain Broccolichi, "Orientations et ségrégations nouvelles dans l'enseignement secondaire," *Sociétés contemporaines* 21 (1995): 15–27.
23. See Georges Felouzis and Joëlle Perroton, "Les 'marchés scolaires': Une analyse en termes d'économie de la qualité," *Revue française de sociologie* 48, no. 4 (2007): 693–722.
24. Hood, "The 'New Public Management' in the 1980s."
25. Peter T. Ewell, "The Evolution of Longitudinal Student Tracking Databases," *New Directions for Institutional Research* 87 (1995): 7–19.
26. See Carolyn L. Wiener, *The Elusive Quest: Accountability in Hospitals* (New York: Aldine de Gruyter, 2000).
27. This obligation has applied to all French public hospitals since 1994.
28. See Lise Demailly et al., *Évaluer les établissements scolaires: Enjeux, expériences, débats* (Paris: L'Harmattan, 1998).
29. See the analysis by Trudy Lieberman, who was one of the first U.S. consumer reporters, in "The Rise and Fall of Consumer Journalism," *American History of Business Journalism*, March 2013, https://ahbj.sabew.org/story/04042013-the-rise-and-fall-of-consumer-journalism/.
30. Robert Morse, Skype interview by the author, January 8, 2015.
31. See Lucas Graves, *Deciding What's True: The Rise of Political Fact-Checking in American Journalism* (New York: Columbia University Press, 2016).
32. Pierre Falga, interview by the author, Paris, March 11, 2015.
33. Patricia M. McDonough et al., "College Rankings: Democratized College Knowledge for Whom?," *Research in Higher Education* 39, no. 5 (1998): 514.
34. Anne Machung, "Playing the Ranking Game," *Change* 30, no. 4 (1998): 16.
35. Morse, interview.
36. Theodore M. Porter, *Trust in Numbers: The Pursuit of Objectivity in Science and Public Life* (Princeton, NJ: Princeton University Press, 1996).
37. This model was reconstructed from the details on methodology published in each "America's Best Colleges" issue of *U.S. News & World Report*. The coefficients changed annually.
38. Morse, interview.
39. Quoted in Deirdre Carmody, "Ranking of 'Best Colleges' Rankles Many Educators," *New York Times*, October 25, 1989.
40. Quoted in Mel Elfin, "Letters to the Editor," *Pittsburgh Post-Gazette*, November 28, 1996.
41. Barbara Lundberg, "To Find Right College, Do Your Homework: In Making a Choice, Don't Rely Only on a Magazine's 'Ranking,'" *Christian Science Monitor*, December 1, 1994.
42. Machung, "Playing the Ranking Game."
43. See National Opinion Research Center, *A Review of the Methodology for the US News & World Report Rankings of Undergraduate Colleges and Universities* (Chicago: National Opinion Research Center, 1997).

2. RANKINGS

44. Steve Stecklow, "Cheat Sheets: Colleges Inflate SATs and Graduation Rates in Popular Guidebooks," *Wall Street Journal*, April 5, 1995.
45. Lundberg, "To Find Right College."
46. Don Hossler, "The Problem with College Rankings," *About Campus*, March–April 2000, quoted in Luke Myers and Jonathan Roe, *College Rankings: History, Criticism, and Reform* (Washington, DC: Center for College Affordability and Productivity, 2008), 30.
47. James Monks and Ronald G. Ehrenberg, "*U.S. News & World Report*'s College Rankings: Why They Do Matter," *Change: The Magazine of Higher Learning* 31, no. 6 (1999): 42–51.
48. Espeland and Sauder, "Rankings and Reactivity."
49. This confrontation was also very intense in France, although it materialized differently, with major actors in education and health care arguing that the general public should not have access to evaluations.
50. In *The Audit Society: Rituals of Verification* (Oxford: Oxford University Press, 1997), Michael Power highlights the role of this rhetoric in improving performance calculations.
51. Sanoff, "The *US News* College Rankings."
52. American journalism's professional organizations formally recognized transparency as a key ethical principle in the late 1990s (Tim P. Vos and Stephanie Craft, "The Discursive Construction of Journalistic Transparency," *Journalism Studies* 18, no. 12 [2017]: 1505–22). Nevertheless, the underlying norm emerged earlier as a consequence of the "critical culture" that has shaped American and French journalism since the 1960s (Michael Schudson, *Discovering the News: A Social History of American Newspapers* [1978; reprint, New York: Basic, 1981]). As journalists became more critical of institutions, media organizations could not escape criticism as institutions. As a result, the need to disclose the various aspects of the news-production process became a regulating principle of journalistic work. Cyril Lemieux identifies this trend in the case of French journalism in *Mauvaise presse*, 94–96.
53. For France, see Philippe Ponet, "Les logiques d'une consécration journalistique: L'exemple des '50 meilleurs hôpitaux de France,'" *Questions de communication* 11 (2007): 91–110.
54. Sanoff, "The *US News* College Rankings."
55. Christian Baudelot, quoted in "Les lycées sous le feu de l'évaluation," *Supplément à la lettre d'information de Pénombre* 2, no. 4 (1999): 24.
56. Morse, interview.
57. Machung, "Playing the Ranking Game."
58. In the case of the British *Times*, see David Jobbins, "The *Times* / the *Times Higher Education Supplement*—League Tables in Britain: An Insider's View," *Higher Education in Europe* 27, no. 4 (2002): 383–88.
59. Morse, interview.
60. Stecklow, "Cheat Sheets."

2. RANKINGS

61. These professionals were part of the "institutional research" sector, which is a distinctive feature of American higher education. This area of applied research emerged in the 1950s to advise university management. See Marvin W. Peterson, "Institutional Research: An Evolutionary Perspective," in *Institutional Research in Transition: New Directions for Institutional Research*, ed. Mary Corcoran and Marvin W. Peterson (San Francisco: Jossey-Bass, 1985), 5–15.
62. Morse, interview.
63. See, for example, Loïc Ballarini, "Le rôle des 'palmarès des hôpitaux' dans le débat sur la qualité des soins," *Revue d'études politiques des assistants parlementaires*, no. 4 (2009): 26–27.

3. REBOOTING JOURNALISM

1. For a discussion of how the crisis in journalism has influenced the context of digital innovation in the news industry, see Nikki Usher, *Interactive Journalism: Hackers, Data, and Code* (Urbana: University of Illinois Press, 2016).
2. This network includes computer programs specially designed for data journalism as well as conferences, workshops, and professional training courses.
3. There is no official count of data journalists in the United States, but a query on LinkedIn shows approximately two thousand people featuring "data journalism" in their job title or as a skill.
4. A similar query on LinkedIn shows approximately two hundred people in France featuring "data journalism" in their job title or as a skill.
5. Henrik Örnebring, "Technology and Journalism-as-Labour: Historical Perspectives," *Journalism* 11, no. 1 (2010): 57–74.
6. The same observation was made in relation to French journalism in Denis Ruellan, *Les "pro" du journalisme: De l'état au statut, la construction d'un espace professionnel* (Rennes, France: Presses universitaires de Rennes, 1997).
7. Rue Bucher and Anselm Strauss, "Professions in Process," *American Journal of Sociology* 66, no. 4 (1961): 325–34.
8. In a similar vein, Seth Lewis and Rodrigo Zamith have called for an interactionist perspective to think about the emergence of these technology-supported journalistic specialties. See their essay "On the Worlds of Journalism," in *Remaking the News: Essays on the Future of Journalism Scholarship in the Digital Age*, ed. Pablo J. Boczkowski and C. W. Anderson (Cambridge, MA: MIT Press, 2017), 111–28. Following Howard Becker, they have supported the concept of a "world," defined as a set of "social actors, labor activities, material infrastructures, and patterns of production that collectively enable and legitimize particular forms of journalism" (112). I prefer the concept of a "segment," although it shares many similarities with "world," because it places greater emphasis on the processual nature of these areas of specialization.

3. REBOOTING JOURNALISM

9. I interviewed not only professionals who presented their work as data journalism, irrespective of their job title or the news organizations for which they worked (legacy or independent), but also individuals with a background in computer science, web development, or web activism who became involved in data journalism projects.
10. See Pablo J. Boczkowski, *Digitizing the News: Innovation in Online Newspapers* (Cambridge, MA: MIT Press, 2005).
11. In the second half of the 1990s, early online U.S. newsrooms hired computer programmers because most journalists were reluctant to handle news-editing tasks. See Jane B. Singer, Martha P. Tharp, and Amon Haruta, "Online Staffers: Superstars or Second-Class Citizens?," *Newspaper Research Journal* 20, no. 3 (1999): 29–47.
12. On how technologies contribute to politics—in other words, to the ordering of beings and things—see Andrew Barry, *Political Machines: Governing a Technological Society* (New York: A&C Black, 2001), 1–33. For an internal presentation of the movement toward seeing and using data infrastructure as a political technology and of some emblematic projects conducted in the United States, see Daniel Lathrop and Laurel Ruma, *Open Government: Collaboration, Transparency, and Participation in Practice* (Sebastopol, CA: O'Reilly, 2010).
13. See Harlan Yu and David G. Robinson, "The New Ambiguity of Open Government," *UCLA Law Review Discourse* 59 (2011): 178.
14. Initiated in the 1990s, the Human Genome Project is one of the most spectacular achievements of the open-data movement. See Bruno J. Strasser, "The Experimenter's Museum: Genbank, Natural History, and the Moral Economies of Biomedicine," *Isis* 102, no. 1 (2011): 60–96.
15. In France, the Law on Authors' Rights and Related Rights in the Information Society was adopted in June 2006, and the Supreme Authority for the Distribution and Protection of Intellectual Property on the Internet was adopted in May 2009.
16. See Valérie Peugeot, "Les enjeux publics, économiques et citoyens de l'ouverture des données: L'expérience britannique," paper presented at the conference "Document Numérique et société," Aix-en-Provence, France, November 15–16, 2010.
17. Charles Arthur and Michael Cross, "Give Us Back Our Crown Jewels," *Guardian*, March 9, 2006, https://www.theguardian.com/technology/2006/mar/09/education.epublic.
18. On the importance of these ideals in the history of the internet, see Fred Turner, *From Counterculture to Cyberculture: Stewart Brand, the Whole Earth Network, and the Rise of Digital Utopianism* (Chicago: University of Chicago Press, 2006); and Patrice Flichy, *The Internet Imaginaire* (Cambridge, MA: MIT Press, 2007).
19. Open Government Working Group, "The Annotated 8 Principles of Open Government Data," 2007, https://opengovdata.org/.
20. Daniel X. O'Neil, interview by the author, Chicago, September 8, 2010.
21. For the French case, see Samuel Goëta and Clément Mabi, "L'open data peut-il (encore) servir les citoyens?," *Mouvements* 3 (2014): 81–91.

22. Andrew Abbott, *The System of Professions: An Essay on the Division of Expert Labor* (Chicago: University of Chicago Press, 2014), 92.
23. Pamela Licalzi O'Connell, "Do-It-Yourself Cartography," *New York Times*, December 11, 2005.
24. The application Faces of the Fallen, for instance, was launched in 2006. It consisted of a browsable database of U.S. service members who died in Iraq and Afghanistan.
25. Seth C. Lewis, "Journalism Innovation and Participation: An Analysis of the Knight News Challenge," *International Journal of Communication* 5 (2011): 1623–48.
26. Adrian Holovaty, "A Fundamental Way Newspaper Sites Need to Change," *Adrian Holovaty* (blog), September 6, 2006, emphasis in original, http://www.holovaty.com/writing/fundamental-change/.
27. See in particular the "semantic web" theory proposed by the inventor of the web, Tim Berners-Lee, in Tim Berners-Lee, James Hendler, and Ora Lassila, "The Semantic Web," *Scientific American* 284, no. 5 (2001): 34–43.
28. Holovaty, "A Fundamental Way Newspaper Sites Need to Change," emphasis in original.
29. Eric Klinenberg, *Fighting for Air: The Battle to Control America's Media* (New York: Metropolitan Books, 2007).
30. Holovaty, "A Fundamental Way Newspaper Sites Need to Change."
31. Sylvain Parasie and Éric Dagiral, "Data-Driven Journalism and the Public Good: 'Computer-Assisted-Reporters' and 'Programmer-Journalists' in Chicago," *New Media & Society* 15, no. 6 (2013): 853–71; Cindy Royal, "The Journalist as Programmer: A Case Study of the *New York Times* Interactive News Technology Department," *International Symposium on Online Journalism* 2, no. 1 (2012): 5–24.
32. As Nicolas Auray and Michaël Vicente have shown, many open-source developers seek to balance their professional and personal lives either by starting their own business or by looking for a job that gives them time for their own open-source projects. See their working paper "Free Software and the Double Life of Computing Professionals: Some Biographical Insights in the Life Courses of Some Elder Developers," working paper, 2006, http://ses-perso.telecom-paristech.fr/auray/AurayVicente.pdf.
33. Tasneem Raja, interview by the author, San Francisco, September 13, 2012.
34. Raja, interview.
35. Michel Callon, "The Role of Hybrid Communities and Socio-technical Arrangements in the Participatory Design," *Journal of the Center for Information Studies* 5, no. 3 (2004): 3–10.
36. In 2010 and 2011, the Online News Association awarded OWNI for General Excellence in Online Journalism.
37. Pierre Romera, interviewed by the author, Paris, August 3, 2012.
38. This questionnaire, which I designed with the data journalist Alexandre Léchenet, received sixty-six responses. A comparison with the results from the queries on LinkedIn mentioned in notes 3 and 4 suggests that we contacted between a third and a quarter of the data journalism segment in France.

3. REBOOTING JOURNALISM

39. Several journalists in the United States and Great Britain, including Emily Bell, the former editor in chief of the *Guardian* and a journalism teacher at Columbia, have denounced the underrepresentation of women and minorities in the professional segment. See Emily Bell, "Journalism Startups Aren't a Revolution If They're Filled with All These White Men," *Guardian*, March 12, 2014.
40. The figures for the French professional group come from Christine Leteinturier, "La formation des journalistes français: Quelles évolutions? Quels atouts à l'embauche? Le cas des nouveaux titulaires de la carte de presse 2008," *Les cahiers du journalisme* 21 (2010): 110–34.
41. See, for example, Katherine Fink and Christopher W. Anderson, "Data Journalism in the United States: Beyond the 'Usual Suspects,'" *Journalism Studies* 16, no. 4 (2015): 467–81; Constance Tabary, Anne-Marie Provost, and Alexandre Trottier, "Data Journalism's Actors, Practices, and Skills: A Case Study from Quebec," *Journalism* 17, no. 1 (2016): 66–84; and Eddy Borges-Rey, "Unravelling Data Journalism: A Study of Data Journalism Practice in British Newsrooms," *Journalism Practice* 10, no. 7 (2016): 833–43.
42. As Lucas Grave and his colleagues have shown for fact-checking, the rise of recent journalistic practices can be explained first of all by journalists' attachment to the ideals of the profession. See Lucas Graves, Brendan Nyhan, and Jason Reifler, "Understanding Innovations in Journalistic Practice: A Field Experiment Examining Motivations for Fact-Checking," *Journal of Communication* 66, no. 1 (2016): 102–38.
43. See Ignacio Siles and Pablo J. Boczkowski, "Making Sense of the Newspaper Crisis: A Critical Assessment of Existing Research and an Agenda for Future Work," *New Media & Society* 14, no. 8 (2012): 1375–94.
44. I interviewed fifteen data journalists in the United States and ten in France. They were working for legacy news organizations (*Chicago Tribune, Libération, Le Monde, Mother Jones, New Scientist*), nonprofit organizations (Center for Investigative Reporting), news agencies (Agence France Presse), and news start-ups (OWNI, Journalism++).
45. Jules Bonnard, interview by the author, Paris, December 29, 2015.
46. Michael Corey, interview by the author, San Francisco, August 24, 2012.
47. Agustin Armendariz, interview by the author, Berkeley, CA, September 12, 2012.
48. Damien Brunon, interview by the author, Paris, January 6, 2016.
49. Nicolas Kayser-Bril, interview by the author, Paris, January 18, 2010.
50. Xavier Ternisien, "Les forçats de l'info," *Le Monde*, May 25, 2009, https://www.lemonde.fr/actualite-medias/article/2009/05/25/les-forcats-de-l-info_1197692_3236.html.
51. Sarah Cohen, James T. Hamilton, and Fred Turner, "Computational Journalism," *Communications of the ACM* 54, no. 10 (2011): 66–71.
52. Peter Aldhous, interview by the author, San Francisco, September 7, 2012.
53. Bonnard, interview.
54. Bonnard, interview.

4. A TALE OF TWO CULTURES?

1. This distinction can be found in landmark studies of journalism: Herbert J. Gans, *Deciding What's News: A Study of CBS Evening News, NBC Nightly News, Newsweek, and Time*, 25th anniversary ed., with a new preface by the author (Evanston, IL: Northwestern University Press, 2004); Michael Schudson, "The Objectivity Norm in American Journalism," *Journalism* 2, no. 2 (2001): 149–70; Jean K. Chalaby, "Journalism as an Anglo-American Invention: A Comparison of the Development of French and Anglo-American Journalism, 1830s–1920s," *European Journal of Communication* 11, no. 3 (1996): 303–26; Jean-Gustave Padioleau, *Le Monde et le Washington Post: Précepteurs et mousquetaires* (Paris: Presses universitaires de France, 1985).
2. Cyril Lemieux, "Les formats de l'égalitarisme: Transformations et limites de la figure du journalisme-justicier dans la France contemporaine," *Quaderni* 45, no. 1 (2001): 53–68.
3. Dominique Marchetti, "The Revelations of Investigative Journalism in France," *Global Media and Communication* 5, no. 3 (2009): 368–88.
4. Michèle Lamont and Laurent Thévenot, eds., *Rethinking Comparative Cultural Sociology: Repertoires of Evaluation in France and the United States* (Cambridge: Cambridge University Press, 2000).
5. See Michael Schudson, *Discovering the News: A Social History of American Newspapers* (1978; reprint, New York: Basic, 1981); Gans, *Deciding What's News*; Chalaby, "Journalism as an Anglo-American Invention."
6. Chalaby, "Journalism as an Anglo-American Invention."
7. Chalaby, "Journalism as an Anglo-American Invention," 320.
8. Gans, *Deciding What's News*, 275.
9. Chalaby, "Journalism as an Anglo-American Invention"; Schudson, "The Objectivity Norm in American Journalism."
10. Padioleau, *Le Monde et le Washington Post*.
11. Padioleau, *Le Monde et le Washington Post*, 31.
12. Schudson, "The Objectivity Norm in American Journalism."
13. Schudson, "The Objectivity Norm in American Journalism."
14. Angèle Christin, *Metrics at Work: Journalism and the Contested Meaning of Algorithms* (Princeton, NJ: Princeton University Press, 2020).
15. Rodney Benson, *Shaping Immigration News: A French–American Comparison* (Cambridge: Cambridge University Press, 2013).
16. Marchetti, "The Revelations of Investigative Journalism in France."
17. Chalaby, "Journalism as an Anglo-American Invention."
18. Lemieux, "Les formats de l'égalitarisme."
19. Cyril Lemieux and John Schmalzbauer, "Involvement and Detachment Among French and American Journalists: To Be or Not to Be a 'Real' Professional," in *Rethinking Comparative Cultural Sociology*, ed. Thévenot and Lamont, 148–69.
20. See Lamont and Thévenot, *Rethinking Comparative Cultural Sociology*.

4. A TALE OF TWO CULTURES?

21. Michel Callon, "The Sociology of an Actor-Network: The Case of the Electric Vehicle," in *Mapping the Dynamics of Science and Technology*, ed. Michel Callon, John Law, and Arie Rip (London: Palgrave Macmillan, 1986), 19–34.
22. See Gans, *Deciding What's News*; Cyril Lemieux, *Mauvaise presse: Une sociologie compréhensive du travail journalistique et de ses critiques* (Paris: Métailié, 2000).
23. Harold Garfinkel, *Studies in Ethnomethodology* (Englewood Cliffs, NJ: Prentice-Hall, 1967), 33.
24. By adopting the so-called sunshine laws, the State of Florida was a pioneer in this movement, which largely explains why the first major journalistic investigations based on the collection and analysis of digital government data were conducted in that state, as early as the 1970s. See Sandra F. Chance and Christina Locke, "The Government-in-the-Sunshine Law Then and Now: A Model for Implementing New Technologies Consistent with Florida's Position as a Leader in Open Government," *Florida State University Law Review* 35 (2008): 245–70.
25. The U.S. Census Bureau has been publishing statistics on the web since 1994, as have the FBI and other federal agencies. In 1997, the federal government launched FedStats.gov, which provides access to a large number of databases.
26. On resistance to requests for access, see David E. Pozen and Michael Schudson, eds., *Troubling Transparency: The History and Future of Freedom of Information* (New York: Columbia University Press, 2018). On the low quality of data, see Daniel Lathrop and Laurel Ruma, *Open Government: Collaboration, Transparency, and Participation in Practice* (Sebastopol, CA: O'Reilly, 2010).
27. In *Computer-Assisted Reporting* (2nd ed., Mahwah, NJ: Lawrence Erlbaum, 1998), Bruce Garrison provides a list of the major federal databases that were available on the web in the second half of the 1990s (147–50).
28. See Jean K. Chalaby, "Scandal and the Rise of Investigative Reporting in France," *American Behavioral Scientist* 47, no. 9 (2004): 1194–207.
29. With the Law of 17 July 1978, France was the fifth country in the world to adopt legislation of this type, after Finland (1951), the United States (1967), Denmark (1970), Norway (1970), and Austria (1973). See Jean Laveissière, "L'accès aux documents administratifs," in *Information et transparence administratives*, ed. François Rangeon, Jean Laveissière, and Philippe Belin (Paris: Presses universitaires de France, 1988), 11–35.
30. See Joumana Boustany, "Accès et réutilisation des données publiques," *Les cahiers du numérique* 9, no. 1 (2013): 21–37.
31. As an example of the primacy given to privacy protection, the French Parliament passed a law in 1999 that deprived journalists of access to French hospitals' official performance database on the grounds that journalists could use it to identify patients' names. See Frédéric Pierru, "Les clairs-obscurs de la forme palmarès: L'exemple de la carrière des palmarès hospitaliers," working paper, Maison des sciences de l'homme, 2009, https://www.meshs.fr/datas/files/docs/sem/2009-10/perru.pdf.
32. Directive 2003/98/EC on the reuse of public information, known as the Public Sector Information Directive.

4. A TALE OF TWO CULTURES?

33. In its benchmark report published in 2018, however, the Open Knowledge Foundation ranked France fourth in the world for the publication of open data, ahead of the United States (eleventh). See Open Knowledge Foundation, Global Open Data Index, "Place Overview," 2017, https://index.okfn.org/place/.
34. Jean-Luc Nevache, quoted in Alexandre Léchenet and Gabriel Zignani, "Accès aux documents: Les collectivités n'appliquent pas bien la réglementation," *La gazette des communes*, December 2, 2020, https://www.lagazettedescommunes.com/710586/acces-aux-documents-les-collectivites-nappliquent-pas-bien-la-reglementation-jean-luc-nevache/.
35. Theodore M. Porter, *Trust in Numbers: The Pursuit of Objectivity in Science and Public Life* (Princeton, NJ: Princeton University Press, 1996), 143–45.
36. Jacques Donzelot, Catherine Mével, and Anne Wyvekens, *Faire société: La politique de la ville aux États-Unis et en France* (Paris: Le Seuil, 2003), 344.
37. See Michael Schudson, "Political Observatories, Databases, & News in the Emerging Ecology of Public Information," *Daedalus* 139, no. 2 (2010): 100–109.
38. As mentioned in chapter 1, David Burnham started building a data infrastructure, the Transactional Records Access Clearing House, in the late 1980s to monitor the fairness and effectiveness of federal tax policy through systematic FOIA requests of IRS databases.
39. For a comparative analysis of the role of think tanks, a particular form of such political or citizen observatories, in France, see Catherine Fieschi and John Gaffney, "French Think Tanks in Comparative Perspective," in *Think Tanks Across Nations: A Comparative Approach*, ed. Diane Stone, Andrew Denham, and Mark Garnett (Manchester, U.K.: Manchester University Press, 1998), 105–20.
40. See Pierre Rosanvallon and Arthur Goldhammer, *Counter-Democracy: Politics in an Age of Distrust* (Cambridge: Cambridge University Press, 2008).
41. Alain Touraine was the French theorist of these new social movements, notably in his book *La voix et le regard* (Paris: Seuil, 1978).
42. This limited access is illustrated in Daniel Béland and Jean-Philippe Viriot Durandal's study of retiree movements in France and the United States, "L'expertise comme pouvoir: Le cas des organisations de retraités face aux politiques publiques en France et aux États-Unis," *Lien social et politiques* 50 (2003): 105–23.
43. In the late 1990s, each major U.S. newspaper assigned an average of eleven people to computer-assisted reporting tasks, compared with four for smaller newspapers. See Bruce Garrison, "Newspaper Size as Factor in Use of Computers for Newsgathering," *Newspaper Research Journal* 20, no. 3 (1999): 72–85.
44. In actor-network theory, the concept of translation refers to the activity of defining roles for a set of entities by presenting them with a technology as being tailored to their own interests. The success of a translation depends on the actor-network's ability to define and enroll entities that are likely to challenge these definitions and enrollments (Michel Callon, "Actor-Network Theory—the Market Test," *Sociological Review* 47, no. 1 [1999]: 181–95).

5. THE TENSIONS FACING DATA JOURNALISM

45. In the late 1990s, this investigation was cited as an example of the possibilities afforded by the web in Garrison's handbook on computer-assisted reporting (*Computer-Assisted Reporting* [1998], 68).
46. In the 1990s, most computer-assisted reporters preferred data from statistical institutions and some federal or state agencies, which they received in the form of CD-ROMs. For example, I found that as early as 1996 *Chicago Tribune* reporters considered that the data put online by the Chicago Police Department was systematically manipulated and unsuitable for journalistic use.
47. George Landau, "Objects in Mirror Are Closer Than They Appear," in *When Nerds and Words Collide: Reflections on the Development of Computer Assisted Reporting*, ed. Nora Paul (St. Petersburg, FL: Poynter Institute of Media Studies, 1999), 29–30.
48. The information on Little comes from Darnell Little, interview by the author, Chicago, September 10, 2010.
49. The information on Falga comes from Pierre Falga, interview by the author, Paris, March 11, 2015.
50. In the late 1990s, prominent computer-assisted reporters recognized that the spread of computer-assisted reporting to Mexico and Denmark faced major obstacles (see, in general, Paul, *When Nerds and Words Collide*).
51. The rise of "data-harvest" conferences, which have been held in Brussels since the late 2000s, has played an important role in bringing together investigative journalists and coders around projects involving European Union data. Brigitte Alfter, a German Danish journalist, has been instrumental in building a framework for collaboration among European investigative journalists. See her book *Cross-Border Collaborative Journalism: A Step-by-Step Guide* (New York: Routledge, 2019).

5. THE TENSIONS FACING DATA JOURNALISM

1. According to Nate Silver, the FiveThirtyEight site had thirty-seven staff members and 10.7 million unique visitors per month in 2016. It was purchased by ABC News in 2018.
2. A few scholars have documented some of the ethical tensions in the practice of data journalism. See, for example, Ester Appelgren, "An Illusion of Interactivity: The Paternalistic Side of Data Journalism," *Journalism Practice* 12, no. 3 (2018): 308–25; and Sylvain Parasie, "Data-Driven Revelation? Epistemological Tensions in Investigative Journalism in the Age of 'Big Data,'" *Digital Journalism* 3, no. 3 (2015): 364–80.
3. Building on science studies and pragmatic sociology, this theory considers disputing processes as collective actions that transform social order. See Luc Boltanski and Laurent Thévenot, *On Justification: Economies of Worth* (Princeton, NJ: Princeton University Press, 2006); Luc Boltanski and Laurent Thévenot. "The Sociology of Critical Capacity," *European Journal of Social Theory* 2, no. 3 (1999): 359–77; and Cyril Lemieux, "À quoi sert l'analyse des controverses?," *Mil neuf cent* 25, no. 1 (2007): 191–212.

5. THE TENSIONS FACING DATA JOURNALISM

4. Since the early 1980s, investigative reporting has become an established journalistic genre in France, to the extent that investigative reporters have become the symbol of the profession in the eyes of the public and especially of newcomers to the profession. See Jean K. Chalaby, "Scandal and the Rise of Investigative Reporting in France," *American Behavioral Scientist* 47, no. 9 (2004): 1194–207; Dominique Marchetti, "The Revelations of Investigative Journalism in France," *Global Media and Communication* 5, no. 3 (2009): 368–88.
5. See Gary Chapman and Angela Newell, "The Transformation of Public Information in the United States," in *Everyday Information: The Evolution of Information Seeking in America*, ed. William Aspray and Barbara M. Hayes (Cambridge, MA: MIT Press, 2011), 256.
6. In France, the proportion of requests made by journalists is not public information.
7. Published in 2012, *The Data Journalism Handbook* encouraged reporters to use freedom-of-information laws in their countries. See Jonathan Gray, Lucy Chambers, and Liliana Bounegru, *The Data Journalism Handbook: How Journalists Can Use Data to Improve the News* (Sebastopol, CA: O'Reilly, 2012).
8. Or to a "new enlightenment," as some authors have suggested. See Nicolas Auray, "De l'éthique à la politique: L'institution d'une cité libre," *Multitudes* 1 (2002): 171–80.
9. See Christopher Hood, "From FOI World to Wikileaks World: A New Chapter in the Transparency Story?," *Governance* 24, no. 4 (2011): 635–38.
10. See Elizabeth B. Hindman and Ryan J. Thomas, "When Old and New Media Collide: The Case of WikiLeaks," *New Media & Society* 16, no. 4 (2014): 541–58.
11. In the early 2010s, the French data journalism website OWNI partnered with WikiLeaks to disseminate the Iraq Warlog, which earned it an award from the Online News Association in 2010 (see chapter 3).
12. See Daniel Lathrop and Laura Ruma, eds., *Open Government: Collaboration, Transparency, and Participation in Practice* (Sebastopol, CA: O'Reilly, 2010).
13. See Harlan Yu and David G. Robinson, "The New Ambiguity of Open Government," *UCLA Law Review Discourse* 59 (2011): 178–208.
14. Derek Willis was one of the first reporters to use scraping. In 2007, he designed an application for the *Washington Post* that provided access to all bills and votes on bills in the U.S. Senate.
15. Alexandre Léchenet, quoted in Gray, Chambers, and Bounegru, *The Data Journalism Handbook*, 131.
16. As Nicolas Dodier has shown, workers' virtuosity can be recognized only when they are confronted with material objects and call their own abilities into question in front of their colleagues. See Dodier, *Les hommes et les machines: La conscience collective dans les sociétés technicisées* (Paris: Métailié, 1995), 261–68.
17. Alexandre Léchenet, quoted in Gray, Chambers, and Bounegru, *The Data Journalism Handbook*, 131.
18. See James Surowiecki, *The Wisdom of Crowds* (Palatine, IL: Anchor, 2005); Yochai Benkler, *The Wealth of Networks: How Social Production Transforms Markets and Freedom* (New Haven, CN: Yale University Press, 2006).

5. THE TENSIONS FACING DATA JOURNALISM

19. For an overview of crowdsourcing for data, see Tanja Aitamurto, "Crowdsourcing as a Knowledge-Search Method in Digital Journalism," *Digital Journalism* 4, no. 2 (2015): 280–97.
20. For a sociological definition of public accountability and transparency, see Mark Bovens, Thomas Schillemans, and Robert E. Goodin, "Public Accountability," in *The Oxford Handbook of Public Accountability*, ed. Mark Bovens, Robert E. Goodin, and Thomas Schillemans (Oxford: Oxford University Press, 2014), 1–22.
21. The sociologists Jérôme Denis and Samuel Goëta have shown that the dissemination of data by administrations requires significant work, without which these data would be unintelligible for the actors likely to use them. See their article "Rawification and the Careful Generation of Open Government Data," *Social Studies of Science* 47, no. 5 (2017): 604–29.
22. Ben Welsh and Doug Smith, "Highest Crime Rate in L.A.? No, Just an LAPD Map Glitch," *Los Angeles Times*, April 5, 2009, http://www.latimes.com/local/la-me-geocoding-errors5-2009apr05-story.html.
23. Ben Welsh, "Q&A: EveryBlock's Adrian Holovaty on the LAPD and Accuracy Standards," *Los Angeles Times*, April 6, 2009, http://latimesblogs.latimes.com/lanow/2009/04/adrian-holovaty-everyblock.html.
24. Historians have analyzed the rise of news practices in U.S. journalism, which were less centered on facts and more focused on interpretation. See Katherine Fink and Michael Schudson, "The Rise of Contextual Journalism, 1950s–2000s," *Journalism* 15, no. 1 (2014): 3–20; and Kevin G. Barnhurst, "The Interpretive Turn in News," in *Journalism and Technological Change: Historical Perspectives, Contemporary Trends*, ed. Martin Schreiber and Clemens Zimmermann (Frankfort-am-Main, Germany: Campus-Verlag, 2014), 111–41.
25. Jason Grotto, interview by the author, Chicago, September 16, 2010.
26. Owen Youngman, interview by the author, Chicago, September 16, 2010.
27. Launched in 2010, the *Bay Citizen* merged with the Center for Investigative Reporting in 2013.
28. Nate Silver, quoted in Joe Coscarelli, "Nate Silver on the Launch of ESPN's New FiveThirtyEight, Burritos, and Being a Fox," *New York Magazine*, March 13, 2014.
29. Nate Silver, *The Signal and the Noise: Why so Many Predictions Fail—but Some Don't* (New York: Penguin Press, 2012). Amazon nominated this book as best nonfiction book of 2012.
30. See Cyril Lemieux and John Schmalzbauer, "Involvement and Detachment Among French and American Journalists: To Be or Not to Be a 'Real' Professional," in *Rethinking Comparative Cultural Sociology: Repertoires of Evaluation in France and the United States*, ed. Michèle Lamont and Laurent Thévenot (Cambridge: Cambridge University Press, 2000), 148–69.
31. According to Lorraine Daston, this form of objectivity "strives to eliminate all forms of human intervention in the observation of nature, either by using machines, such as self-inscription devices or the camera, or by mechanizing scientific procedures, as in

5. THE TENSIONS FACING DATA JOURNALISM

deploying statistical techniques to choose the best of a set of observations" ("The Moral Economy of Science," *Osiris* 10 [1995]: 19).

32. See Harvey Molotch and Marilyn Lester, "News as Purposive Behavior: On the Strategic Use of Routine Events, Accidents, and Scandals," *American Sociological Review* 39, no. 1 (1974): 101–12. For a critical analysis of how public institutions influence crime news, see Stuart Hall et al., *Policing the Crisis: Mugging, the State, and Law and Order* (London: Macmillan International Higher Education, 1978).
33. See Mary Lynn Young and Alfred Hermida, "From Mr. and Mrs. Outlier to Central Tendencies: Computational Journalism and Crime Reporting at the *Los Angeles Times*," *Digital Journalism* 3, no. 3 (2015): 381–97.
34. Jill Leovy, quoted in Kevin Roderick, "Homicide Report Gets New Life at the *LA Times*," *LA Observed*, March 2013, http://www.laobserved.com/archive/2013/03/homicide_report_gets_new.php.
35. Nate Silver, "What the Fox Knows," FiveThirtyEight, March 17, 2014, http://fivethirtyeight.com/features/what-the-fox-knows/.
36. The algorithms used by Silver rely on Bayesian inference. In a nutshell, this means that every normative assumption integrated into the model is subject to change as new facts become known. For a history of Bayesian algorithms, see Sharon B. McGrayne, *The Theory That Would Not Die: How Bayes' Rule Cracked the Enigma Code, Hunted Down Russian Submarines, & Emerged Triumphant from Two Centuries of Controversy* (New Haven, CN: Yale University Press, 2011).
37. Leon Wieseltier, "The Emptiness of Data Journalism: Nate Silver Could Learn a Lot from Those Op-Ed Columnists He Maligns," *New Republic*, March 19, 2014, http://www.newrepublic.com/article/117068/nate-silvers-fivethirtyeight-emptiness-data-journalism. On the history of the separation between science and politics and the role of scientific facts in modernity, see Bruno Latour, *We Have Never Been Modern*, trans. Catherine Porter (1993; reprint, Cambridge, MA: Harvard University Press, 2012), 13–48.
38. Alberto Cairo, "Data Journalism Needs to Up Its Own Standards," *Nieman Lab*, July 9, 2014, http://www.niemanlab.org/2014/07/alberto-cairo-data-journalism-needs-to-up-its-own-standards/.
39. Allison Schrager, "The Problem with Data Journalism," *Quartz*, March 19, 2014, https://qz.com/189703/the-problem-with-data-journalism/.
40. Paul Krugman, "Sergeant Friday Was Not a Fox," *New York Times*, March 18, 2014, https://krugman.blogs.nytimes.com/2014/03/18/sergeant-friday-was-not-a-fox/?_r=0.
41. Seth C. Lewis and Nikki Usher, "Open Source and Journalism: Toward New Frameworks for Imagining News Innovation," *Media, Culture, & Society* 35, no. 5 (2013): 608.
42. Brian Boyer, interview by the author, Chicago, September 9, 2010.
43. Pierre Romera, interview by the author, Paris, August 3, 2012.
44. Nathaniel Kelso, interview by the author, San Francisco, September 11, 2012.

5. THE TENSIONS FACING DATA JOURNALISM

45. Simon Rogers, "Hey Wonk Reporters, Liberate Your Data! Data Journalism Only Matters When It's Transparent," *Mother Jones*, April 24, 2014, http://www.motherjones.com/media/2014/04/vox-538-upshot-open-data-missing.
46. On the history of the transparency standard in Western journalism, see Cyril Lemieux, *Mauvaise presse: Une sociologie compréhensive du travail journalistique et de ses critiques* (Paris: Métailié, 2000).
47. On how U.S. journalists have used social media and online technology to increase the transparency of news production, see Jane B. Singer, "The Political J-Blogger: Normalizing a New Media Form to Fit Old Norms and Practices," *Journalism* 6, no. 2 (2005): 173–98; and Dominic L. Lasorsa, Seth C. Lewis, and Avery E. Holton, "Normalizing Twitter: Journalism Practice in an Emerging Communication Space," *Journalism Studies* 13, no. 1 (2011): 19–36. On how French journalists have done this, see Éric Dagiral and Sylvain Parasie, "Vidéo à la une! L'innovation dans les formats de la presse en ligne," *Réseaux* 2 (2010): 101–32.
48. On the struggle against informational rents in the open-source movement, see Ursula Holtgrewe and Raymund Werle, "De-commodifying Software? Open Source Software Between Business Strategy and Social Movement," *Science Studies* 14, no. 2 (2001): 43–65; Nicolas Auray, "Pirates en réseau: Détournement, prédation et exigence de justice," *Esprit* 7 (2009): 168–79.
49. In their study on the publication of data and algorithms, Nicholas Diakopoulos and Michael Koliska found that American media professionals view it mostly as an ethical obligation. See their article "Algorithmic Transparency in the News Media," *Digital Journalism* 5, no. 7 (2017): 809–28.
50. Boyer, interview.
51. Daniel X. O'Neil, interview by the author, Chicago, September 8, 2010.
52. Tasneem Raja, interview by the author, San Francisco, September 13, 2012.
53. Mallary J. Tenore, "*Texas Tribune* Databases Drive Majority of Site's Traffic, Help Citizens Make Sense of Government Data," Poynter, March 2, 2011, https://www.poynter.org/2011/texas-tribune-databases-drive-majority-of-sites-traffic-help-citizens-make-sense-of-government-data/121281/.
54. In 2011, *Libération* published an online map of toxic loans contracted by French cities (http://so.libe.com/fremen/maps/carte-emprunts-toxiques/).
55. See David J. Goodman, "Outcry Over Newspaper's Map of Handgun Permit Holders," *City Room* (*New York Times* blog), December 26, 2012, https://cityroom.blogs.nytimes.com/2012/12/26/a-newspaper-publishes-names-of-gun-permit-holders-sparking-outrage/.
56. Jeff Sonderman, "Programmers Explain How to Turn Data Into Journalism and Why That Matters," Poynter, January 10, 2013, emphasis in original, http://www.poynter.org/2013/programmers-explain-how-to-turn-data-into-journalism-why-that-matters-after-gun-permit-data-publishing/199834/.
57. Steve Doig, quoted in Samantha Sunne, "The Challenges and Possible Pitfalls of Data Journalism, and How You Can Avoid Them," American Press Institute, March 9, 2016,

5. THE TENSIONS FACING DATA JOURNALISM

https://www.americanpressinstitute.org/publications/reports/strategy-studies/challenges-data-journalism/.

58. Matt Waite, quoted in Sonderman, "Programmers Explain How to Turn Data Into Journalism."
59. See Tracy Powell, "Mug-Shot Websites Move Beyond Journalism to Mainstream Profiteers," Poynter, September 12, 2012, https://www.poynter.org/reporting-editing/2012/mug-shot-websites-move-beyond-journalism-to-mainstream-profiteers/.
60. Albert O. Hirschman analyzed the risks that exit strategies present for organizations in his book *Exit, Voice, and Loyalty: Responses to Decline in Forms, Organizations, and States* (Cambridge, MA: Harvard University Press, 1970).
61. O'Neil, interview.
62. Boyer, interview.
63. Michael Schudson, *The Good Citizen: A History of American Civic Life* (New York: Free Press, 1998), 310–12. See also Daniel Kreiss, "Beyond Administrative Journalism: Civic Skepticism and the Crisis in Journalism," in *The Crisis of Journalism Reconsidered: Democratic Culture, Professional Codes, Digital Future,* ed. Jeffrey C. Alexander, Elizabeth Butler Breese, and María Luengo (Cambridge: Cambridge University Press, 2016), 59–76.

6. THE MAKING OF A REVELATION

This chapter is a revised version of Sylvain Parasie, "Data-Driven Revelation? Epistemological Tensions in Investigative Journalism in the Age of 'Big Data,'" *Digital Journalism* 3, no. 3 (2015): 364–80. The fieldwork was done in collaboration with Éric Dagiral.

1. Robert J. Rosenthal, "Reinventing Journalism: An Unexpected Personal Journey from Journalist to Publisher," California Watch, October 4, 2011, https://knightfoundation.org/wp-content/uploads/2011/10/CIR_IndustryReport_FINAL.pdf.
2. Investigative Reporters and Editors, "2011 IRE Award Winners," 2011, https://www.ire.org/archives/29421.
3. Rosenthal, "Reinventing Journalism."
4. For example, Herbert J. Gans, *Deciding What's News: A Study of* CBS Evening News, NBC Nightly News, Newsweek, *and* Time, 25th anniversary ed., with a new preface by the author (Evanston, IL: Northwestern University Press, 2004), originally published in 1979.
5. For example, Pablo J. Boczkowski, *News at Work: Imitation in an Age of Information Abundance* (Chicago: University of Chicago Press, 2010); Chris A. Paterson and David Domingo, eds., *Making Online News: The Ethnography of New Media Production* (Bern, Switzerland: Peter Lang, 2008); and Angèle Christin, *Metrics at Work: Journalism and the Contested Meaning of Algorithms* (Princeton, NJ: Princeton University Press, 2020).

6. THE MAKING OF A REVELATION

6. Bruno Latour and Steve Woolgar, *Laboratory Life: The Construction of Scientific Facts* (Princeton, NJ: Princeton University Press, 2013).
7. Corey Johnson, Skype interview by the author, August 31, 2012; all quotations from Corey Johnson in this chapter come from this interview.
8. On how American investigative reporters assess the value of a tip, see James S. Ettema and Theodore L. Glasser, "On the Epistemology of Investigative Journalism," in *Journalism: The Democratic Craft*, ed. G. Stuart Adam and Roy Peter Clark (New York: Oxford University Press), 126–40.
9. A description of California Watch's original business model is given in Jim Barnett, "California Watch's Revenue Model: Charge News Outlets, Target Donors," Nieman Lab, November 17, 2009, https://www.niemanlab.org/2009/11/california-watchs-revenue-model-charge-news-outlets-target-donors/.
10. James S. Ettema and Theodore L. Glasser, *Custodians of Conscience: Investigative Journalism and Public Virtue* (New York: Columbia University Press, 1998).
11. Agustin Armendariz, interview by the author, Berkeley, CA, September 12, 2012; all quotes from Agustin Armendariz in this chapter come from this interview.
12. Harold Garfinkel, *Studies in Ethnomethodology* (Englewood Cliffs, NJ : Prentice-Hall 1967), 186–207.
13. The literature on "data science" practitioners includes many warnings against objectivist attitudes. See, for instance, Cathy O'Neil and Rachel Schutt, *Doing Data Science: Straight Talk from the Frontline* (Sebastopol, CA: O'Reilly, 2013), 41–46.
14. Lucy Suchman, "Supporting Articulation Work," in *Computerization and Controversy: Value Conflicts and Social Choices*, 2nd ed., ed. Rob Kling (San Diego: Academic Press, 1996), 407–23. The original concept of "articulation work" comes from Anselm Strauss, "The Articulation of Project Work: An Organizational Process," *Sociological Quarterly* 29, no. 2 (1988): 163–78.
15. Kendall Taggart, interview by the author, San Francisco, September 6, 2012; all quotations from Kendall Taggart in this chapter come from this interview.
16. See Ettema and Glasser, *Custodians of Conscience*, 139–43.
17. Data exploratory analysis was founded by John W. Tukey and explained in his article "The Future of Data Analysis," *Annals of Mathematical Statistics* 33, no. 1 (1962): 1–67. See also Éric Dagiral and Sylvain Parasie, "La science des données à la conquête des mondes sociaux: Ce que le Big Data doit aux épistémologies locales," in *Big Data, entreprises et sciences sociales*, ed. Pierre-Michel Menger and Simon Paye (Paris: Editions du Collège de France, 2017), 85–104.
18. Ettema and Glasser, *Custodians of Conscience*, 131–53.
19. Madeleine Akrich, "The Description of Technical Objects," in *Shaping Technology, Building Society: Studies in Sociotechnical Change*, ed. Wiebe Bijker and John Law (Cambridge, MA: MIT Press, 1992), 205–23.
20. Ken Doctor, "The Newsonomics of a Single Investigative Story," Nieman Lab, April 21, 2011, http://www.niemanlab.org/2011/04/the-newsonomics-of-a-single-investigative-story/.

7. HOW NOT TO GET ACADEMIC

1. Meyer published his first academic paper in *Public Opinion Quarterly* in 1969.
2. See Elihu Katz, "Journalists as Scientists: Notes Toward an Occupational Classification," *American Behavioral Scientist* 33, no. 2 (1989): 238–46; and James T. Hamilton and Fred Turner, "Accountability Through Algorithm: Developing the Field of Computational Journalism," Report from the Center for Advanced Study in the Behavioral Sciences, Summer Workshop, Stanford University, 2009.
3. Christopher W. Anderson, *Apostles of Certainty: Data Journalism and the Politics of Doubt* (Oxford: Oxford University Press, 2018); Denis Ruellan, *Les "pro" du journalisme: De l'état au statut, la construction d'un espace professionnel* (Rennes, France: Presses universitaires de Rennes, 1997).
4. Anderson, *Apostles of Certainty*, 50.
5. Cyril Lemieux, *Mauvaise presse: Une sociologie compréhensive du travail journalistique et de ses critiques* (Paris: Métailié, 2000).
6. In 2017, *Paris Match* sold approximately 570,000 copies each week. Although predominantly female, its audience is representative of all the categories that make up French society. On the type of stories it carries, see , ed. Christian Delporte, Claire Blandin, and François Robinet, *Histoire de la presse en France: XXe–XXIe siècles* (Paris: Armand Colin, 2016), 211–27.
7. On several occasions since the 1980s, the magazine has been accused of violating professional ethics by publishing stolen photographs, covering news stories in a sensationalist way, and complacently portraying government officials. For an analysis of these criticisms in the French context, see Lemieux, *Mauvaise presse*, 322–66.
8. Adrien Gaboulaud, interview by the author, Paris, June 8, 2020; all quotations from Adrien Gaboulaud in this chapter come from this interview.
9. Anne-Sophie Lechevallier, interview by the author, Paris, June 9, 2020; all quotations from Anne-Sophie Lechevallier in this chapter come from this interview.
10. Mike Bostock, Shan Carter, and Matthew Ericson, "At the National Conventions, the Words They Used: A Comparison of How Often Speakers at the Two Presidential Nominating Conventions Used Different Words and Phrases, Based on an Analysis of Transcripts from the Federal News Service," *New York Times*, September 6, 2012, https://archive.nytimes.com/www.nytimes.com/interactive/2012/09/06/us/politics/convention-word-counts.html?_r=0.
11. Since the early 2000s, the social sciences have taken on greater importance in the training of French journalists (Ivan Chupin, "Sciences sociales et formations en journalisme: Émergence d'un nouvel enjeu de distinction," *Questions de communication* 16 [2009]: 45–70). It is estimated that about 60 percent of French journalists have received social science training (Christine Leteinturier, "La formation des journalistes français: Quelles évolutions? Quels atouts à l'embauche? Le cas des nouveaux titulaires de la carte de presse 2008," *Les cahiers du journalisme* 21 [2010]: 110–34).

7. HOW NOT TO GET ACADEMIC

12. As Cyril Lemieux's research has shown, the ethics of journalism require journalists to fully engage with their respondents when they are in a private context. By following the rules of a "natural grammar," journalists are more likely to gather secret information that can then be revealed to the public (Lemieux, *Mauvaise presse*, 125–82).
13. Damon Mayaffre, phone interview by the author, June 17, 2020; all quotations from Damon Mayaffre in this chapter come from this interview.
14. See Vincent Goulet and Philippe Ponet, "Journalists and Sociologists: Reviewing the Battles Over Ways of 'Giving an Account of Society,'" *Questions de communication* 16 (2009): 2–15.
15. After doing their research, the journalists opted for a service offered by a British start-up that used machine-learning algorithms trained on European Parliament speeches.
16. In the 1990s, Pierre Bourdieu pointed out the growing importance of the media in the evaluation of scientists in France since the 1980s. See his book *On Television*, trans. Priscilla Parkhurst Ferguson (New York: New Press, 1998), 54–64.
17. One could argue, however, that these practices have existed for quite a long time, citing several sociologists to whom journalists have provided data. See, for example, Luc Boltanski's study on public denunciation, *Love and Justice as Competences: Three Essays on the Sociology of Action* (Cambridge: Polity, 2012), which was based on a corpus of letters collected by a journalist from *Le Monde*.
18. See Herbert J. Gans, *Deciding What's News: A Study of* CBS Evening News, NBC Nightly News, Newsweek, *and* Time, 25th anniversary ed., with a new preface by the author (Evanston, IL: Northwestern University Press, 2004); Lemieux, *Mauvaise presse*.
19. The reference used by the journalists was the volume of speeches delivered by one of the candidates, François Fillon, who, because he was personally affected by a political scandal, reacted by speaking much less than the others.
20. For a discussion on quantitative textual-analysis methods in political science, see Justin Grimmer and Brandon M. Stewart. "Text as Data: The Promise and Pitfalls of Automatic Content Analysis Methods for Political Texts," *Political Analysis* 21, no.3 (2013): 267–97.
21. As noted in Adrien Gaboulaud et al., "Qu'est-ce que 'Le poids des mots'?," *Paris Match*, January 1, 2019, https://www.parismatch.com/Le-Poids-des-Mots.
22. Steven Lebolloch, Zoom interview by the author, July 8, 2020.
23. See Pablo J. Boczkowski, *News at Work: Imitation in an Age of Information Abundance* (Chicago: University of Chicago Press, 2010).
24. See Tony Harcup and Deirdre O'Neill, "What Is News? News Values Revisited (Again)," *Journalism Studies* 23, no. 1 (2016): 1–19. Barbie Zelizer has also analyzed the many understandings of temporality in news media, pointing out that immediacy is not always the dominant consideration. See her article "Epilogue: Timing the Study of News Temporality," *Journalism* 19, no. 1 (2018): 111–21.
25. My analysis is consistent with the framework recently articulated by Mike Ananny and Megan Finn, who argue that to understand news rhythms, scholars must consider the

7. HOW NOT TO GET ACADEMIC

"materials, practices, and values of hybrid, time-setting sociotechnical systems" ("Anticipatory News Infrastructures: Seeing Journalism's Expectations of Future Publics in Its Sociotechnical Systems," *New Media & Society* 22, no. 9 [2020]: 1600).

26. Eric Hacquemand, "Mélenchon: Adieu 'camarades,' bonjour 'les gens'!," *Paris Match*, April 4, 2017, https://www.parismatch.com/Actu/Politique/Melenchon-adieu-camarades-bonjour-les-gens-1226144.

27. Adrien Gaboulaud, "Qui est ce candidat qui utilise régulièrement le verbe 'emmerder'?," *Paris Match*, April 16, 2017, https://www.parismatch.com/Actu/Politique/Qui-est-ce-candidat-qui-utilise-regulierement-le-verbe-emmerder-1234163.

28. Adrien Gaboulaud and Anne-Sophie Lechevallier, with Nicolas Certes, Marine Jeannin, and Caroline Petit, "Exclusif: Les mots du débat le plus dur de la Ve République," *Paris Match*, May 5, 2017, https://www.parismatch.com/Actu/Politique/Exclusif-Les-mots-du-debat-le-plus-dur-de-la-Ve-Republique-1249400.

29. Nicolas Certes and Marine Jeannin, "Les deux premiers discours du président Macron analyses," *Paris Match*, May 8, 2017, https://www.parismatch.com/Actu/Politique/Les-deux-premiers-discours-du-president-Macron-analyses-1250927.

30. Lebolloch, interview.

8. THE ART OF BRINGING ABOUT PUBLICS

This chapter is a revised version of Jean-Philippe Cointet and Sylvain Parasie, "Comment se forment les publics d'une carte de crimes? Une analyse computationnelle de traces textuelles," *Réseaux* 2 (2019): 209–50. The analysis was conducted in close collaboration with Jean-Philippe Cointet.

1. In 2019, the homicide rate in the United States was 5 per 100,000 people (U.S. Department of Justice, FBI, "2019 Crime in the United States," Fall 2020, https://ucr.fbi.gov/crime-in-the-u.s/2019/crime-in-the-u.s.-2019/topic-pages/murder), compared to 1.26 per 100,000 in France (Ministère de l'Intérieur, "Insécurité et délinquance en 2019: Bilan statistique," September 2020, https://www.interieur.gouv.fr/Interstats/Themes/Homicides/Insecurite-et-delinquance-en-2018-premier-bilan-statistique-Fiche-Homicides2).

2. See Bob Roshier, "The Selection of Crime News by the Press," in *The Manufacture of News: Deviance, Social Problems, and the Mass Media*, ed. Stanley Cohen and Jock Young (Beverly Hills, CA: Sage, 1973), 28–39; and Jack Katz, "What Makes Crime 'News'?," *Media, Culture, and Society* 9 (1987): 47–75.

3. See Wesley Lowery, "A Reckoning Over Objectivity, Led by Black Journalists," *New York Times*, June 23, 2020, https://www.nytimes.com/2020/06/23/opinion/objectivity-black-journalists-coronavirus.html. See also Candis Callison and Mary Lynn Young, *Reckoning: Journalism's Limits and Possibilities* (Oxford: Oxford University Press, 2020).

4. See Sara Morrison, "For 7 Years, *L.A. Times*' Homicide Report Has Wrested Stories from Grim Data," Poynter, February 20, 2014, https://www.poynter.org/reporting-editing/2014/since-2007-l-a-times-homicide-report-has-wrested-stories-from-data/.

8. THE ART OF BRINGING ABOUT PUBLICS

5. Alastair Reid, "How Homicide Report Tells the 'True Story' of LA's Violent Crime," Journalism.co.uk, January 28, 2014, https://www.journalism.co.uk/news/how-the-homicide-report-tells-the-true-story-of-la-s-violent-crime/s2/a555713/.
6. Both movements saw reducing the gatekeeping power of journalists as a way to strengthen journalism's contribution to democracy. See Patrick Ferrucci, Jacob L. Nelson, and Miles P. Davis, "From 'Public Journalism' to 'Engaged Journalism': Imagined Audiences and Denigrating Discourse," *International Journal of Communication* 14 (2020): 1586–604.
7. Cass R. Sunstein, *#Republic: Divided Democracy in the Age of Social Media* (Princeton, NJ: Princeton University Press, 2018).
8. Gabriel Tarde was the first sociologist to highlight this phenomenon in 1901, which was more fully evidenced later by research on agenda setting. See Maxwell McCombs, *Setting the Agenda: The Mass Media and Public Opinion* (Cambridge: Polity, 2004).
9. John Dewey, *The Public and Its Problems: An Essay in Political Inquiry* (1927; reprint, Chicago: Gateway Books, 1946), 179–80. To understand how U.S. journalism evolved in response to what was perceived as a "crisis of facts," see Michael Schudson, *Discovering the News: A Social History of American Newspapers* (1978; reprint, New York: Basic, 1981), 134–59.
10. Francisque Sarcey, journalist at *Le Temps*, quoted in Bernard Voyenne, *Les journalistes français* (Paris: CFPJ-Retz, 1985), 151. To understand how French journalists evolved in response to this challenge, see Cyril Lemieux, *Mauvaise presse: Une sociologie compréhensive du travail journalistique et de ses critiques* (Paris: Métailié, 2000), 38–54.
11. Mary Lynn Young and Alfred Hermida, "From Mr. and Mrs. Outlier to Central Tendencies: Computational Journalism and Crime Reporting at the *Los Angeles Times*," *Digital Journalism* 3, no. 3 (2015): 381–97. ·
12. Megan Garvey, quoted in Reid, "How Homicide Report Tells the 'True Story' of LA's Violent Crime."
13. See Roshier, "The Selection of Crime News by the Press"; and Katz, "What Makes Crime 'News'?"
14. For all homicides listed in the Homicide Report database for these two years, Jean-Philippe Cointet and I manually checked how many had resulted in a story in the print edition.
15. Young and Hermida, "From Mr. and Mrs. Outlier to Central Tendencies."
16. Ben Welsh, quoted in Young and Hermida, "From Mr. and Mrs. Outlier to Central Tendencies."
17. Jill Leovy, quoted in Kevin Roderick, "L.A. Gets a Homicide Blog," *LA Observed*, February 5, 2007, http://www.laobserved.com/archive/2007/02/la_gets_a_homicide_blog.php.
18. Jill Leovy, quoted in Kevin Roderick, "Homicide Report Gets New Life at the *LA Times*," *LA Observed*, March 18, 2013, http://www.laobserved.com/archive/2013/03/homicide_report_gets_new.php.
19. Ken Schwencke, quoted in Reid, "How Homicide Report Tells the 'True Story' of LA's Violent Crime."

8. THE ART OF BRINGING ABOUT PUBLICS

20. See Luc Boltanski, *Love and Justice as Competences: Three Essays on the Sociology of Action* (Cambridge: Polity, 2012).
21. See Stuart Hall, "Encoding/Decoding," in *The Cultural Studies Reader*, ed. Simon During (New York: Routledge, 1999), 507–17; and David G. Morley, *The Nationwide Audience: Structure and Decoding* (London: British Film Institute, 1980).
22. David Lazer et al., "Computational Social Science," *Science* 323, no. 5915 (2009): 721–22; Noortje Marres, *Digital Sociology: The Reinvention of Social Research* (Cambridge: Polity, 2017).
23. Justin Grimmer and Brandon M. Stewart, "Text as Data: The Promise and Pitfalls of Automatic Content Analysis Methods for Political Texts," *Political Analysis* 21, no. 3 (2013): 267–97; Jean-Philippe Cointet and Sylvain Parasie, "What Big Data Does to the Sociological Analysis of Texts: A Review of Recent Research," *Revue francaise de sociologie* 59, no. 3 (2018): 533–57; James A. Evans and Pedro Aceves, "Machine Translation: Mining Text for Social Theory," *Annual Review of Sociology* 42 (2016): 21–50.
24. Jean-Philippe Cointet, the computational social scientist with whom I conducted this study, developed the web-mining algorithms that we used.
25. Over the past decade, a fair amount of research in communication and computer science has studied user comments in journalism. However, automatic tools, in particular machine-learning techniques, have rarely been used to capture the way people interpret events. For an overview of these studies, see Julius Reimer et al., "Content Analyses of User Comments in Journalism: A Systematic Literature Review Spanning Communication Studies and Computer Science," *Digital Journalism*, online only, 2021, 1–25, doi:10.1080/21670811.2021.1882868.
26. See Lada A. Adamic and Bernardo Huberman, "Power–Law Distribution of the World Wide Web," *Science* 287, no. 5461 (2000): 2115.
27. See Boltanski, *Love and Justice as Competences*.
28. Looking at a three-year period, Jean-Philippe Cointet and I performed two statistical regressions to identify under which conditions a homicide got covered in the print edition of the *Los Angeles Times* and under which conditions it received a high number of comments on Homicide Report (see appendix 2 at the end of the chapter).
29. Roshier, "The Selection of Crime News by the Press"; Katz, "What Makes Crime 'News'?"
30. Online forums almost always include a minority of highly involved users. See Todd Graham and Scott Wright, "Discursive Equality and Everyday Talk Online: The Impact of 'Superparticipants,'" *Journal of Computer-Mediated Communication* 19, no. 3 (2014): 625–42.
31. See Joëlle Zask, "Le public chez Dewey: Une union sociale plurielle," *Tracés* 15 (2008): 169–89.
32. This approach aligns with the sociological tradition that emphasizes the ability of social movements to build "cognitive frames," which offer coherent ways of making sense of occurrences. See Robert D. Benford and David A. Snow, "Framing Processes and Social Movements: An Overview and Assessment," *Annual Review of Sociology* 26, no. 1

CONCLUSION: AN ETHICS OF REFLEXIVITY

(2000): 611–39; and Dietram A. Scheufele, "Framing as a Theory of Media Effects," *Journal of Communication* 49, no. 1 (1999): 103–22. This is especially applicable to the internet and social media platforms. See W. Lance Bennett and Alexandra Segerberg, *The Logic of Connective Action: Digital Media and the Personalization of Contentious Politics* (Cambridge: Cambridge University Press, 2013); and Merlyna Lim, "Clicks, Cabs, and Coffee Houses: Social Media and Oppositional Movements in Egypt, 2004–2011," *Journal of Communication* 62, no. 2 (2012): 231–48.

33. Although there is no evidence on this, we can posit that members of this "loving relatives" public use some of the interactive possibilities offered by the platform, such as name searches and map browsing. The driving force behind this public's contribution to the platform is indeed the close relationship between comment authors and victims.

34. As suggested by ethnographic research conducted in central Los Angeles neighborhoods, these interpretations may be built on a set of shared norms within Black communities. See João H. Costa Vargas, *Catching Hell in the City of Angels: Life and Meanings of Blackness in South Central Los Angeles* (Minneapolis: University of Minnesota Press, 2006).

35. On the role of anonymity in online forums, see Sylvain Parasie, Jean-Philippe Cointet, and Michael O'Mahony, "Online Press Serving Local Democracy," *Revue française de science politique* 62, no. 1 (2012): 45–70.

36. Ken Schwencke, quoted in Reid, "How Homicide Report Tells the 'True Story' of LA's Violent Crime."

37. Ken Schwencke, comment posted on Homicide Report, May 3, 2010, https://homicide.latimes.com/post/trevon-coats/.

38. Megan Garvey, comment posted on Homicide Report, May 27, 2010, https://homicide.latimes.com/post/savoy-ewell/#c29327.

39. The article is cited in Reid, "How Homicide Report Tells the 'True Story' of LA's Violent Crime."

CONCLUSION: AN ETHICS OF REFLEXIVITY

1. See Oscar Westlund and Alfred Hermida, "Data Journalism and Misinformation," in *The Routledge Companion to Media Misinformation and Populism*, ed. Howard Tumber and Silvio Waisbord (London: Routledge, 2021), 142–50.

2. William R. Chase, "Why I'm Not Making COVID19 Visualizations, and Why You (Probably) Shouldn't Either," *William R. Chase* (blog), March 31, 2020, https://www.williamrchase.com/post/why-i-m-not-making-covid19-visualizations-and-why-you-probably-shouldn-t-either/.

3. The research here echoes that of Jonathan Stray, who notes that the use of artificial intelligence remains rather limited in journalism despite the enthusiastic rhetoric around it. See Stray, "Making Artificial Intelligence Work for Investigative Journalism," *Digital Journalism* 7, no. 8 (2019): 1076–97.

4. Nicholas Diakopoulos similarly argues that journalists should embrace algorithmic transparency as an ethical principle. See Diakopoulos, *Automating the News: How Algorithms Are Rewriting the Media* (Cambridge, MA: Harvard University Press, 2019), 234–39.
5. This concept was forged by Peter Galison in his article "Computer Simulations and the Trading Zone," in *From Science to Computational Science: Studies in the History of Computing and Its Influence on Today's Sciences*, ed. Gabriele Gramelsberger (Zürich: Diaphanes, 2011), 118–57.

BIBLIOGRAPHY

Abbott, Andrew. *The System of Professions: An Essay on the Division of Expert Labor*. Chicago: University of Chicago Press, 2014.
Adamic, Lada A., and Bernardo Huberman. "Power–Law Distribution of the World Wide Web." *Science* 287, no. 5461 (2000): 2115.
Aitamurto, Tanja. "Crowdsourcing as a Knowledge-Search Method in Digital Journalism." *Digital Journalism* 4, no. 2 (2015): 280–97.
Akrich, Madeleine. "The Description of Technical Objects." In *Shaping Technology, Building Society: Studies in Sociotechnical Change*, ed. Wiebe Bijker and John Law, 205–23. Cambridge, MA: MIT Press, 1992.
Aldridge, Alan. "The Construction of Rational Consumption in *Which?* Magazine: The More Blobs the Better?" *Sociology* 28, no. 4 (1994): 899–912.
Alfter, Brigitte. *Cross-Border Collaborative Journalism: A Step-by-Step Guide*. New York: Routledge, 2019.
Ananny, Mike, and Kate Crawford. "A Liminal Press: Situating News App Designers Within a Field of Networked News Production." *Digital Journalism* 3, no. 2 (2015): 192–208.
Ananny, Mike, and Megan Finn. "Anticipatory News Infrastructures: Seeing Journalism's Expectations of Future Publics in Its Sociotechnical Systems." *New Media & Society* 22, no. 9 (2020): 1600–618.
Anderson, Christopher W. *Apostles of Certainty: Data Journalism and the Politics of Doubt*. Oxford: Oxford University Press, 2018.
———. *Rebuilding the News: Metropolitan Journalism in the Digital Age*. Philadelphia, PA: Temple University Press, 2013.

BIBLIOGRAPHY

Appelgren, Ester. "An Illusion of Interactivity: The Paternalistic Side of Data Journalism." *Journalism Practice* 12, no. 3 (2018): 308–25.

Aspray, William. "One Hundred Years of Car Buying." In *Everyday Information: The Evolution of Information Seeking in America*, ed. William Aspray and Barbara M. Hayes, 9–70. Cambridge, MA: MIT Press, 2011.

Aucoin, James. *The Evolution of American Investigative Journalism.* Columbia: University of Missouri Press, 2007.

Auray, Nicolas. "De l'éthique à la politique: L'institution d'une cité libre." *Multitudes* 1 (2002): 171–80.

———. "Pirates en réseau: Détournement, prédation et exigence de justice." *Esprit* 7 (2009): 168–79.

Auray, Nicolas, and Michaël Vicente. "Free Software and the Double Life of Computing Professionals: Some Biographical Insights in the Life Courses of Some Elder Developers." Working paper, 2006. http://ses-perso.telecom-paristech.fr/auray/AurayVicente.pdf.

Baack, Stefan. "Practically Engaged: The Entanglements Between Data Journalism and Civic Tech." *Digital Journalism* 6, no. 6 (2018): 673–92.

Ball, Terence. "American Political Science in Its Postwar Political Context." In *Discipline and History: Political Science in the United States*, ed. James Farr and Raymond Seidelman, 207–21. Ann Arbor: University of Michigan Press, 1993.

Ballarini, Loïc. "Le rôle des 'palmarès des hôpitaux' dans le débat sur la qualité des soins." *Revue d'études politiques des assistants parlementaires*, no. 4 (2009): 26–27.

Ballion, Robert. *La bonne école: Évaluation et choix du collège et du lycée.* Paris: Hatier, 1991.

Barnhurst, Kevin G. "The Interpretive Turn in News." In *Journalism and Technological Change: Historical Perspectives, Contemporary Trends*, ed. Martin Schreiber and Clemens Zimmermann, 111–41. Frankfort-am-Main, Germany: Campus-Verlag, 2014.

Barry, Andrew. *Political Machines: Governing a Technological Society.* New York: A&C Black, 2001.

Barthe, Yannick, Damien de Blic, Jean-Philippe Heurtin, Éric Lagneau, Cyril Lemieux, Dominique Linhardt, Cédric Moreau de Bellaing, Catherine Rémy, and Danny Trom. "Pragmatic Sociology: A User's Guide." *Politix* 3 (2013): 175–204.

Beiler, Markus, Felix Irmer, and Adrian Breda. "Data Journalism at German Newspapers and Public Broadcasters: A Quantitative Survey of Structures, Contents, and Perceptions." *Journalism Studies* 21, no. 11 (2020): 1571–89.

Béland, Daniel, and Jean-Philippe Viriot Durandal. "L'expertise comme pouvoir: Le cas des organisations de retraités face aux politiques publiques en France et aux États-Unis." *Lien social et politiques* 50 (2003): 105–23.

Benford, Robert D., and David A. Snow. "Framing Processes and Social Movements: An Overview and Assessment." *Annual Review of Sociology* 26, no. 1 (2000): 611–39.

Benkler, Yochai. *The Wealth of Networks: How Social Production Transforms Markets and Freedom.* New Haven, CN: Yale University Press, 2006.

BIBLIOGRAPHY

Bennett, W. Lance, and Alexandra Segerberg. *The Logic of Connective Action: Digital Media and the Personalization of Contentious Politics.* Cambridge: Cambridge University Press, 2013.

Benson, Rodney. *Shaping Immigration News: A French-American Comparison.* Cambridge: Cambridge University Press, 2013.

Berners-Lee, Tim, James Hendler, and Ora Lassila. "The Semantic Web." *Scientific American* 284, no. 5 (2001): 34–43.

Boczkowski, Pablo J. *Digitizing the News: Innovation in Online Newspapers.* Cambridge, MA: MIT Press, 2005.

———. *News at Work: Imitation in an Age of Information Abundance.* Chicago: University of Chicago Press, 2010.

Boltanski, Luc. *Love and Justice as Competences: Three Essays on the Sociology of Action.* Cambridge: Polity, 2012.

Boltanski, Luc, and Laurent Thévenot. *On Justification: Economies of Worth.* Princeton, NJ: Princeton University Press, 2006.

———. "The Sociology of Critical Capacity." *European Journal of Social Theory* 2, no. 3 (1999): 359–77.

Borges-Rey, Eddy. "Data Journalism in Latin America: Community, Development, and Contestation." In *Data Journalism in the Global South*, ed. Bruce Mutsvairo, Saba Bebawi, and Eddy Borges-Rey, 257–83. Cham, Switzerland: Palgrave Macmillan, 2019.

———. "Unravelling Data Journalism: A Study of Data Journalism Practice in British Newsrooms." *Journalism Practice* 10, no. 7 (2016): 833–43.

Bouchard, Julie. "La fabrique d'un classement médiatique de l'enseignement supérieur et de la recherche: Le cas du *Monde de l'éducation* (1976–1988)." *Quaderni* 77, no. 1 (2012): 25–40.

Bourdieu, Pierre. *On Television.* Trans. Priscilla Parkhurst Ferguson. New York: New Press, 1998.

Boustany, Joumana. "Accès et réutilisation des données publiques." *Les cahiers du numérique* 9, no. 1 (2013): 21–37.

Bovens, Mark, Thomas Schillemans, and Robert E. Goodin. "Public Accountability." In *The Oxford Handbook of Public Accountability*, ed. Mark Bovens, Robert E. Goodin, and Thomas Schillemans, 1–22. Oxford: Oxford University Press, 2014.

Bowker, Geoffrey C., and Susan Leigh Star. *Sorting Things Out: Classification and Its Consequences.* Cambridge, MA: MIT Press, 2000.

Bradsher, James G. "A Brief History of the Growth of Federal Government Records, Archives, and Information 1789–1985." *Government Publications Review* 13, no. 4 (1986): 491–505.

Broccolichi, Sylvain. "Orientations et ségrégations nouvelles dans l'enseignement secondaire." *Sociétés contemporaines* 21 (1995): 15–27.

Bruno, Isabelle, and Emmanuel Didier. *Benchmarking: L'état sous pression statistique.* Paris: Zones, 2015.

BIBLIOGRAPHY

Bruno, Isabelle, Emmanuel Didier, and Tommaso Vitale. "Statactivism: Forms of Action Between Disclosure and Affirmation." *Partecipazione e conflitto: The Open Journal of Sociopolitical Studies* 7, no. 2 (2014): 198–220.

Bucher, Rue, and Anselm Strauss. "Professions in Process." *American Journal of Sociology* 66, no. 4 (1961): 325–34.

Bucher, Taina. "'Machines Don't Have Instincts': Articulating the Computational in Journalism." *New Media & Society* 19, no. 6 (2017): 918–33.

Burnham, David. *A Law Unto Itself: Power, Politics, and the IRS*. 1989. Reprint. New York: Open Road Media, 2015.

———. *The Rise of the Computer State*. New York: Random House, 1983.

Callison, Candis, and Mary Lynn Young. *Reckoning: Journalism's Limits and Possibilities*. Oxford: Oxford University Press, 2020.

Callon, Michel. "Actor-Network Theory—the Market Test." *Sociological Review* 47, no. 1 (1999): 181–95.

———. "The Role of Hybrid Communities and Socio-technical Arrangements in the Participatory Design." *Journal of the Center for Information Studies* 5, no. 3 (2004): 3–10.

———. "The Sociology of an Actor-Network: The Case of the Electric Vehicle." In *Mapping the Dynamics of Science and Technology*, ed. Michel Callon, John Law, and Arie Rip, 19–34. London: Palgrave Macmillan, 1986.

Cardon, Dominique. "Inside the Mind of PageRank: A Study of Google's Algorithm." *Réseaux* 1, no. 177 (2013): 63–95.

Cardon, Dominique, and Fabien Granjon. *Médiactivistes*. Paris: Presses de Sciences Po, 2010.

Carlson, Matt. "News Algorithms, Photojournalism, and the Assumption of Mechanical Objectivity in Journalism." *Digital Journalism* 7, no. 8 (2019): 1117–33.

Chalaby, Jean K. "Journalism as an Anglo-American Invention: A Comparison of the Development of French and Anglo-American Journalism, 1830s–1920s." *European Journal of Communication* 11, no. 3 (1996): 303–26.

———. "Scandal and the Rise of Investigative Reporting in France." *American Behavioral Scientist* 47, no. 9 (2004): 1194–207.

Chance, Sandra F., and Christina Locke. "The Government-in-the-Sunshine Law Then and Now: A Model for Implementing New Technologies Consistent with Florida's Position as a Leader in Open Government." *Florida State University Law Review* 35 (2008): 245–70.

Chapman, Gary, and Angela Newell. "The Transformation of Public Information in the United States." In *Everyday Information: The Evolution of Information Seeking in America*, ed. William Aspray and Barbara M. Hayes, 249–76. Cambridge, MA: MIT Press, 2011.

Cheruiyot, David, Stefan Baack, and Raul Ferrer-Conill. "Data Journalism Beyond Legacy Media: The Case of African and European Civic Technology Organizations." *Digital Journalism* 7, no. 9 (2019): 1215–29.

Christians, Clifford. *Normative Theories of the Media: Journalism in Democratic Societies*. Urbana: University of Illinois Press, 2009.

Christin, Angèle. *Metrics at Work: Journalism and the Contested Meaning of Algorithms*. Princeton, NJ: Princeton University Press, 2020.

BIBLIOGRAPHY

Chupin, Ivan. "Sciences sociales et formations en journalisme: Émergence d'un nouvel enjeu de distinction." *Questions de communication* 16 (2009): 45–70.

Coddington, Mark. "Clarifying Journalism's Quantitative Turn: A Typology for Evaluating Data Journalism, Computational Journalism, and Computer-Assisted Reporting." *Digital Journalism* 3, no. 3 (2015): 331–48.

Cohen, Sarah, James T. Hamilton, and Fred Turner. "Computational Journalism." *Communications of the ACM* 54, no. 10 (2011): 66–71.

Cointet, Jean-Philippe, and Sylvain Parasie. "Comment se forment les publics d'une carte de crimes? Une analyse computationnelle de traces textuelles." *Réseaux* 2 (2019): 209–50.

———. "What Big Data Does to the Sociological Analysis of Texts: A Review of Recent Research." *Revue française de sociologie* 59, no. 3 (2018): 533–57.

Costa Vargas, João H. *Catching Hell in the City of Angels: Life and Meanings of Blackness in South Central Los Angeles*. Minneapolis: University of Minnesota Press, 2006.

Dagiral, Éric, and Sylvain Parasie. "Presse en ligne: Où en est la recherche?" *Réseaux* 2 (2010): 13–42.

———. "La science des données à la conquête des mondes sociaux: Ce que le Big Data doit aux épistémologies locales." In *Big Data, entreprises et sciences sociales*, ed. Pierre-Michel Menger and Simon Paye, 85–104. Paris: Editions du Collège de France, 2017.

———. "Vidéo à la une! L'innovation dans les formats de la presse en ligne." *Réseaux* 2 (2010): 101–32.

Daston, Lorraine. "The Moral Economy of Science." *Osiris* 10 (1995): 2–24.

Daston, Lorraine, and Peter Galison. *Objectivity*. New York: Zone, 2007.

DeFleur, Margaret H. *Computer-Assisted Investigative Reporting: Development and Methodology*. New York: Routledge, 2013.

Delporte, Christian, Claire Blandin, and François Robinet. *Histoire de la presse en France. XXe–XXIe siècles*. Paris: Armand Colin, 2016.

De Maeyer, Juliette, Manon Libert, David Domingo, François Heinderyckx, and Florence Le Cam. "Waiting for Data Journalism: A Qualitative Assessment of the Anecdotal Take-Up of Data Journalism in French-Speaking Belgium." *Digital Journalism* 3, no. 3 (2015): 432–66.

Demailly, Lise, Nicole Gadrey, Philippe Deubel, and Juliette Verdière. *Evaluer les établissements scolaires: Enjeux, expériences, débats*. Paris: L'Harmattan, 1998.

Denis, Jérôme, and Samuel Goëta. "Rawification and the Careful Generation of Open Government Data." *Social Studies of Science* 47, no. 5 (2017): 604–29.

Desrosières, Alain. *Pour une sociologie historique de la quantification: L'argument statistique I*. Paris: Presses des Mines, 2013.

Dewey, John. *The Public and Its Problems: An Essay in Political Inquiry*. 1927. Reprint. Chicago: Gateway Books, 1946.

Diakopoulos, Nicholas. *Automating the News: How Algorithms Are Rewriting the Media*. Cambridge, MA: Harvard University Press, 2019.

Diakopoulos, Nicholas, and Michael Koliska. "Algorithmic Transparency in the News Media." *Digital Journalism* 5, no. 7 (2017): 809–28.

BIBLIOGRAPHY

Dodier, Nicolas. *Les hommes et les machines: La conscience collective dans les sociétés technicisées.* Paris: Métailié, 1995.

Donzelot, Jacques, Catherine Mével, and Anne Wyvekens. *Faire société: La politique de la ville aux États-Unis et en France.* Paris: Le Seuil, 2003.

Espeland, Wendy Nelson, and Michael Sauder. "Rankings and Reactivity: How Public Measures Recreate Social Worlds." *American Journal of Sociology* 113, no. 1 (2007): 1–40.

Espeland, Wendy Nelson, and Mitchell L. Stevens. "A Sociology of Quantification." *European Journal of Sociology / Archives européennes de sociologie* 49, no. 3 (2008): 401–36.

Ettema, James S., and Theodore L. Glasser. *Custodians of Conscience: Investigative Journalism and Public Virtue.* New York: Columbia University Press, 1998.

———. "On the Epistemology of Investigative Journalism." In *Journalism: The Democratic Craft*, ed. G. Stuart Adam and Roy Peter Clark, 126–40. New York: Oxford University Press.

Evans, James A., and Pedro Aceves. "Machine Translation: Mining Text for Social Theory." *Annual Review of Sociology* 42 (2016): 21–50.

Ewell, Peter T. "The Evolution of Longitudinal Student Tracking Databases." *New Directions for Institutional Research* 87 (1995): 7–19.

Felouzis, Georges, and Joëlle Perroton. "Les 'marchés scolaires': Une analyse en termes d'économie de la qualité." *Revue française de sociologie* 48, no. 4 (2007): 693–722.

Ferrucci, Patrick, Jacob L. Nelson, and Miles P. Davis. "From 'Public Journalism' to 'Engaged Journalism': Imagined Audiences and Denigrating Discourse." *International Journal of Communication* 14 (2020): 1586–604.

Fieschi, Catherine, and John Gaffney. "French Think Tanks in Comparative Perspective." In *Think Tanks Across Nations: A Comparative Approach*, ed. Diane Stone, Andrew Denham, and Mark Garnett, 105–20. Manchester, U.K.: Manchester University Press, 1998.

Fink, Katherine, and Christopher W. Anderson. "Data Journalism in the United States: Beyond the 'Usual Suspects.'" *Journalism Studies* 16, no. 4 (2015): 467–81.

Fink, Katherine, and Michael Schudson. "The Rise of Contextual Journalism, 1950s–2000s." *Journalism* 15, no. 1 (2014): 3–20.

Flichy, Patrice. *The Internet Imaginaire.* Cambridge, MA: MIT Press, 2007.

Galison, Peter. "Computer Simulations and the Trading Zone." In *From Science to Computational Science: Studies in the History of Computing and Its Influence on Today's Sciences*, ed. Gabriele Gramelsberger, 118–57. Zürich: Diaphanes, 2011.

Gans, Herbert J. *Deciding What's News: A Study of CBS Evening News, NBC Nightly News, Newsweek, and Time.* 25th anniversary ed., with a new preface by the author. Evanston, IL: Northwestern University Press, 2004.

———. "What Can Journalists Actually Do for American Democracy?" *Harvard International Journal of Press/Politics* 3, no. 4 (1998): 6–12.

Garfinkel, Harold. *Studies in Ethnomethodology.* Englewood Cliffs, NJ: Prentice-Hall, 1967.

Garrison, Bruce. *Computer-Assisted Reporting.* Mahwah, NJ: Lawrence Erlbaum, 1995.

———. *Computer-Assisted Reporting.* 2nd ed. Mahwah, NJ: Lawrence Erlbaum, 1998.

———. "Newspaper Size as Factor in Use of Computers for Newsgathering." *Newspaper Research Journal* 20, no. 3 (1999): 72–85.

BIBLIOGRAPHY

Goëta, Samuel, and Clément Mabi. "L'open data peut-il (encore) servir les citoyens?" *Mouvements* 3 (2014): 81–91.

Goulet, Vincent, and Philippe Ponet. "Journalists and Sociologists: Reviewing the Battles Over Ways of 'Giving an Account of Society.'" *Questions de communication* 16 (2009): 2–15.

Graham, Todd, and Scott Wright. "Discursive Equality and Everyday Talk Online: The Impact of 'Superparticipants.'" *Journal of Computer-Mediated Communication* 19, no. 3 (2014): 625–42.

Graves, Lucas. *Deciding What's True: The Rise of Political Fact-Checking in American Journalism*. New York: Columbia University Press, 2016.

Graves, Lucas, Brendan Nyhan, and Jason Reifler. "Understanding Innovations in Journalistic Practice: A Field Experiment Examining Motivations for Fact-Checking." *Journal of Communication* 66, no. 1 (2016): 102–38.

Gray, Jonathan, Lucy Chambers, and Liliana Bounegru. *The Data Journalism Handbook: How Journalists Can Use Data to Improve the News*. Sebastopol, CA: O'Reilly, 2012.

Grimmer, Justin, and Brandon M. Stewart. "Text as Data: The Promise and Pitfalls of Automatic Content Analysis Methods for Political Texts." *Political Analysis* 21, no. 3 (2013): 267–97.

Gutiérrez, Miren. *Data Activism and Social Change*. London: Palgrave Macmillan, 2018.

Hall, Stuart. "Encoding/Decoding." In *The Cultural Studies Reader*, ed. Simon During, 507–17. New York: Routledge, 1999.

Hall, Stuart, Chas Critcher, Tony Jefferson, John Clarke, and Brian Roberts. *Policing the Crisis: Mugging, the State, and Law and Order*. London: Macmillan International Higher Education, 1978.

Hallin, Daniel. *We Keep America on Top of the World: Television Journalism and the Public Sphere*. London: Routledge, 2005.

Hamilton, James T. *Democracy's Detectives: The Economics of Investigative Journalism*. Cambridge, MA: Harvard University Press, 2017.

Hamilton, James T., and Fred Turner. "Accountability Through Algorithm: Developing the Field of Computational Journalism." Report from the Center for Advanced Study in the Behavioral Sciences, Summer Workshop, Stanford University, 2009.

Harcup, Tony, and Deirdre O'Neill. "What Is News? News Values Revisited (Again)." *Journalism Studies* 23, no. 1 (2016): 1–19.

Helberger, Natali. "On the Democratic Role of News Recommenders." *Digital Journalism* 7, no. 8 (2019): 993–1012.

Hermida, Alfred, and Mary Lynn Young. "Finding the Data Unicorn: A Hierarchy of Hybridity in Data and Computational Journalism." *Digital Journalism* 5, no. 2 (2017): 159–76.

Hindman, Elizabeth B., and Ryan J. Thomas. "When Old and New Media Collide: The Case of WikiLeaks." *New Media & Society* 16, no. 4 (2014): 541–58.

Hirschman, Albert O. *Exit, Voice, and Loyalty: Responses to Decline in Forms, Organizations, and States*. Cambridge, MA: Harvard University Press, 1970.

BIBLIOGRAPHY

Holtgrewe, Ursula, and Raymund Werle. "De-commodifying Software? Open Source Software Between Business Strategy and Social Movement." *Science Studies* 14, no. 2 (2001): 43–65.

Hood, Christopher. "From FOI World to Wikileaks World: A New Chapter in the Transparency Story?" *Governance* 24, no. 4 (2011): 635–38.

———. "The 'New Public Management' in the 1980s: Variations on a Theme." *Accounting, Organizations, and Society* 20, nos. 2–3 (1995): 93–109.

Houston, Brand. "Changes in Attitudes, Changes in Latitude." In *When Nerds and Words Collide: Reflections on the Development of Computer-Assisted Reporting*, ed. Nora Paul, 6–7. St. Petersburg, FL: Poynter Institute for Media Studies, 1999.

———. *Computer-Assisted Reporting: A Practical Guide*. New York: St. Martin's, 1996.

———. "A Summary of Problems Using Nine-Track Tapes." NICAR Tipsheet no. 136 (1993). https://www.ire.org/resources/.

Jaspin, Elliot, and Mark Sableman. "News Media Access to Computer Records: Updating Information Laws in the Electronic Age." *Saint Louis University Law Journal* 36, no. 2 (1992): 349–408.

Jobbins, David. "The *Times* / the *Times Higher Education Supplement*—League Tables in Britain: An Insider's View." *Higher Education in Europe* 27, no. 4 (2002): 383–88.

Katz, Elihu. "Journalists as Scientists: Notes Toward an Occupational Classification." *American Behavioral Scientist* 33, no. 2 (1989): 238–46.

Katz, Jack. "What Makes Crime 'News'?" *Media, Culture, and Society* 9 (1987): 47–75.

Kinzie, Jillian, Megan Palmer, John Hayek, Don Hossler, Stacy A. Jacob, and Heather Cummings. *Fifty Years of College Choice: Social, Political, and Institutional Influences on the Decision-Making Process*. Indianapolis, IN: Lumina Foundation for Education, 2004.

Klinenberg, Eric. *Fighting for Air: The Battle to Control America's Media*. New York: Metropolitan Books, 2007.

Knight, Megan. "Data Journalism in the UK: A Preliminary Analysis of Form and Content." *Journal of Media Practice* 16, no. 1 (2015): 55–72.

Knorr Cetina, Karin. *Epistemic Cultures: How the Sciences Make Knowledge*. Cambridge, MA: Harvard University Press, 1999.

Kreiss, Daniel. "Beyond Administrative Journalism: Civic Skepticism and the Crisis in Journalism." In *The Crisis of Journalism Reconsidered: Democratic Culture, Professional Codes, Digital Future*, ed. Jeffrey C. Alexander, Elizabeth Butler Breese, and María Luengo, 59–76. Cambridge: Cambridge University Press, 2016.

Lamont, Michèle, and Laurent Thévenot, eds. *Rethinking Comparative Cultural Sociology: Repertoires of Evaluation in France and the United States*. Cambridge: Cambridge University Press, 2000.

Landau, George. "Objects in Mirror Are Closer Than They Appear." In *When Nerds and Words Collide: Reflections on the Development of Computer Assisted Reporting*, ed. Nora Paul, 28–30. St. Petersburg, FL: Poynter Institute of Media Studies, 1999.

Lasorsa, Dominic L., Seth C. Lewis, and Avery E. Holton. "Normalizing Twitter: Journalism Practice in an Emerging Communication Space." *Journalism Studies* 13, no. 1 (2011): 19–36.

BIBLIOGRAPHY

Lathrop, Daniel, and Laurel Ruma. *Open Government: Collaboration, Transparency, and Participation in Practice.* Sebastopol, CA: O'Reilly, 2010.

Latour, Bruno. *We Have Never Been Modern.* Trans. Catherine Porter. 1993. Reprint. Cambridge, MA: Harvard University Press, 2012.

Latour, Bruno, and Steve Woolgar. *Laboratory Life: The Construction of Scientific Facts.* Princeton, NJ: Princeton University Press, 2013.

Laveissière, Jean. "L'accès aux documents administratifs." In *Information et transparence administratives*, ed. François Rangeon, Jean Laveissière, and Philippe Belin, 11–35. Paris: Presses universitaires de France, 1988.

Lazer David, Alex S. Pentland, Lada Adamic, and Sinan Aral. "Computational Social Science." *Science* 323, no. 5915 (2009): 721–22.

Lemieux, Cyril. "À quoi sert l'analyse des controverses?" *Mil neuf cent* 25, no. 1 (2007): 191–212.

———. "Les formats de l'égalitarisme: Transformations et limites de la figure du journalisme-justicier dans la France contemporaine." *Quaderni* 45, no. 1 (2001): 53–68.

———. *Mauvaise presse: Une sociologie compréhensive du travail journalistique et de ses critiques.* Paris: Métailié, 2000.

Lemieux, Cyril, and John Schmalzbauer, "Involvement and Detachment Among French and American Journalists: To Be or Not to Be a 'Real' Professional." In *Rethinking Comparative Cultural Sociology: Repertoires of Evaluation in France and the United States*, ed. Michèle Lamont and Laurent Thévenot, 148–69. Cambridge: Cambridge University Press, 2000.

Leteinturier, Christine. "La formation des journalistes français: Quelles évolutions? Quels atouts à l'embauche? Le cas des nouveaux titulaires de la carte de presse 2008." *Les cahiers du journalisme* 21 (2010): 110–34.

Lewis, Norman P., and Eisa Al Nashmi. "Data Journalism in the Arab Region: Role Conflict Exposed." *Digital Journalism* 7, no. 9 (2019): 1200–214.

Lewis, Seth C. "Journalism Innovation and Participation: An Analysis of the Knight News Challenge." *International Journal of Communication* 5 (2011): 1623–48.

Lewis, Seth C., and Nikki Usher. 2013. "Open Source and Journalism: Toward New Frameworks for Imagining News Innovation." *Media, Culture, & Society* 35, no. 5: 602–19.

Lewis, Seth C., and Rodrigo Zamith. "On the Worlds of Journalism." In *Remaking the News: Essays on the Future of Journalism Scholarship in the Digital Age*, ed. Pablo J. Boczkowski and C. W. Anderson, 111–28. Cambridge, MA: MIT Press, 2017.

Lieberman, Trudy. "The Rise and Fall of Consumer Journalism." *American History of Business Journalism*, March 2013. https://ahbj.sabew.org/story/04042013-the-rise-and-fall-of-consumer-journalism/.

Lim, Merlyna. "Clicks, Cabs, and Coffee Houses: Social Media and Oppositional Movements in Egypt, 2004–2011." *Journal of Communication* 62, no. 2 (2012): 231–48.

Loeb, Penny. "Tips on Computer-Assisted Reporting." NICAR Tipsheet no. 160 (1993). https://www.ire.org/resources/.

Machung, Anne. "Playing the Ranking Game." *Change* 30, no. 4 (1998): 12–16.

BIBLIOGRAPHY

Maier, Scott R. "The Digital Watchdog's First Byte: Journalism's First Computer Analysis of Public Records." *American Journalism* 17, no. 14 (2000): 75–91.

Marchetti, Dominique. "The Revelations of Investigative Journalism in France." *Global Media and Communication* 5, no. 3 (2009): 368–88.

Marcus-Steiff, Joachim. "L'information comme mode d'action des organisations de consommateurs." *Revue française de sociologie* 18 (1977): 85–107.

Marres, Noortje. *Digital Sociology: The Reinvention of Social Research.* Cambridge: Polity, 2017.

McCombs, Maxwell. *Setting the Agenda: The Mass Media and Public Opinion.* Cambridge: Polity, 2004.

McDonough, Patricia M., Anthony L. Antonio, MaryBeth Walpole, and Leonor X. Perez. "College Rankings: Democratized College Knowledge for Whom?" *Research in Higher Education* 39, no. 5 (1998): 513–37.

McGrayne, Sharon B. *The Theory That Would Not Die: How Bayes' Rule Cracked the Enigma Code, Hunted Down Russian Submarines, & Emerged Triumphant from Two Centuries of Controversy.* New Haven, CN: Yale University Press, 2011.

Meyer, Philip. *Paper Route: Finding My Way to Precision Journalism.* Bloomington, IN: iUniverse, 2012.

———. *Precision Journalism: A Reporter's Introduction to Social Science Methods.* Bloomington: Indiana University Press, 1973.

Milan, Stefania, and Lonneke Van der Velden. "The Alternative Epistemologies of Data Activism." *Digital Culture & Society* 2, no. 2 (2016): 57–74.

Ministère de l'Intérieur (France). "Insécurité et délinquance en 2019: Bilan statistique." September 2020. https://www.interieur.gouv.fr/Interstats/Themes/Homicides/Insecurite-et-delinquance-en-2018-premier-bilan-statistique-Fiche-Homicides2.

Molotch, Harvey, and Marilyn Lester. "News as Purposive Behavior: On the Strategic Use of Routine Events, Accidents, and Scandals." *American Sociological Review* 39, no. 1 (1974): 101–12.

Monks, James, and Ronald G. Ehrenberg. "*U.S. News & World Report*'s College Rankings: Why They Do Matter." *Change: The Magazine of Higher Learning* 3, no. 6 (1999): 42–51.

Morley, David G. *The Nationwide Audience: Structure and Decoding.* London: British Film Institute, 1980.

Moyo, Last. "Data Journalism and the Panama Papers: New Horizons for Investigative Journalism in Africa." In *Data Journalism in the Global South*, ed. Bruce Mutsvairo, Saba Bebawi, and Eddy Borges-Rey, 23–38. Cham, Switzerland: Palgrave Macmillan.

Myers, Luke, and Jonathan Roe. *College Rankings: History, Criticism, and Reform.* Washington, DC: Center for College Affordability and Productivity, 2008.

Noble, Safiya Umoja. *Algorithms of Oppression: How Search Engines Reinforce Racism.* New York: New York University Press, 2018.

O'Neil, Cathy, and Rachel Schutt. *Doing Data Science: Straight Talk from the Frontline.* Sebastopol, CA: O'Reilly, 2013.

Örnebring, Henrik. "Technology and Journalism-as-Labour: Historical Perspectives." *Journalism* 11, no. 1 (2010): 57–74.

BIBLIOGRAPHY

Padioleau, Jean-Gustave. Le Monde *et le* Washington Post: *Précepteurs et mousquetaires*. Paris: Presses universitaires de France, 1985.

———. "Systèmes d'interaction et rhétoriques journalistiques." *Sociologie du travail* 3 (1976): 256–82.

Parasie, Sylvain. "Data-Driven Revelation? Epistemological Tensions in Investigative Journalism in the Age of 'Big Data.'" *Digital Journalism* 3, no. 3 (2015): 364–80.

Parasie, Sylvain, Jean-Philippe Cointet, and Michael O'Mahony. "Online Press Serving Local Democracy." *Revue française de science politique* 62, no. 1 (2012): 45–70.

Parasie, Sylvain, and Éric Dagiral. "Data-Driven Journalism and the Public Good: 'Computer-Assisted-Reporters' and 'Programmer-Journalists' in Chicago." *New Media & Society* 15, no. 6 (2013): 853–71.

Park, Robert E. "News as a Form of Knowledge: A Chapter in the Sociology of Knowledge." *American Journal of Sociology* 45, no. 5 (1940): 669–86.

Paterson, Chris A., and David Domingo, eds. *Making Online News: The Ethnography of New Media Production*. Bern, Switzerland: Peter Lang, 2008.

Paul, Nora, ed. *When Nerds and Words Collide: Reflections on the Development of Computer Assisted Reporting*. St. Petersburg, FL: Poynter Institute of Media Studies, 1999.

Peterson, Marvin W. "Institutional Research: An Evolutionary Perspective." In *Institutional Research in Transition: New Directions for Institutional Research*, ed. Mary Corcoran and Marvin W. Peterson, 5–15. San Francisco: Jossey-Bass, 1985.

Pierru, Frédéric. "Les clairs-obscurs de la forme palmarès: L'exemple de la carrière des palmarès hospitaliers." Working paper, Maison des sciences de l'homme, 2009. https://www.meshs.fr/datas/files/docs/sem/2009-10/perru.pdf.

———. "La fabrique des palmarès: Genèse d'un secteur d'action publique et renouvellement d'un genre journalistique. Le cas du palmarès des hôpitaux." In *La presse écrite: Objets délaissés*, ed. Jean-Baptiste Legavre, 247–70. Paris: L'Harmattan, 2004.

Ponet, Philippe. "Les logiques d'une consécration journalistique: L'exemple des '50 meilleurs hôpitaux de France.'" *Questions de communication* 11 (2007): 91–110.

Port, Bob. "The Contraption." In *When Nerds and Words Collide: Reflections on the Development of Computer Assisted Reporting*, ed. Nora Paul, 37–39. St. Petersburg, FL: Poynter Institute of Media Studies, 1999.

Porter, Theodore M. *Trust in Numbers: The Pursuit of Objectivity in Science and Public Life*. Princeton, NJ: Princeton University Press, 1995.

Power, Michael. *The Audit Society: Rituals of Verification*. Oxford: Oxford University Press, 1997.

Pozen, David E., and Michael Schudson, eds. *Troubling Transparency: The History and Future of Freedom of Information*. New York: Columbia University Press, 2018.

Prior, Markus. *Post-broadcast Democracy: How Media Choice Increases Inequality in Political Involvement and Polarizes Elections*. Cambridge: Cambridge University Press, 2007.

Reid, Alastair. "How Homicide Report Tells the 'True Story' of LA's Violent Crime." Journalism.co.uk, January 28, 2014. https://www.journalism.co.uk/news/how-the-homicide-report-tells-the-true-story-of-la-s-violent-crime/s2/a555713/.

Reimer, Julius, Marlo Häring, Wiebke Loosen, Walid Maalej, and Lisa Merten. "Content Analyses of User Comments in Journalism: A Systematic Literature Review Spanning Communication Studies and Computer Science." *Digital Journalism*, online only, 2021: 1–25. doi:10.1080/21670811.2021.1882868.

Rogers, Simon. *Facts Are Sacred*. London: Faber and Faber, 2013.

Rosanvallon, Pierre, and Arthur Goldhammer. *Counter-Democracy: Politics in an Age of Distrust*. Cambridge: Cambridge University Press, 2008.

Roshier, Bob. "The Selection of Crime News by the Press." In *The Manufacture of News: Deviance, Social Problems, and the Mass Media*, ed. Stanley Cohen and Jock Young, 28–39. Beverly Hills, CA: Sage, 1973.

Royal, Cindy. "The Journalist as Programmer: A Case Study of the *New York Times* Interactive News Technology Department." *International Symposium on Online Journalism* 2, no. 1 (2012): 5–24.

Ruellan, Denis. *Les "pro" du journalisme: De l'état au statut, la construction d'un espace professionnel*. Rennes, France: Presses universitaires de Rennes, 1997.

———. *Le professionnalisme du flou: Identité et savoir-faire des journalistes français*. Grenoble: Presses universitaires de Grenoble, 1993.

Sanoff, Alvin P. "The *US News* College Rankings: A View from the Inside." In *College and University Ranking Systems*, ed. Institute for Higher Education Policy, 9–21. Washington, DC: Institute for Higher Education Policy, 2007. https://eric.ed.gov/?id=ED497028.

Scheufele, Dietram A. "Framing as a Theory of Media Effects." *Journal of Communication* 49, no. 1 (1999): 103–22.

Schudson, Michael. *Discovering the News: A Social History of American Newspapers*. 1978. Reprint. New York: Basic, 1981.

———. *The Good Citizen: A History of American Civic Life*. New York: Free Press, 1998.

———. "The Objectivity Norm in American Journalism." *Journalism* 2, no. 2 (2001): 149–70.

———. "Political Observatories, Databases, & News in the Emerging Ecology of Public Information." *Daedalus* 139, no. 2 (2010): 100–109.

———. *Why Democracies Need an Unlovable Press*. Cambridge: Polity, 2008.

Sears, D. O., and J. B. McConahay. "Participation in the Los Angeles Riot." *Social Problems* 17, no. 1 (1969): 3–20.

Silber, Norman I. *Test and Protest: The Influence of Consumers Union*. New York: Holmes & Meier, 1983.

Siles, Ignacio, and Pablo J. Boczkowski. "Making Sense of the Newspaper Crisis: A Critical Assessment of Existing Research and an Agenda for Future Work." *New Media & Society* 14, no. 8 (2012): 1375–94.

Silver, Nate. *The Signal and the Noise: Why so Many Predictions Fail—but Some Don't*. New York: Penguin, 2012.

Singer, Jane B. "The Political J-Blogger: Normalizing a New Media Form to Fit Old Norms and Practices." *Journalism* 6, no. 2 (2005): 173–98.

Singer, Jane B., Martha P. Tharp, and Amon Haruta. "Online Staffers: Superstars or Second-Class Citizens?" *Newspaper Research Journal* 20, no. 3 (1999): 29–47.

BIBLIOGRAPHY

Star, Susan L. "The Ethnography of Infrastructure." *American Behavioral Scientist* 43, no. 3 (1999): 377–91.

Strasser, Bruno J. "The Experimenter's Museum: Genbank, Natural History, and the Moral Economies of Biomedicine." *Isis* 102, no. 1 (2011): 60–96.

Strathern, Marilyn. *Audit Cultures: Anthropological Studies in Accountability, Ethics, and the Academy*. Hove, U.K.: Psychology Press, 2000.

Strauss, Anselm. "The Articulation of Project Work: An Organizational Process." *Sociological Quarterly* 29, no. 2 (1988): 163–78.

Stray, Jonathan. "Making Artificial Intelligence Work for Investigative Journalism." *Digital Journalism* 7, no. 8 (2019): 1076–97.

Suchman, Lucy. "Supporting Articulation Work." In *Computerization and Controversy: Value Conflicts and Social Choices*, 2nd ed., ed. Rob Kling, 407–23. San Diego: Academic Press, 1996.

Sunne, Samantha. "The Challenges and Possible Pitfalls of Data Journalism, and How You Can Avoid Them." American Press Institute, March 9, 2016. https://www.americanpress institute.org/publications/reports/strategy-studies/challenges-data-journalism/.

Sunstein, Cass R. *#Republic: Divided Democracy in the Age of Social Media*. Princeton, NJ: Princeton University Press, 2018.

Supplément à la lettre d'information de Pénombre. "Les lycées sous le feu de l'évaluation." 2, no. 4 (1999): 1–35.

Surowiecki, James. *The Wisdom of Crowds*. Palatine, IL: Anchor, 2005.

Susen, Simon, and Bryan S. Turner, eds. *The Spirit of Luc Boltanski: Essays on the "Pragmatic Sociology of Critique."* London: Anthem, 2014.

Tabary, Constance, Anne-Marie Provost, and Alexandre Trottier. "Data Journalism's Actors, Practices, and Skills: A Case Study from Quebec." *Journalism* 17, no. 1 (2016): 66–84.

Tandoc, Edson C., Jr., and Soo-Kwang Oh. "Small Departures, Big Continuities?" *Journalism Studies* 18, no. 8 (2017): 997–1015.

Touraine, Alain. *La voix et le regard*. Paris: Seuil, 1978.

Tuchman, Gaye. "Objectivity as Strategic Ritual: An Examination of Newsmen's Notions of Objectivity." *American Journal of Sociology* 77, no. 4 (1972): 660–79.

Tukey, John W. "The Future of Data Analysis." *Annals of Mathematical Statistics* 33, no. 1 (1962): 1–67.

Turner, Fred. "Actor-Networking the News." *Social Epistemology* 19, no. 4 (2005): 321–24.

———. *From Counterculture to Cyberculture: Stewart Brand, the Whole Earth Network, and the Rise of Digital Utopianism*. Chicago: University of Chicago Press, 2006.

U.S. Department of Justice, FBI. "2019 Crime in the United States." Fall 2020. https://ucr.fbi .gov/crime-in-the-u.s/2019/crime-in-the-u.s.-2019/topic-pages/murder.

Usher, Nikki. *Interactive Journalism: Hackers, Data, and Code*. Urbana: University of Illinois Press, 2016.

Vos, Tim P., and Stephanie Craft, "The Discursive Construction of Journalistic Transparency." *Journalism Studies* 18, no. 12 (2017): 1505–22.

Voyenne, Bernard. *Les journalistes français*. Paris: CFPJ-Retz, 1985.

BIBLIOGRAPHY

Wallace, Lewis Raven. *The View from Somewhere: Undoing the Myth of Journalistic Objectivity.* Chicago: University of Chicago Press, 2019.

Ward, Stephen J. A. *Disrupting Journalism Ethics: Radical Change on the Frontier of Digital Media.* London: Routledge, 2019.

Weaver, David H., and Maxwell E. McCombs. "Journalism and Social Science: A New Relationship?" *Public Opinion Quarterly* 44, no. 4 (1980): 477–94.

Westlund, Oscar, and Alfred Hermida. "Data Journalism and Misinformation." In *The Routledge Companion to Media Misinformation and Populism*, ed. Howard Tumber and Silvio Waisbord, 142–50. London: Routledge, 2021.

Wiener, Carolyn L. *The Elusive Quest: Accountability in Hospitals.* New York: Aldine de Gruyter, 2000.

Young, Mary Lynn, and Alfred Hermida. "From Mr. and Mrs. Outlier to Central Tendencies: Computational Journalism and Crime Reporting at the *Los Angeles Times*." *Digital Journalism* 3, no. 3 (2015): 381–97.

Yu, Harlan, and David G. Robinson. "The New Ambiguity of Open Government." *UCLA Law Review Discourse* 59 (2011): 178–208.

Zask, Joëlle. "Le public chez Dewey: Une union sociale plurielle." *Tracés* 15 (2008): 169–89.

Zelizer, Barbie. "Epilogue: Timing the Study of News Temporality." *Journalism* 19, no. 1 (2018): 111–21.

Zhang, Shuling, and Jieyun Feng. "A Step Forward? Exploring the Diffusion of Data Journalism as Journalistic Innovations in China." *Journalism Studies* 20, no. 9 (2019): 1281–300.

INDEX

Abbott, Andrew, 86
accountability, increasing, 127–34
actor-network theory, 112
advertising, revenues from, 108
air quality data, 142–43, *143f*
Akrich, Madeleine, 173
Aldhous, Peter, 100
Alfter, Brigitte, 265n51
algorithms, 250n50
Amazon (firm), 83
Ananny, Mike, 273–74n25
Anderson, Christopher, 11, 28, 178
application programming interfaces (APIs), 82–83
Armendariz, Agustin, 99, 157–64, 167, 168, 172–73, 239
articulation work, 162, 271n14
artificial intelligence, 277n3
Assange, Julian, 94–95
Aucoin, James, 30
Auray, Nicolas, 260n32

Barlett, Donald, 29
Baudelot, Christian, 72–73
Bayesian analysis, 268n26
Bell, Emily, 248n30, 261n39
Benson, Rodney, 109
Boltanski, Luc, 211
Bonnard, Jules, 97, 100–101
Bostock, Mike, 181
Bourdieu, Pierre, 273n16
Boyer, Brian, 92, 93; on map-based data, 147; on public access to data, 139, 141
Brunet, Etienne, 188
Brunon, Damien, 99
Burnham, David, 29, 39, 48, 264n38

Cairo, Alberto, 137–38
California, earthquake-proofing schools in, 153–75
California Geological Survey, 160
California Watch (of Center for Investigative Reporting), 153–54, 156,

INDEX

California Watch (*continued*)
  162–71, 271n9; ethical issues in
  algorithms of, 171–74, *174f*
Callon, Michel, 93
Carter, Shan, 181
Census Bureau, U.S., 114, 263n25
Center for Investigative Reporting
  (organization), 1, 23; on earthquake
  standards for schools in California, 153–75
Center for Responsive Politics
  (organization), 117
ChicagoCrime.org (website), 88, 98
Chicago Tribune, 91–92
Christin, Angèle, 109
Ciot, Jean-David, 86, *87f*
citizen organizations, 117–19
climate change, 8
Cohen, Sarah, 45
Cointet, Jean-Philippe, 203–4, 209, 228, 229
colleges and universities, 59; increases in
  enrollment in, 58; public reporting of
  data on, 59; rankings of, 51–55, 61, 63–70,
  66f; transparency and fairness in
  rankings of, 59
Commission for the Access to
  Administrative Records (CADA;
  France), 114
computational journalism, 3–4
computer-assisted reporters, 42–45
computer-assisted reporting, 19–20, 27–28,
  37–38, 80, 119–22, 242; in France, 50; to
  investigate injustice, 30–31; selling benefits
  of, *43f*; standards and norms of, 46–49
computer-assisted reporting movement, 119
computer cowboys, 48
computers, history of use in journalism of,
  28–29
constructivist approach, 47
consumer journalism, 56–57; decline in, 61
Consumer Reports (magazine), 56
copyright laws, 85
Corey, Michael, 98

Cota, David, 220
counterpublics, 214
COVID-19 pandemic, 235–36
crime: applications reporting on, 147;
  erroneous data on, 131–32; Homicide
  Report on, *207f*; homicides, 135, 201,
  274n1; mugshots of people arrested, 146;
  public data on, 115–16; *See also* Homicide
  Report
crowdsourcing, 130

Daston, Loraine, 5, 267–68n31
data: application programming interfaces
  for, 83; assuring accuracy of, 47; civic
  potential of, 84–87; does not speak for
  themselves, 136–38; governmental, in
  France, 113–16; obtaining from
  government agencies, 40, *41f*, 127–28,
  128f; in rankings, quality of, 74–75;
  structured, 90
data activism, 10
data analysis, 138
database journalism, 80
databases: accuracy of, 47; of earthquake
  risks to California schools, 157–61, *158f*,
  166–68; of homicides, 205–13, *206f*, *207f*;
  news data stored in, 90; scraping
  government data into, 129–30
Data.gov (website), 84
data-harvest conferences, 265n51
data journalism, 3–7, 80–81, 102; as career
  path, 99–100; ethics of, 13–14, 265n2;
  ethics of reflexivity in, 17–19; in France,
  94–97; government data necessary for,
  113; to help readers make informed
  choices, 141–48; increasing government
  accountability for, 127–34; international
  spread of, 123; objectivity and, 238–40; in
  Paris Match, 180–83; Philip Meyer
  Journalism Award for, 199; problems
  with, 7–10; relationships between
  journalists and scientists in, 178; in

INDEX

United States, 91–93; verifiability of news in, 138–42
data journalists, 79; numbers of, 258nn3–4
Data Match (*Paris Match*), 180–81, 185
data reporters, 164–65
Dedman, Bill, 27, *28f*, 37
Denis, Jérôme, 267n21
Dewey, John, 203, 216
Diakopoulos, Nicholas, 278n4
Division of State Architects (DSA; California), 153–58, 170, 172
Django (software), 88
Dodier, Nicolas, 266n16
Doig, Stephen, 30, 48, 146
Donzelot, Jacques, 116

education: earthquake-proofing schools in California, 153–75; public reporting of data on, 60; *See also* colleges and universities
Education, Department of (California), 158
Ehrenberg, Ronald G., 69
engaged journalism, 202, 204
Environment Defense (organization), 117
Ericson, Matthew, 181
Espeland, Wendy, 11, 69
ethical issues: in algorithms of California Watch, 171–74, *174f*; in data journalism, 132, 265n2; in journalism, 13–14; in journalism's dependence on values, 134–38; privacy as, 145–46; in reflexivity, 17–19, 240–43; in relationships between journalists and scientists, 178; transparency as, 257n52; verifiability of news as, 139
Ettema, James, 170
EveryBlock.com (website), 88, 131–33, 143, 144

Falga, Pierre, 62, 122
Field Act (California, 1933), 153
Fillon, François, 196
Finn, Megan, 273–74n25
FiveThirtyEight (website), 8, 125–26, 265n1

Florida, 263n24
France: accessing government data in, 113–16; computer-assisted reporting in, 50; data journalism in, 80, 94–97, 102–3, 123–24, 258n4; education market in, 58; election of 2017 in, 181–200; history of journalism in, 105–6; investigative reporting in, 266n4; journalism in U.S. compared with, 14–17, *15f*; objectivity in journalism of, 106–11; open-data movement in, 84–85; public data in, 86; public reporting of health-care data in, 59–60; rankings in, 62
Freedom of Information Act (FOIA; U.S.; 1966), 30, 35, 84; for governmental data, 113; to increase government accountability, 127–28
French National Institute of Statistics and Economic Studies, 114–15

Gaboulaud, Adrien, 180–84, 187–88, 190, 191, 193–96, 198
Galison, Peter, 5, 278n5
Gans, Herbert, 108
Garfinkel, Harold, 112, 159
Garvey, Megan, 205, 223–24
gatekeeping, 135
gender: of early computer-assisted reporters, 44–45; of French data journalists, 96
Germuska, Joe, 92
GitHub (software-development platform), 139–40
Glasser, Theodore, 170
Goëta, Samuel, 267n21
Google (firm), 83
Graves, Lucas, 261n41
Great Britain: data journalism in, 94; open data movement in, 85
Guardian (newspaper, Great Britain), 247n19; "data journalism" coined by, 80, 94, 123; in open data movement, 85
gun permits, 145

295

INDEX

hacker journalism, 80
health care system, 58; public reporting of data on, 59–60
Hermida, Alfred, 205
high schools, 72–73
Hirschman, Albert, 9
Holovaty, Adrian, 87–91, 98, 122; EveryBlock.com website created by, 131, 132
Homicide Report (*Los Angeles Times*), 24, 202–8; comments by relatives and friends on, 219–22; comments on, 209–13, *210f*, *212f*, *214f*, 216–19, *217f*, *221f*, *225f*, 229–33; individual record in, *207f*; interactive map in, *206f*; publics for, 208–9, 213–16, 222–26; South Vermont Avenue in, 224, *225f–227f*
homicides, 6–7, 135, 201; U.S. rate of, 274n1
hospitals: public reporting of data on, 59; public reporting of data on, in France, 263n31; rankings of, 51–53, 55–56
Human Genome Project, 259n14
Hurricane Andrew, 30, 48
hybrid communities, 93

ideologies, 134
Information System Medicalization Program (France), 58–59
infrastructure, development of, 37–42
injustice, computers used in investigation of, 29–31
institutional research professionals, 258n61
International Consortium of Investigative Journalists (organization), 3
Investigative Reporters and Editors (organization), 39, 120, 199
investigative reporting: data journalism and, 100; in France, 50, 106, 109–10, 266n4; history of, 30

Jaspin, Elliot, 34, 38–40, 44, 48–49
Johnson, Corey, 156–64, 166, 167

Jones, Clarence, 35–36
journalism: artificial intelligence used in, 277n3; boundary between social sciences and, 177–78; crisis in, 97–101; data journalism, 91–93; dependence on values, 134–38; ethics of, 13–14; in France, history of, 105–6; French-U.S. comparison, 14–17; history of use of computers in, 28–29; public journalism, 202; rebooting, 79–82; sociology of, 10–11
journalists: Burnham on, 39; data journalists, 79; division of labor between programmers and, 87–91; newsworthiness for, 195–99; scientists and, 178; trade-offs between scientists and, 190–95

Kayser-Bril, Nicolas, 94, 99
Kelso, Nathaniel, 140
Kline, Scott, 93
Klinenberg, Eric, 90
Knight Foundation, 89
Krugman, Paul, 138

Landau, George, 44, 120–21
Law on Authors' Rights and Related Rights in the Information Society (France; 2006), 259n15
leaks of government data, 129
Lebolloch, Steven, 184, 194, 197–98
Lechevallier, Anne-Sophie, 180–96
Lemieux, Cyril, 110, 178, 273n12
Le Monde: data journalism by, 95; proportion of articles using percentage figures, *15f*
Leovy, Jill, 135, 202, 205, 207
Le Petit Parisien (French newspaper), 108
Lewis, Seth, 89, 139, 258n8
Little, Darnell, 121–22
Loeb, Penny, 46
Long, Susan, 39

INDEX

Los Angeles Police Department (LAPD), 132, 206–7
Los Angeles Times: on homicides, 6–7, 135; *See also* Homicide Report
Lowery, Wesley, 7–8

Macron, Emmanuel, 179, 196, 198
mainframe computers, 34
Mayaffre, Damon, 185–93, 195
McCormick, Erin, 253n51
mechanical objectivity, 5
Mélenchon, Jean-Luc, 196
Mével, Catherine, 116
Meyer, Philip, 177, 199; on computer cowboys, 48; criticisms of, 61; on Detroit riots, 27, 29, 36; statistical analysis used by, 31–34
money laundering, 247–48n20
Monks, James, 69
Morse, Robert, 61, 63, 65, 74, 75
Mother Jones (magazine), 92
mugshots, 146

National Institute for Computer-Assisted Reporting (NICAR), 38–42
new media, 81
New Public Management, 52, 59
New Public Management (France), 115
new social movements, 118
New York Times: on political conventions of 2012, 181; proportion of articles using percentage figures, *15f*
Nextdoor.com (website), 131
NineTrack Express (software), 38
nonprofit organizations, 117–19; think tanks, 264n39

Obama administration, 84
objectivity, 237, 246n8; data journalism and, 238–40; in French journalism, 106–11; problems with, 7; in social sciences, 10–13

Objet web non identifié (OWNI; Unidentified Web Object; organization), 94–95
O'Neil, Daniel, 143–44, 147
O'Neil, Daniel X., 85
open-data movement, 84–86
Open Government Chicago (organization), 92
open-government movement, 84
opensecrets.org (website), 117
open-source movement, 140
Örnebring, Henrik, 81
OWNI (Objet web non identifié; Unidentified Web Object; organization), 94–95

Paris Match (magazine), 23–24: data journalism in, 180–83, 199; on French presidential election of 2016–2017, 178–79; readership of, 272n6; science in coverage of election of 2017 in, 183–85; symmetrical relationship between scientists and, 186–90; "Weight of Words" infrastructure in, 196–97, *197f*
Philip Meyer Journalism Award, 32, 199
Pierru, Frederic, 55
Pilhofer, Aron, 87–88
pipelines, 82
Plichon, Dévrig, 180
political science, 31
politics: of computation, 45–49, 120; in French journalism, 108
PolitiFact (website), 146
Porter, Theodore, 10, 63, 115, 123
precision journalism, 19–20, 27, 80
privacy issues, 145–46
programmers, 87–91
ProPublica (website), 52, 91
public journalism, 202, 204
publics, 201, 204, 222–26; in comments on Homicide Report, 215, 216; emergence of, 208–13

297

INDEX

Raja, Tasneem, 92, 93, 144
ranker journalists, 52–53, 62, 69–70
rankings, 11, 20, 255n15; of colleges, 51–53; criticisms of, 61–63; maintaining distance from institutions in, 73–76; as movement among U.S. and French journalists, 53–56; transparency and fairness in, 70–73; by *U.S. News & World Report*, 63–70, 66f
reflexivity, 240–43
Rogers, Simon, 4, 140
Romera, Pierre, 95, 139
Royal, Cindy, 91
Royant, Olivier, 180
Russia, money laundering by oligarchs from, 247–48n20

Sanoff, Alvin P., 54, 58, 71, 72
Sarkozy, Nicolas, 186–87
Sauder, Michael, 11, 69
Schmalzbauer, John, 110
Schrager, Allison, 8, 138
Schudson, Michael, 6, 117, 148
Schwencke, Ken, 205, 208, 223
Science & Avenir (French magazine), 53, 55
science journalism, 100
scientists: journalists and, 178; in *Paris Match* coverage of election of 2017, 183–85; *Paris Match*'s symmetrical relationship with, 186–90; trade-offs between journalists and, 190–95
ScoreCard.org (website), 117
scraping government data, 129–30
Silber, Norman I., 56, 57
Silver, Nate, 5, 134; on Bayesian analysis, 268n26; on causality, 135–37; FiveThirtyEight website of, 125–26
Smith, Doug, 132
social sciences, 10–13, 31, 102; boundary between journalism and, 177–78; Meyer's use of, 32, 33; in training of French journalists, 272n11

sociology: of disputing processes, 126, 265n3; of journalism, 10–11; of quantification, 11
statistics: contexts of, 137; on crime, public availability of, 115–16; data analysis of, 168–69; epidemiological, 235; limitations on reporting of, 36; Meyer on use and abuse of, 32; social, 10; transparency in, 71, 257n52
Steele, James, 29
St. Paul Pioneer Press, 120
Strauss, Anselm, 81
Stray, Jonathan, 277n3
structured data, 90
Student Right-to-Know and Campus Security Act (U.S.), 59
Suchman, Lucy, 162
Sunstein, Cass, 202
Supreme Authority for the Distribution and Protection of Intellectual Property (France; 2009), 259n15

Taggart, Kendall, 164–66, 168
Tarde, Gabariel, 275n8
tax evasion, 247–48n20
technology: in generation of story ideas, 46; in journalism, 241–42; in rebooting journalism, 79
Texas Tribune, 144
think tanks, 264n39
Transactional Records Access Clearing House (TRAC; organization), 39, 264n38
translators (in actor-network theory), 119–22, 264n44
transparency: in accessing government data, 131–34; as ethical principle, 257n52; of news production, 138–42; in rankings, 71
Tukey, John W., 271n17
Turner, Fred, 44

United States: citizen observatories in, 117–19; data journalism in, 80, 102–3, 258n3; government data in, 113–14;

298

INDEX

homicide rate in, 274n1; journalism in France compared with, 14–17, *15f*; objectivity in journalism of, 106; open-data movement in, 84
Usher, Nikki, 139
U.S. News & World Report: air quality data published by, 142; "America's Best Colleges" published in, 53–55, 61, 63–70, *66f*; maintaining distance in, 73–74; transparency and fairness in, 70–73

values, minimizing journalism's dependence on, 134–38
verifyability, of news, 138–42
Vicente, Michael, 260n32

Waite, Matt, 87–88, 146
Warlog Irak application, 95

web-development frameworks, 83
web journalism, 99–100
Weil, Richard, 44
Welsh, Ben, 87–88; in computer-assisted reporting movement, 122; on errors in LAPD data, 132; Homicide Report by, 205–7
Wieseltier, Leon, 137
WikiLeaks (website), 129
women, as early computer-assisted reporters, 45, 253n51
Wyvekens, Anne, 116

Young, Mary Lynn, 204–5
Youngman, Owen, 133

Zamith, Rodrigo, 258n8
Zelizer, Barbie, 273n24

GPSR Authorized Representative: Easy Access System Europe, Mustamäe tee 50, 10621 Tallinn, Estonia, gpsr.requests@easproject.com